W9-APW-828

# Harlan Miners Speak

*Report on Terrorism in the Kentucky Coal Fields*

A Da Capo Press Reprint Series

# CIVIL LIBERTIES IN AMERICAN HISTORY

GENERAL EDITOR: LEONARD W. LEVY

*Brandeis University*

# Harlan Miners Speak

*Report on Terrorism in the Kentucky Coal Fields*
*Prepared by Members of the National Committee*
*for the Defense of Political Prisoners*

THEODORE DREISER

LESTER COHEN          ANNA ROCHESTER
MELVIN P. LEVY          ARNOLD JOHNSON
CHARLES R. WALKER          JOHN DOS PASSOS
ADELAIDE WALKER          BRUCE CRAWFORD
JESSIE WAKEFIELD          BORIS ISRAEL
SHERWOOD ANDERSON

VON CANON LIBRARY
SOUTHERN SEMINARY
BUENA VISTA, VIRGINIA 24416

25145

DA CAPO PRESS · NEW YORK · 1970

A Da Capo Press Reprint Edition

This Da Capo Press edition of *Harlan Miners Speak*
is an unabridged republication of the first
edition published in New York in 1932.

HD 8039. M62 U6465 1970

*Library of Congress Catalog Card Number 70-107410*

SBN 306-71889-8

Copyright, 1932, by Harcourt, Brace and Company, Inc.

Published by Da Capo Press
A Division of Plenum Publishing Corporation
227 West 17th Street, New York, N.Y. 10011
All Rights Reserved

Manufactured in the United States of America

# Harlan Miners Speak

# Harlan Miners Speak

REPORT ON

TERRORISM IN THE KENTUCKY COAL FIELDS

PREPARED BY

MEMBERS OF THE NATIONAL COMMITTEE

FOR THE DEFENSE OF POLITICAL PRISONERS

---

THEODORE DREISER

LESTER COHEN            ANNA ROCHESTER

MELVIN P. LEVY          ARNOLD JOHNSON

CHARLES R. WALKER       JOHN DOS PASSOS

ADELAIDE WALKER         BRUCE CRAWFORD

JESSIE WAKEFIELD        BORIS ISRAEL

SHERWOOD ANDERSON

---

HARCOURT, BRACE AND COMPANY

NEW YORK

COPYRIGHT, 1932, BY

HARCOURT, BRACE AND COMPANY, INC.


*All rights reserved, including
the right to reproduce this book
or portions thereof in any form.*


*first edition*

PRINTED IN THE UNITED STATES OF AMERICA
BY QUINN & BODEN COMPANY, INC., RAHWAY, N. J.

*Typography by Robert S. Josephy*

## AUNT MOLLY JACKSON'S
## KENTUCKY MINERS' WIVES
## RAGGED HUNGRY BLUES

### I

I'm sad and weary; I've got the hungry ragged blues;
I'm sad and weary; I've got the hungry ragged blues;
Not a penny in my pocket to buy the thing I need to use.

### 2

I woke up this morning with the worst blues I ever had in my
    life;
I woke up this morning with the worst blues I ever had in my
    life;
Not a bite to cook for breakfast, a poor coal miner's wife.

### 3

When my husband works in the coal mines, he loads a car on
    every trip,
When my husband works in the coal mines, he loads a car on
    every trip,
Then he goes to the office that evening and gits denied of scrip.

### 4

Just because it took all he had made that day to pay his mine
    expense,
Just because it took all he had made that day to pay his mine
    expense,
A man that'll work for coal-light and carbide, he ain't got a
    speck of sense.

v

### 5

*All the women in the coal camps are a-sitting with bowed-down
　　heads,
All the women in the coal camps are a-sitting with bowed-down
　　heads,
Ragged and barefooted, the children a-crying for bread.*

### 6

*No food, no clothes for our children, I'm sure this ain't no lie,
No food, no clothes for our children, I'm sure this ain't no lie,
If we can't git more for our labor, we will starve to death and
　　die.*

### 7

*Listen, friends and comrades, please take a friend's advice,
Listen, friends and comrades, please take a friend's advice,
Don't load no more that dirty coal till you git a living price.*

### 8

*Don't go under the mountains with the slate a-hanging over
　　your heads,
Don't go under the mountains with the slate a-hanging over
　　your heads,
And work for just coal-light and carbide and your children
　　a-crying for bread.*

### 9

*This mining town I live in is a sad and lonely place,
This mining town I live in is a sad and lonely place,
Where pity and starvation is pictured on every face.*

### 10

*Ragged and hungry, no slippers on our feet,
Ragged and hungry, no slippers on our feet,
We're bumming around from place to place to get a little bite
　　to eat.*

11

*All a-going round from place to place bumming for a little food*
    *to eat.*
*Listen, my friends and comrades, please take a friend's advice,*
*Don't put out no more of your labor, till you get a living price.*

12

*Some coal operators might tell you the hungry blues are not*
    *bad;*
*Some coal operators might tell you the hungry blues are not*
    *bad;*
*They are the worst blues this poor woman ever had.*

# A STATEMENT OF THE PURPOSES
# OF THE NATIONAL COMMITTEE
# FOR THE
# DEFENSE OF POLITICAL PRISONERS

THE National Committee for the Defense of Political Prisoners has been formed at a time of panic and despair among the owning and directing classes of this country, and of brutal poverty, oppression, and growing unrest among the working men and women. On the side of the great financial and industrial corporations are the machinery of the press, politics, organized charity and the law. Through these means every effort is made to stifle protest, to destroy or to prevent organization. Against the workers who demand for themselves and their families the basic human rights and decent conditions of life and work, there is a constant attack directed by the employing and owning class and carried on through every available channel of education, publicity and law.

The National Committee for the Defense of Political Prisoners has been formed to aid workers to organize and to defend themselves against terror and suppression, whether extra-legal or carried on in the frame-work of the legal system, either through alien deportation, criminal syndicalism, sedition, anti-labor laws, or through perversion of murder, vagrancy or other laws. The National Committee recognizes the right of workers to organize, strike and picket, their right to freedom of speech, press and assembly, and it will aid in combating any violation of those rights, through legal means, and above all, by stimulating a wide public interest and protest. By these means the National Committee will act to aid in repealing all anti-labor laws, to fight the deportation of foreign-born workers, and the use of lynch law or special disqualification of any sort against Negroes, finally to assist in the defense of workers prosecuted for their activities in organizing to demand civil rights or better living conditions.

Membership in the National Committee for the Defense of Political Prisoners is nation-wide. The Committee invites, too, writers, artists, scientists, teachers and professional people from other countries than the United States to join its ranks and aid its work.

# CONTENTS

# Harlan Miners Speak

# I. INTRODUCTION

## by *Theodore Dreiser*

THE reason that I personally went to the Harlan coal district
in Kentucky was because from about June to November, 1931,
the newspapers of America carried more or less continuous reports of outrages upon the rights of not only the striking miners
in that region, but apparently those of all sorts of other people
inside and outside the State who sought to interfere in their
behalf. I recall reading that representatives of different newspapers and press agencies, the United Press, the Federated
Press, and individual newspaper men such as Bruce Crawford,
of Norton, Virginia, were attacked, and in Crawford's particular
case, shot in the leg, the others threatened and ordered from
the State, as though a portion of any State, apart from the
State itself, as illustrated by this Harlan County coal district,
had authority, let alone the right, to set up a military law of
its own and order citizens from other States to observe it, all
Constitutional guarantees to the contrary notwithstanding.

I really did not pay so much attention to this particular
situation at first, because mining wars of this character in
America have been a part of my life's entire experience. As
a newspaper man in Chicago, St. Louis, Pittsburgh and other
places, I was early drawn into this sort of thing and as early,
of course, witnessed the immense injustice which property in
America has not only always sought to but has succeeded in in-
flicting upon labor. Besides, in July of this same summer, I
personally was asked by the National Miners Union to come
to Pittsburgh and witness for myself the cruelties being inflicted
upon the strikers of that region—Eastern Ohio, Northwest
West Virginia and Pennsylvania. What I saw there of murder,
starvation, extortion and the like practiced upon the coal miners
by the coal operators was sufficient to cause me to openly indict

the American Federation of Labor, which resulted in nothing more than a glossy and self-exculpatory denial from William Green, the present President of the A. F. of L.

In late October, however, I was presented with a thirty-two page document or indictment compiled apparently by the International Labor Defense from various sources, but all relating to crimes and abuses inflicted on the striking miners in the Harlan district by, obviously, the coal operators' association of the same area. This document contained from three to five indictments to the page and covered, as usual, everything from unpunished murders (eleven all told) to the dynamiting of soup kitchens, the unwarranted search of strikers' homes, the denial of their right to join any union except the United Mine Workers of America of which they were heartily sick and to which they did not want to belong, also the denial of free speech, of the right of representatives from outside newspapers or organizations to come there and see for themselves what was going on.

Because the International Labor Defense confessed itself as in no position to evoke public interest in this wholesale brutality, it wanted to know if I, as Chairman of the National Committee for the Defense of Political Prisoners, would not organize a Committee out of the membership of the general committee of that body and proceed to Kentucky not only to question authority there as to their actions, but to see if by so doing we could not center possible attention and so modify if not dispel some of the ills being suffered by the miners there.

My objection to this was that a more or less lay Committee such as I could organize would not prove effective and that it might be met, if not with the same brutality, at least with the same irritating indifference which had followed efforts on the part of different newspapers not only to gather data, but arouse public sentiment. A counter proposal of mine was that instead of the National Committee for the Defense of Political Prisoners organizing such a visit, I, as Chairman of that body, invite, rather, various representative Americans already known for their courage and their public-spirited interest in the Con-

stitutional rights of Americans everywhere, to volunteer as
members of such an invading body and, once there, to hold
such meetings and interview such people, officials, miners, coal
operators and citizens, who could testify to the truth of these
various charges, and, in that way, definitely inform the American public as to what was going on and also, by the same process,
to persuade the officials and operators of Kentucky to a more
equitable course of action.

To that end, and since the International Labor Defense was
anxious for action in any form, the following telegram was
sent to the names listed below it:

ALL CONSTITUTIONAL AND CIVIL RIGHTS AS WELL AS ORDINARY
HUMAN RIGHTS DENIED TO EIGHTEEN THOUSAND AMERICAN
MINERS AND FAMILIES HELD IN GRIP OF FRIGHTFUL REIGN OF
TERROR IMPOSED BY THUGS AND JAILBIRDS WHICH NEW YORK
TIMES DESCRIBES QUOTE HARLAN COAL FIELDS FACE CIVIL WAR
KENTUCKY COUNTY ARMED CAMP UNQUOTE LEGALIZED GUNMEN
HAVE SHOT TWO NEWSPAPERMEN TO PREVENT PUBLICATION OF
TRUTH AND KIDNAPED OTHER INVESTIGATORS DYNAMITED RELIEF
AGENTS CAR DYNAMITED RELIEF KITCHEN SHOT DOWN UNARMED
MEN STOP GUNMEN AND CONVICTS ARE ARBITRATING LABOR DIS-
PUTE WHILE WOMEN AND CHILDREN ARE SUFFERING CRUEL
EVICTIONS AND HUNGER DISEASE OF BLEEDING BOWELS STOP
THIRTY FOUR MINERS CHARGED WITH MURDER ON RIDICULOUS
EVIDENCE TRANSPORTED FOR TRIAL TO COUNTIES TWO HUNDRED
MILES AWAY DEPRIVED OF DEFENSE SINCE PENNILESS THEY
CANNOT PAY TO TRANSPORT WITNESSES STOP FREE SPEECH FREE
ASSEMBLY UNITED STATES CONSTITUTION SUSPENDED CALLING
FOR DELEGATION TO GO TO HARLAN TO INVESTIGATE STOP
NATIONAL COMMITTEE FOR DEFENSE OF POLITICAL PRISONERS
INVITES YOU TO JOIN OUR INVESTIGATION STOP DELEGATION
MEETING IN LEXINGTON KENTUCKY NOVEMBER FIFTH PRO-
CEEDING TO HARLAN NOVEMBER SIXTH TO MAKE FREE OPEN
INQUIRY FOR BESIEGED COMMUNITY INVITATION EXTENDED TO
SENATORS LAFOLLETTE COUZENS NORRIS SHIPSTEAD AND ROY
HOWARD COLONEL ANDERSON CHARLES CLAYTON MORRISON

BISHOP DUBOSE FELIX FRANKFURTER CHARLES TAFT WILLIAM
ALLEN WHITE E LINDEMAN REVEREND FORTUNE ARTHUR BRA-
DEN WILLIAM HUTCHINS DANIEL WILLARD STOP LETTER FOL-
LOWS KINDLY TELEGRAPH REPLY HOTEL ANSONIA NEW YORK
THEODORE DREISER CHAIRMAN

Senator Robert M. LaFollette
Senator Henrik Shipstead
Senator George W. Norris
Senator James Couzens
Roy Howard, Scripps-Howard Newspapers
Daniel Willard, President, B. & O. R. R.
William Allen White, Emporia (Kansas) *Gazette*
Felix Frankfurter, Harvard Law School
Col. Henry W. Anderson, member Wickersham Committee
Charles Taft, 2nd, former Prosecuting Attorney Hamilton
Co., Ohio
E. C. Lindeman, Director, Willard Straight Foundation
Charles Clayton Morrison, Editor, *Christian Century*, Chi-
cago, Ill.
Arthur Braden, President, Transylvania College, Lexing-
ton, Ky.
A. W. Fortune, Pastor, Central Christian Church, Lexing-
ton, Ky.
Wm. J. Hutchins, President, Berea College, Berea, Kentucky
Bruce Crawford, Publisher, *Crawford's Weekly*, Norton, Va.
Bishop Wm. H. DuBose, Sewanee, Tennessee
D. F. Meeman [then] editor, Knoxville *News-Sentinel*,
Knoxville, Tenn.

With one or two exceptions, all replied; some critically, some
genially, but, with the exception of Bruce Crawford, all de-
clined for various reasons a few of which are quoted here-
with:

I AM SORRY THAT HEALTH DOES NOT PERMIT ME TO JOIN
DELEGATION.

PRIOR ARRANGEMENTS MAKE IT IMPOSSIBLE FOR ME TO GO.

BELIEVING PROPOSED COMMITTEE CANNOT ACHIEVE DESIRED
RESULT CANNOT ACCEPT INVITATION.

Having thus signally failed to interest the few Americans
whom I thought we might look to in connection with such a
crisis as this, and the International Labor Defense continuing
to point out the cruel and unpublicized inequity of the process
still going on, I finally called a meeting of the National Committee for the Defense of Political Prisoners and asked for
volunteers from among its membership. The following responded:

John Dos Passos
Charles Rumford Walker
Mrs. Adelaide Walker
Bruce Crawford
Samuel Ornitz
Lester Cohen
Melvin P. Levy

Then, as a Committee, we first gave notice to the press
that we would invade Harlan County and the Eastern coal district of Kentucky, seeking, if possible, to do what the more
general committee just mentioned was asked to do. Also, as a
Committee, we wired Flem D. Sampson, Governor of Kentucky, for military protection. Yet, without waiting for his
reply, we proceeded to Pineville in Bell County, the country
that lies just west of Harlan, one of the counties in which
various offenses have been committed and there, as well as in
Harlan County, proceeded to take testimony and to make
inquiry. As a Committee, we invited not only the Sheriff, District Attorney and the County Judge, but the local representatives of the Harlan County Coal Operators' Association,
as well as representatives of the National Miners Union, and
many striking miners in Evarts, Straight Creek, and elsewhere,
to testify concerning the crimes that had been committed against
them as well as the ills, economic, political, social and otherwise, to which they had been and were being subjected by the

operators and officials who were said to be making war upon them.

Also, such meetings as were held in the Harlan district were thrown open to the public, the press, the local officials, and whomsoever would, without let or hindrance. Since the press was fully represented, a portion of the testimony we took and the data we unearthed for ourselves was given to the country; not always, however, in the spirit and the intention of the witnesses, nor with the confirming data included. Rather, a large portion of the press, particularly that represented by the Associated Press, appeared to be determined to either modify, limit or ignore such facts as were testified to, and, worse, to make light of and discredit the significance if not the ambitions of the Committee. Not only that, but while I personally, on my arrival, was greeted by the Mayor of Pineville and by Judge Jones, who assured me that I would find no evidence of the presence there of deputies nor any ill-treatment of the miners, their wives and children by the officials of the district, nevertheless and thereafter, the Committee was subjected to as many embarrassments and delays as possible. For instance, the witnesses called by us were spied upon, as they themselves testified, by the very deputies whom Judge Jones had told me were not only inoperative but not to be found. Not only that, but apart from injustices previously practiced upon them, they had been more recently threatened with future trouble if they testified in this instance, and those who came insisted upon some form of protection, not only protection personally guaranteed by the local officials, but by the Governor as well. To effect this, the Committee wired several local officials as well as the Governor. The only person who responded with a promise of protection to these witnesses was the Governor; not any local official, and by these I mean Judge D. C. Jones, District Attorney W. A. Brock, and Sheriff John Henry Blair. More, as we proceeded from Pineville to Harlan, as well as from Harlan County to Evarts, Straight Creek, etc., in the adjoining area, the cars containing our members were followed, as some of the local newspaper men reported, and as I for one saw for myself, by an automobile containing at least four of those hired deputies paid for by the coal operators' association, but deputized by Sheriff Blair.

Not only that, but it having previously been announced that this Committee would attempt to call public meetings of the strikers in order to test whether they would be allowed to exercise the right of free speech, I was handed a note, in Pineville, near the hotel where I was staying, by some one whom I did not know, which note read as follows:

*If any meeting is held at Wallins Creek on Sunday afternoon, there will be trouble.*

The government having sent a Major and several military assistants to attend us on our various pilgrimages, I handed this note to this same Major who replied: "Go ahead and hold the meeting. There will be no trouble." The meeting was held and there was no trouble, although there were Harlan County as well as other political representatives and an official stenographer, evidently appointed by somebody—either some Harlan County official or the coal operators—to report such speeches as were made. It was assumed afterwards by this Committee that it was due to the testimony taken on this occasion by this official stenographer for either the coal operators or the officials of Harlan County, that the charges of criminal syndicalism which were followed by State indictments for the same, were filed and officially acted upon.

I myself as I afterwards also learned was spied upon and after I had left the State was charged with adultery in the Continental Hotel at Pineville at which hotel Judge Jones of Harlan County was also stopping at the time.

I trouble to enter upon all of these details because as I personally noticed, the attitude of all of the officials of Bell and Harlan Counties, as well as those of other districts, and some elements of the public, the small trading world in particular, were especially inimical. It was made perfectly clear by all that the Committee was not wanted there, that its members were looked upon as unauthorized and unaccredited

interlopers without authority from some governmental body
and hence, without any right to inquire into any, let alone all,
of the crimes that were alleged. Judge Jones, for instance,
after assuring me on my arrival that he would be willing and
glad to answer any and all questions which might be asked of
him, refused the next day to be either seen or questioned in any
manner whatsoever.

Apparently Sheriff Blair had not been reached in time or
persuaded to the proper course of action in this matter, for
he alone of the officials permitted the Committee to invade his
office and there answered all of the questions, which testimony
will be found in the report of the Committee. Subsequently,
by calling on W. A. Brock, the District Attorney, we persuaded him that it would be best for all if he talked about
what had been going on in the county and his testimony as
recorded in the report of the Committee, throws a very clear
light on what is considered right and fair by small American
officials and the mine owners' associations in this typical labor
war.

My personal conclusion, after the various individuals had
been examined and the mining districts visited, was that this
was a very remarkable struggle of the American worker against
the usual combination of power and wealth in America which
for so long has held him in subjection. As a matter of fact,
there, I found the same line-up of petty officials and business
interests on the side of the coal operators and as against the
miners, as I have discovered in almost every other labor war
or controversy that I have had the opportunity to observe.
The small town bankers, grocers, editors and lawyers, the
police, the sheriff, if not the government, were all apparently
subservient to the money and corporate masters of the area.
It was their compulsion, if possibly not always their desire, to
stand well with these who had the power to cause them material or personal difficulties and, as against those, the underpaid and even starving workers, who could do nothing for
themselves.

Possibly this practice springs from the asinine notion in

America that every one has an equal opportunity to become a money master, a Morgan or a Rockefeller, although the data concerning America's economic life today show that no more than three hundred and fifty families control 95 per cent of the wealth of the country. Also, that almost every man, short of the officers and owners of our great and all-controlling corporations today, must wear the collar of one or another of these great combinations, and it is only through their favor and power that there is a chance for him or any one to improve his economic state or his social position. He must wear the collar marked with the name of his owner.

This criticism also goes for the press, the church and the public officials elected by those very people who suffer so very greatly at their hands. It is possible that here and there you may find a starving, struggling or unimportant editor who dares to exercise freedom of opinion in connection with just such things as have occurred and to this hour are still occurring in Harlan and elsewhere, but he never succeeds in prospering thereby.

In general, in so far as America is concerned, you can go into any town or city, comment vigorously on inequity in favor of the few and you will very soon find out how unprofitable that really is. Here, as elsewhere, I found, and not to my amazement any longer, the church as well as the press and public charity in all of its forms, and by that I mean the Red Cross, the Salvation Army, the Y.M.C.A. and any such related bodies as may exist, entirely on the side of the corporations as opposed to the workers.

Thus, since the corporations did not desire the miners to strike for more wages or to join a labor union which was not, as is the A. F. of L., directed by the corporations, or to read a paper such as the *Daily Worker*, which does not set forth the usual corporation blah in regard to what is necessary for the welfare of the country, these organizations, particularly where workers were on strike and in need of aid, were not willing to assist them in any way unless they were willing to bow to the demands of the corporations, i.e., in this instance, that they refuse to have anything to do with the National Miners Union, and at once ally themselves with the United Mine Workers of America, a branch of the A. F. of L.; that they cease reading the *Daily Worker* and substitute for it, let us say, the *Harlan Daily Clarion* or the *Louisville Courier Journal* and that they return to work at such wages as the A. F. of L. through its traitor union, the United Mine Workers of America, would arrange for them. Failing this, no food, no clothing, no medicine, no this, no that, for any mine worker. Rather, as I have said, jail, espionage, the blacklist, hunger, even death. In fact, this has become the accepted order in America. The corporation, organized as it is in various nation wide tie-ups, all of the industries in a given line, textile operators' association, coal operators' association, the metal manufacturers' association, and the like, seek to and do, especially for the humbler forms of labor, create a kind of slavery. The purpose of all such organizations everywhere is to prevent unionization of every kind where possible, and where this is not possible, to control such unions with a view to low, and not high, wages, with a view to company stores, even company controlled towns, and certainly company controlled notions and even religious views.

So thoroughly had all this been brought about in this particular region that the right of public meeting had certainly been denied until we arrived there. Also, the right to collect food and clothing and to distribute the same independent of the Red Cross, the Salvation Army and the Y.M.C.A. which were either indifferent to or arbitrary in their demands upon the striking miners. As a matter of fact, what followed is amply set forth in the testimony taken and the data presented in this volume by other members of the Committee.

In conclusion, however, I should like to add that what I cannot understand is why the American people which has been drilled from the beginning in the necessity and the advantage of the individual and his point of view, does not now realize how complete is the collapse of that idea as a working social formula.

For while, on the one hand, we have arrogated to each of ourselves the right to be a giant individual if we can, we have not seen how impossible it is for more than a very few, if so many, to achieve this. Also that, should it be achieved by so much as one, the rest of us would be mere robots functioning at the will and under the direction of that particular individual. It would follow, then, if we had the mental strength to grasp it, that it is really not complete individualism for anybody that we need or want or can endure even, but a limited form of individualism which will guarantee to all, in so far as possible, the right, if there is such a right, to life, liberty, and the pursuit of happiness, and also an equitable share in the economic results of any such organization as the presence and harmony of numerous individuals presupposes and compels.

As it is now, we have gotten no further than the right of the most cunning and strong individuals among us to aggrandize ourselves, leaving the rest of us here in America, as elsewhere, to subsist on what is left after they are through. And if you will examine our American economic arrangement, you will find that they are not through, since by now, three hundred and fifty families control 95 per cent of the wealth of the country, and these families, their trusts and holding companies, are now not only not distributing that wealth in any equitable ratio, but even if they were so minded, they are not capable of so doing. Taken collectively, they do not constitute any central authority. And except through the functions of government which they seek to and do direct for their own private aggrandizement, they have no means, let alone any intention of so doing. More, the government which is supposed to represent all the individualistic ambitions of all of our people, is in no position to do that. It, too, in its turn, has become one of the instruments of this central group of individuals which now directs all of its functions to its particular and very special advantage. That leaves the American citizen, one hundred and twenty-five million strong, with his faith in individualism and what it will do for him, mainly without his rent, his job, a decent suit of clothes, a pair of shoes, or food. His faith in this free-for-all individualism has now led him to the place where his fellow individualists of greater strength, cunning and greed, are in a position to say for how much, or rather, for how little, he shall work, for how long, and whether he shall be allowed to make any complaint or even seek redress in case he is unhappy or dissatisfied, ill-treated, deprived, or even actually starved. In fact, his faith in this individualism as a solvent for all his ills, has caused him to slumber, while his fellow individualists of greater greed and cunning have been seizing his wealth, his church, his press, his courts, his judges, his legislators, his police, and quite all of his originally agreed upon Constitutional privileges so that, today, he walks practically in fear of his own shadow. He cannot now any longer openly say that he is dissatisfied with his government, or that he thinks it is wrong; nor that he thinks individualism is wrong, if actually, he as yet now thinks it is wrong; nor can he any longer organize in unions which are not suborned and so controlled by the very individuals from whose economic pressure he is seeking to escape. He cannot turn to his church, because his church will not listen to his economic ills here on earth; it calls his attention to a Paradise which is to come hereafter. The present earthly Paradise, in its economic form, at least, the church blandly concedes to the very individualists of whom he now complains. Nor can he turn to his press which, by reason of economic advantages, which only those great individualists whom he has so much admired have in their keeping and can bestow, turns not to him but to these his masters. And for that reason he may not be heard. Personally, as poor as he is now, he cannot bring to the door of the press that cash return which they now demand in order to do justice to those millions whose minute and underpaid labors still constitute the source of the wealth of the treasuries which his giant overlords, once lesser individuals like himself, now control.

In sum, by his worship of his own private rights to individual advancement, as opposed to the rights and welfare of every other, he sees himself, if he is really poor and as he really is, an Ishmael in the land as well as the prosperity of the land which he creates. Actually, as a worker, he is laughed at and, in times of unrest and contest, spit upon as a malcontent, a weakling, a radical, an undesirable citizen, one who has not the understanding and hence not the right to complain of the ills by which he finds himself beset. Herded, in so far as the majority of him is concerned, in work-warrens called towns, watched over as the slaves of the South were watched over in the days before the Civil War, by the spies and agents of the immense coöperative associations of wealth, in the factories and mines and mills for which he now works, warred upon by the veritable armies of mercenaries employed by these giants whom he still so much admires, in order to overawe him and subdue him; he finds himself discharged, starved, and then blacklisted and shot down when he strikes; he finds himself, as I have said before, frustrated, ignored, and denied by his church, his press, his paid officials and his supine and traitor government.

Americans today should make an intensive study of individualism as such. They will find its best exemplar in the jungle, where every individual is for itself, prowls to sustain itself, and deals death to the weakest at every turn.

The cries of the jungle today are no more and no worse than the cries of the miners in Harlan, or of the cotton mill workers of Gastonia, or the textile workers of Lawrence, or the agricultural workers of Imperial Valley, or of the masses in general. They, like the zebra in the jaws of the lion, are the economic victims of these giant corporations, *still posing as individuals*, although armed to the teeth with purchased laws, hired officials, and over-awed or controlled courts. These latter are their teeth and their claws, and with these they strike, and their dead are everywhere, defeated and starved.

Again I say, Americans should mentally follow individualism to its ultimate conclusion, for society is not and cannot be a jungle. It should be and is, if it is a social organism worthy of the name, an escape from this drastic individualism which, for some, means all, and for the many, little or nothing. And consciously or unconsciously, it is by Nature and evolution intended as such, for certainly the thousands-of-years-old growth of organized society augurs desire on the part of Nature to avoid the extreme and bloody individualism of the jungle. In proof of which, I submit that organized society throughout history has indulged in more and more rules and laws, each intended to limit, yet not frustrate, the individual in his relations to his fellows.

In fact, the dream of organized society, conscious or unconscious, has been to make it not only possible but necessary for the individual to live with his fellow in reasonable equity, in order that he may enjoy equity himself.

If that is not so, why then organized society at all? If that is not so, then why the hope and the dream, in every heart, of a State in which the individual may not be too much put upon? And why in the absence of that (this desired State) *Revolution*—the final human expression of its hatred of injustice, cruelty, slavery, usury? Why our present social structure, with its courts, its legislative bodies, executives, its so-called representatives of each and every one?

If these do not indicate or spell a dream of true democracy, of helpful companionship in this all-too-disappointing struggle for existence, what does? And if that is true, then why should not this giant and rapacious individualism here in America, now operating for the whim and the comfort of a few, and the debasement and defilement of the many, be curbed or, as I would have it, set aside entirely?

*New York, N. Y.*
*December 23, 1931*

# II. BLOODY GROUND

## by Lester Cohen

KENTUCKY is an Indian name. It means "the dark and bloody ground." It is a land of wild mountains and sudden, deep valleys. Its history is an endless repetition of wars between the mountain and valley peoples. Its soil is soaked in the blood of the Iroquois, the Shawnees, the Cherokees.

No one knows when the first white man came. Daniel Boone began his explorations in 1769. By 1774 he had founded Boonesborough. Within a few years he was marching into history, blazing the Kentucky trails, beating down the brush of the Wilderness Road, opening the way to the West.

Many men followed him. Some died the pioneer death of Boone, broken and alone on the banks of the Missouri. Others followed Lewis and Clark to Oregon. Still others scattered through the wilderness and settled at the cross-trails. Some stayed right over the great Gap of the Cumberlands, along the trail of Daniel Boone, in what became their native Kentucky.

The people who settled the breaks of the Cumberlands were of four principal stocks—English, English-Irish, Scotch Highlanders and Scotch-Irish. These were the peoples who contributed bold opinion and great brawn to the Anglo-Saxon tradition of human rights. These were the peoples who fought for the Great Charter, fought the English in Scotland, fought the English in Ireland, fought the Catholics, fought nobles and parliaments and kings, fought the French, the Dutch and the Spaniards—

These were the people who fought.

In America they fought the Indians, the wilderness, the French, the British. By 1792 they fought free of "Ferginia," declared themselves citizens of "Kaintuck" and entered the Union as the fifteenth State.

17

And kept on fighting.

They fought for manhood suffrage in a day when the ballot was the privilege of the landed gentry. They fought the Alien and Sedition Laws. They fought Federalism with the Kentucky Resolutions that first enunciated the doctrine of nullification. They fought the "revenoors." They fought the tariffs. They fought the Civil War.

Against the background of the slavery issue and the Civil War, Kentucky presented the tragic aspects of its inherent feudism. Henry Clay, the Kentuckian, torn within himself, made a warlike stand for compromise. When compromise failed, the Kentuckians, Abraham Lincoln and Jefferson Davis, boarded the ships of state. The grassland people were Democrats and Secessionists. The mountain men, then as now, were Union and Republican. But there were many exceptions in this land of exceptions, the records cite many instances of brother fighting against brother.

When they weren't fighting, the Cumberland people lived simple lives in the sparsely settled mountain districts. Because of their isolation, they had been allowed to preserve the last frontier. They were, in their way, lords of creation. They raised their own corn, brought down their own deer, mashed their own "mountain dew" and made their own law.

They remained a primitive people past the turn of the Twentieth Century. They spoke an Elizabethan English. They danced square dances. They gave their settlements such names as "Poorfolk, Poor Due, Looney Creek, Pine Knot, Sourwood, Coalville, Flat Gap, Lookout, Cannel City."

The great change that came upon them did not come through war or the law. It came through modern industrialism. The coal companies offered ready cash for mountaineer lands, and moved the people into the creek bottoms and towns. Soon they were paying rent, buying groceries and wearing "store clothes." When their ready cash dwindled—they went to work in the mines. And a free, primitive people had become the vassals of modern industrialism.

Today Kentucky is again a "dark and bloody ground." Harlan and Bell counties have heard the rattle of machine guns, the roar of dynamite, the curses of thugs, and the multitudinous voices of industrial warfare. And the mountain men, once more Union, Republican, and revolutionary—are leaving their blood to darken upon the ground.

For the pioneer peoples have become the rebellious protestants of His Majesty, King Coal.

# III. CLASS WAR IN KENTUCKY

## by Melvin P. Levy

SOUTH and east of Lexington, Kentucky, in the very corner of the State, shouldering Virginia and, on clear days, within sight of the mountains of Tennessee, the blue grass country crumbles into mountains. Here there are no more orchards, fields, cattle, or cities. On the hillsides are patches, half a city block in size, of corn and sorghums, tilled by men and women whose only tool is the hoe and who "cain't never live in towns because one leg gets shorter than the other from a-walkin' them tall hills." A county seat here, like Hyden, may be merely a court house, a general store, and a wooden house or two at the end of an almost impassable road. In these hills is Harlan County; and it, with part of Bell, part of Knox, a large bit of Hazard and some of Breathitt, composes the Harlan coal fields. In these hills, too, is one of the last strongholds of the pure old-American blood. Some of the first ancestors of the hill people drifted in almost 300 years ago. The greater part were headed through the Gap, into the plains beyond, during the first westward movement after the Revolution. They stopped because the country was full of game, because they liked mountains, because they were of a "droll"—which is to say a solitary—kind. Some stopped because of sickness or death along the way; but the greater part because they were not farmers and did not want to be. They were independent, solitary, pioneer.

Where they stopped they were marooned. No one came in after them, and they did not go out into the world. In these hills, and those of Virginia and Tennessee, is probably the last place in the United States where the Revolution is still vital. The people talk of Daniel Boone as if he were alive, but almost never of Hoover or Laval. Most of them have never seen a map, many never read a book. Among some of the miners Lenin has become a kind of hero. He is the "fellow who organized the miners up there in West Virginia, and he's with us." These are the men who, for generations, were known to the outside world only as feudists—rebels against the organized forms of justice, and as moonshiners in rebellion against the power of the State to tax them or to dictate to them. They are conscious of their dignity and power: they know their rights and what their rights *should* be, and they are quick to fight for them. They are aware of revolution and not afraid of it; and among them now revolution is beginning to boil again—perhaps a second American Revolution, based on coal as surely as the first was on trade, and growing out of a struggle between economic classes sharply defined.

Until 1910 no railway ran into Harlan County, which produces now its 20 million annual tons of high grade bituminous and is a stronghold of the Mellons, the Fords, the Insulls and the Peabodys as surely as of the Duncans, the Blankenships, the Napiers and Snavelys. It is still possible to see it as it must have been twenty years ago by traveling thirty miles past the United States Steel properties at Lynch to Hyden or Hindman, where folk still walk barefooted; ride, two to the horse, along the roads and trails; go out "to shoot a hawg for meat"; and can even dye, card and spin the wool they still use for blankets, if no longer for clothing. A Harlan County mountain man, now a miner who has fought through two strikes and one machine gun battle, who has joined in raiding company stores as one of a starved and embattled working class, has told me of kicking surface coal out of the front yard of his boyhood home while on his way to cut firewood, the only fuel his people knew.

In 1912 there were only five small coal pits in Harlan County, manned, I am told, chiefly by the families of the owners, and trucking the diggings to near-by towns. It was not until 1916 that the great development really began. The movement of capital from a North already showing signs of satiation to the semi-colonial South was accelerated by the War.

A few of the smaller operations here, particularly those outside Harlan County proper, are locally owned, but the greater
number and those representing the largest tonnage are the
property of great American corporations. Some are "captive,"
which is to say that the bulk of their production is not put on
the open market, but used by the parent company in the process
of further production. Others, like the Cincinnati owned Hall
group, are part of great wholesaling and retailing organizations.

With the entry of the great companies into the field, the
character of the country changed. The tiny farm holdings were
merged into great properties. Roads were graded, widened and
in some cases hard surfaced or paved above the streambeds
which had served to transport mountaineers ahorseback or afoot
since their first ancestors drifted into the country from "aholp-
ing General Washington." Railroads were pushed into the hills,
the tracks laid by men who might never have seen a locomo-
tive in their lives. Power lines were strung where kerosene
lamps had hardly penetrated. Great machines were lugged into
places where, a year before, horses could hardly travel, and
set to digging coal to be shipped north and to Europe.

During the five years between 1916 and the first post-war
panic in 1921, the population of Harlan County increased from
35,000 to 65,000 persons. The increase, however, did not come
from an influx of newer European stock, nor even from a
northern American emigration. It was drained from other,
near by, mountain sides and collected in little pools about the
new pit mouths. A Carolinian is still a "foreigner" in the
Harlan fields. In one mining town I was taken to see, as a
curiosity, a man "from Poland or some other far, far place
away." Even now, in spite of the new people in the county,
the effects of generations of clan breeding are visible. In one
place the long, straight noses, general throughout the mountain area are marred by a square rise at the tip; there are little,
local differences in speech.

2

In the first year of great mining operations conditions seem to have been pretty much those of a boom time almost anywhere. There were neither towns nor shops and the companies undertook to supply both. Commissaries were opened for the convenience of the mountain men. Temporary shacks were thrown up. They still remain, many of them untouched from that day to this. They are built of rough nine-inch lumber, some altogether without foundations, others set up on two-by-four stilts above piles of filth or pools of muddy water. All excepting those owned by a few of the larger companies are without paint and always have been. As I write I have a photograph before me of the interior of one of them. There is no furniture excepting one chair, two wooden boxes, a water pail turned end up for a seat, and, in one corner a bedspring without a mattress, covered with one quilt and a pile of old clothing. Here an employed miner, his wife and their two children sleep. In the foreground of the photograph is a pile of dirty clothes—dirty for three weeks, the mine woman told me, because in that time her husband has not made enough above his mine expenses and his cuts—fixed charges—to afford soap at the commissary.

In the beginning, however, conditions were different. Life was rough and hard, but wages were high and the new proletariat, urged to buy phonographs and pretties as well as grits and bacon at the company store, was pleased with possession and the assurance that once the wartime emergency was ended every inconvenience would be rectified. Still, they did become restive. In 1917 the United Mine Workers of America came into Harlan. There was a strike: the blacklist appeared for the first time in the Kentucky hills. But the operators were hungrier for men even than for the railway cars into which they poured the produce of their pits, on its way to Europe or the war-accelerated factories of the Great Lakes. A peace was patched up and contracts drawn between the operators and the union. Checkweighmen were put on every tipple; the right of the miners to trade in the towns springing up about every group of drift mouths was recognized; wages were high—a man could make seven or nine dollars in a ten or twelve hour day.

The condition, however, did not long remain. Almost from the first there was trouble. Checkweighmen, the miners charge, disappeared like magic from the tipples as soon as the strike was well over. Further walkouts were averted only because of the United Mine Workers' anti-strike policy. When the first contract was concluded another was drawn up and signed. But the operators seem to have had no will toward keeping it, nor the union toward enforcing it. It was at this time, or a little later, about 1922, that the first distrust of the Kentucky miners for conservative trade unionism was born. They say now that when a union representative came into the field, the miners never saw him until he had "seen the office." The union died away. It reappeared again in 1924, when United Mine Workers' organizers appeared in the Harlan fields, collected initiation fees from several thousand men and left them, bitter and suspicious, until the spring of 1931.

During these years, though, the operators were also beginning to suffer the results of an expansion made possible only by the War and contradictory to the logic of industrial development. Already in 1914, the use of oil and hydro-electric power was cutting into coal. There were enough pits open then to supply the world's needs for two centuries. But the War cut off the production of the British mines and at the same time increased the demand for fuel, both abroad and in this country. New fields were opened throughout the South, not only in Kentucky, but in West Virginia, Tennessee and Virginia. They were exploited hastily and wastefully. Where the coal appeared in several strata, as it often does here, only the lowest was taken, and still is. This makes for cheap production. It also means that when the operation is "pulled out," the geologic structure above is destroyed. The higher veins are broken. Millions of tons of high grade coal may never be recovered. In the same way, when the seams are mined, only the most accessible fuel is taken. The "pillars" which support the roof are left at the narrowest edge of immediate safety. The floor rises and the top sags; and when the mine is finally "robbed," the whole shaft collapses, making it impossible ever to enter it again, and leaving more millions of tons of coal, forever lost.

In fewer than ten years the Ford Motor Company stripped and destroyed a vast pit at Wallins Creek and left it, with broken upper seams and deserted houses. In such cases—and they have been numerous since 1924—the men and their families must move into other camps, many already overmanned, to enter into competition for what jobs there are, and to allow a steady cutting of wages and laboring conditions. It is impossible for them to return to the primitive mountain life. It is not only that their own pioneer-peasant attitude has been destroyed, but also that their "patches" have been lost or sold, often to coal companies. The prevailing wage scale leaves them penniless. I talked to a mine woman within a dozen miles of Harlan town whose husband had, for two years, been allowed a drawing account at the commissary instead of wages. During that time he had received no accounting of his earnings in the pits. I asked her why they did not leave.

"Man can't walk afar with five childer," she said.

There was a crisis in coal, then, eight years before that general in industry since the fall of 1929. The British mines reopened, to struggle bitterly for their temporarily neglected markets. Germany must pay reparations partly in terms of coal forced into international competition. The use of substitute fuels had advanced tremendously. White coal and petroleum were frequently invincible competitors in industry, on railroads and even in cellar furnaces. A rail-rate differential of thirty-five cents to the Great Lakes had once been an unfortunate incident to the Harlan fields. Now it was a calamity. Some mines shut down. Others worked when they could, absorbing, according to an official of the Harlan County Coal Operators' Association in a private conversation with me, the working population of the dead camps and using the labor surplus to cut wages and to extend hours. The captive mines have managed a fairly steady run. The others engage in a cat-and-dog competition for whatever market still remains. It is notable, however, that the salaries paid for owner-management appear to have remained fairly high, even though profits as such have been cut or even disappeared. It is something of a shock to see the large brick houses of coal operators in Knoxville, Coeburn or Harlan town and to compare them with the hovels, paperplastered against the winter, sometimes floorless, in which the miners live.

3

A definite downtrend in the Harlan coal production was visible in 1924. Three years later there was a threat of closing altogether the fields which should perhaps not have been opened at all, but which had already built towns and destroyed the primitive life of the hills; and into which millions of dollars' worth of equipment, rolling stock, railways and motor roads had already been sunk. Efforts were made to cut costs in the three possible directions: transportation, power and labor. (It is worth noting that no attempt has been made to solve the problem in any other way. No coal is transformed into power at or near the drift mouth. Mr. George Ward, Secretary of the Harlan County Coal Operators' Association, expressed to me complete ignorance of the chemical experiments made by British and some American operators. He also assured me that the only suggestion for cutting overhead past the mine camp has been his own for a coöperative sales organization. And this, he said, has so far failed because of "petty jealousy and mutual distrust.")

Of the three cost cutting paths only one has been found open. The thirty-five cent differential remains, even threatens to increase. Power, purchased from the Insull owned Kentucky Utilities Corporation, has shown little tendency to decrease in price. Wages and living conditions have absorbed the full burden. The man who, during the boom period, could work six days a week, now finds employment for one, two or four.

Wages were cut steadily—in some cases monthly—between 1924 and 1927. They were cut twice in the spring of 1931; and as I write this another cut, probably of twenty-five per cent seems imminent. Many men with families have been reduced to a total income of $4.00 or $5.00 a week. At Stearns, Kentucky, the wage is sixty to seventy cents a day. I have before me here a sheaf of more than one hundred monthly pay statements chiefly from the Old Straight Creek Coal Corporation. They list "cuts" for store, lights, rent, coal, smithing, doctor, burial fund and half a dozen less important items. The highest cash payment for a month's work is $18.82. In several the amount charged against the miner miraculously checks, to the last penny, with his earnings. One lists a deficit. This man, employed by the Clover Fork Coal Co., at Kitts, Harlan County, Kentucky, owed $3.24 for his work during the month of October, 1930. In another camp the miners are allowed a drawing account of $1.00 a day per family at the commissary, regardless of the number of men employed from the family. No wage accountings are rendered here.

But even worse, the miner says, than open wage cuts are those which are concealed in bookkeeping and which, at the same time more subtle and more drastic than the others, have reduced him to a position almost of chattel-slavery—certainly, in many cases, to peonage. There are the cuts which are made before the miner or his family may draw anything for themselves. First are the mine expenses—fuel for the lamp, explosives, and blacksmithing on his tools. Half a week's work may go to pay for these alone. Then there is rent—$2.00 a room, usually, for three, four or five rooms. The doctor bill is $2.00 a month whether the miner is sick or not. A Harlan miner commonly pays ten to twelve per cent of his total income for medical service. There is also a burial fund, usually from fifty cents to $1.00 a month, administered by the company and collected even where, as at a Straight Creek camp, no company funerals have been held for nearly a year. Since there have been no checkweighmen, too, wages have been cut at the drift mouth scales. A miner's daily production, during the boom period, was weighed and paid for at about twenty tons. It now averages ten or eleven in the same working day and, in many cases, in spite of the introduction of machine cutting and the substitution of electric for mule haulage. I have before me, for instance, a copy of a letter written by a miner still in the Harlan fields to another who has left, blacklisted, he tells me, for entering a compensation suit against his former employer over the loss of a finger in the pits.

"You remember those cars," it reads in part, "that used to weigh 2 ton and forty five hundred pound. They have shrunk now friend to about 3400 pound and sometimes just shade a ton."

But above all is the commissary, the company store, and scrip, its complement—a highly inflated private currency issued by the individual operator and valuable only at his commissary, though sometimes saleable to private speculators. In the months between the opening of hostilities between Harlan miners and operators in March, 1931, and the beginning of the winter, scrip fell on the local bourse from eighty or eighty-five cents on the dollar to forty or sixty cents.

The commissary is the center of the mining camp. It is also the center of the troubles which, since March, have led to one pitched battle, the death of a score of men, the beating of another score, more than two hundred arrests, two strikes and now, as I write, the prospect of another strike which will involve some 40,000 miners in Kentucky and others, perhaps, in Tennessee.

Typically, the commissary stands on the hillside at the level of the drift mouth and the tipple. Above it are the houses of the mine bosses and foremen. Below, are the railway siding, an old, bad wagon road and the hundred or two hundred miners' shacks, scattered haphazardly. Among them, perhaps, walks a pig or two and maybe a cow who has not had regular feed for months, who no longer gives milk, and who scratches the bare earth crazily with her snout, seeking to upturn a bit of green, for all the world like a hen scratching for worms. From some of the house chimneys there is smoke; and here youngsters, wearing cotton overalls, a shirt and, commonly enough, neither shoes nor underwear, are gathered against the cold. The store building is large and bare. It contains, beside the commissary, the company offices and the post-office. About it lounge some of the very beautiful, tall miner-mountaineers, with long slender faces and thick blond hair. There is also an occasional woman, belly distended and ugly, walking barefooted until late November, then with a pair of man's shoes tied about her feet.

It is to the store building the miner must come to get his job. If his friends from the outside want to visit him, he comes there for permission to have them. When he suffers a death in his family he must come there to arrange for burial. During elections he comes to the commissary to drop into the old-fashioned ballot box his vote for one of the candidates the companies allow him. If he receives mail, it is from the company clerk; and sometimes, he says, he receives it already opened, or not at all. Whatever he buys to eat or wear must come from the commissary. From my own observation and that of others who have published their findings, as well as from the sworn statements of miners and the admission of operators, company prices may be from thirty to one hundred per cent higher than those prevailing in private shops. A sixty- or sixty-five-cent bag of flour, for instance, is $1.20, or even $1.50 at the commissary. Fat back bacon, a chief article in the miner's diet, sells generally at eight or ten cents the pound. I found it at fifteen, sixteen, eighteen and twenty-seven in the company stores. The ordinary coarse shoes which sell at $1.98 in the towns are $5.00 at the camps. Eggs, at twelve and fifteen cents in the valleys, are twenty-two or thirty on the hillsides.

The miner, however, may spend no great part of his income with private merchants. If he does he is haled before the superintendent and discharged. The rule, it is said, is: "If you can buy cheaper elsewhere go and work there too." In at least one pay office there is a notice promising discharge to any family caught spending money off company grounds. I have here a letter sent from the superintendent of the Insull-Peabody,

Black Mountain Coal Company to one John Burton, a miner in their employ. It says:

DEAR SIR:

On checking our pay rolls and books in the store we find that you are not drawing very much scrip. *This is evidence to us that you are trading with the independent stores.* [The italics, of course, are mine.]

. . . We are furnishing you employment and pay you twice a month for your earned wages. . . .

I am sure that things can be adjusted and you will give us one-hundred per cent of your trade.

Another such letter expresses the wish that "we shall not be forced to discharge you for this cause."

An affidavit submitted to the Harlan investigating committee of which Theodore Dreiser was chairman, declares that in some cases it is possible to pay all the fixed charges of a mining operation through the income of the company store, and with receipts from compensation insurance, for which the miner pays monthly; but which he may not receive on pain of black-listing in the Kentucky fields. In many such cases, however, the injured man or his family receives extra credit at the commissary. In one camp I talked to a woman whose husband had been killed at work. She and her children were allowed $3,000 compensation, payable $33.00 a month, *in goods at the commissary.*

4

With the February, 1931, wage cut in the Harlan fields the miners became rebellious. Many were forced to sell off their furniture at this time or, if the installments were not completely paid, to let it go back to the stores from which it came. Pellagra increased and "flux" or "bleeding bowels" appeared— a form of dysentery to which children are particularly susceptible. The one camp of Cary, in which about 125 families live, averaged seven child deaths a week from this cause during the last summer. In none of the camps is there plumbing. In

some of the smaller there are no outhouses, or they are un-
usable. Here the effects of "flux" are sometimes visible in the
backyards—human excrement flaked with blood.

A few dues-paying members of the United Mine Workers
still remained in the Kentucky fields. With these as a basis,
organization was begun anew, at first without either connection
or aid from the parent organization. On the hillsides, in the
woods, and in the homes of miners, groups of men—white and
Negro—armed with rifles and the pistols which are more common in the Harlan camps than toothbrushes, drifted together
for whispered conferences and to listen to low voiced speeches.
In at least one case a machine gun nest was discovered, covering
the spot planned for a mine meeting. I have in my possession
a photograph of one gathering held in a barn that was blown
to bits by dynamite, not half an hour after the miners had
left it. The operators declared that no union would be allowed
in the Kentucky Hills. Judge D. C. "Baby" Jones, whose wife
is a member of the powerful Hall family of Harlan operators, defined union organization of any kind as a crime under
the Kentucky Criminal Syndicalism Law.

A group of Harlan miners called on William Turnblazer,
Southern Delegate of the United Mine Workers of America,
at his home in Jellico, to acquaint him with the process of
organization and demand assistance from the union, which now
came formally into the Harlan fields again. It was welcomed
by the miners and hated and feared by the operators, to some
of whom even company unions appear a subtle and dangerous
form of bolshevism.

Open union meetings were held. Hundreds of men with
known or suspected union affiliation were discharged and black-
listed. A group of thirty-five privately owned houses into which
they had moved after being "told off" the company property
burned simultaneously. A sealed boxcar came through Evarts
one April night, past the hillside where the pitched Battle of
Evarts would occur a few weeks later and the little, two cage
jail in which even then miners lay, confined by bear chains
about their necks. In the morning the property of the Black

Mountain Coal Company was paraded by a force of one hundred and fifty men, rifle armed.

In the meantime the union organization was proceeding rapidly. The miners demanded an immediate strike call. I talked of this, near Evarts, with a group of miners. One tall fellow made himself spokesman for the rest, as is the habit here, calling for frequent corroboration, interrupted by those who had additional detail. My notebook shows something like this:

"There wa'n't nothing else for us to do. There wa'n't nothing to eat. No man could play shut mouth here and lie by himself, alone and quiet. We was all marked. We made shift to set up nights with our guns out against them that thugged against us. I near to died for sleep.

"It was time for a fight while we still could fight and if we had to get along without the United Union, why then we had."

For the United Mine Workers steadfastly refused to issue the strike call. Relief was promised if the strike did come. In March, 1931, the Harlan miners came out on strike, a purely spontaneous affair, born out of misery and hunger, disease and physical and economic oppression. The United Mine Workers of America "wildcatted" the strike—declared it illegal, that is to say, and without benefit of support by the organization. The Red Cross, distinguishing between a natural calamity and a labor difficulty, moved out of Harlan County.

The decentralized nature of the struggle—which really, perhaps, should be considered many simultaneous strikes rather than one—makes it difficult to say precisely what the demands were. In general, however, these were common: checkweighmen and the testing of the scales at the driftmouth; abolishment of the cut for funeral expenses and, where they existed, the cuts for payment of a minister's salary and that of a school teacher, actually hired out of tax money; the payment in cash of disability insurance; freedom to trade in private stores; the abolishment of scrip; and a retraction of the last wage cut.

As for strike-relief—the men took it into their own hands. One miner found and repaired an ancient automobile and sent it out into Kentucky and the Virginia hills to beg among the farmers. Groups of miners descended on commissaries at night and raided them. One store was emptied three times in as many successive weeks. Sympathetic outsiders began to donate edibles. An Evarts shopkeeper gave the strikers a carload of flour. Immediately a Criminal Syndicalism warrant was sworn out against him and he fled the country.

On May 5 came the Battle of Evarts, in which something between four and eleven men were killed; during which machine gun, rifle and pistol bullets flew for half an hour; and as a result of which thirty-four men, all miners, were arrested and charged with murder.

5

During this whole period leadership was passing from the United Mine Workers. The refusal of the organization to legitimatize the strike or provide relief had, of course, much to do with this. But there are other reasons, some of them inherent in the whole history of the union. During the 1917 strike, as well as that in the spring of 1931, relief had been refused. When, in 1922, the Harlan miners again demanded a walkout, there had been no sanction for it. During the scandalous 1924 convention at Indianapolis, Frank Farrington, President of the Illinois section, openly accused President John L. Lewis of the United Mine Workers of America of having accepted a huge sum of money from Kentucky coal operators to avert the strike. Instead of denying the charge, Mr. Lewis entered a counter charge of bribery against Mr. Farrington in the case of the Vesta Strip Mine Company of Illinois. A Harlan citizen has made an affidavit in which he declares that, in 1928, during the great Pennsylvania-Illinois-Ohio bituminous strike he— then not a coal miner nor a member of any labor union— was paid $75.00 to go to the United Mine Workers' convention for the express purpose of voting Mr. Lewis a $3,000 increase in his annual salary.

And yet it is probable that, more than any of these things,

the entry of the National Miners Union into the Harlan field was responsible for the downfall of the older union there. The National Miners Union is a radical organization, affiliated with the Trade Union Unity League, and under Communist leadership. It entered the Kentucky fields early in June, after the Battle of Evarts, and at the request of a group of miners whose spokesman was one William Duncan, a highly skilled miner who at the time was a local organizer for the United Mine Workers of America. I have talked to Duncan about this.

"I'd go out and get the men into the Union," he said. "Everybody wanted action. Nobody could wait much longer. And every time I'd go to Turnblazer and tell him so he'd say, 'Now, Bill, wait just a little longer. This ain't no time for action, now.' Even after the strike had begun, Turnblazer, he'd just say, 'Not now, Bill. This ain't the time for action now. Just you go out and organize the boys—and don't forget to collect the dues.'

"I'd seen some copies of the *Daily Worker* and the *Southern Worker* (Communist labor publications) and I kinda liked the way they talked. I held a speaking with some other men and we sat down and wrote the *Daily Worker* to ask them for an organizer for us."

Soon after its entry into Kentucky the National Miners Union called a conference of Harlan miners *and their wives*. Here the following objectives were set: a $5.55 wage for day work inside the mines; a sixty-six cent tonnage rate (as compared to the seventy-four cent rate in effect here during the good times); two cents per ton extra for coal mined under difficult conditions or where there is much "dead work" to be done; rent of $1.50 per room per month (as compared to the present $2.00); the right of miners to choose their own doctor when ill; no cuts to be made from pay checks, the company to render bills instead; the maintenance of checkweighmen to be paid by the miners; the right to trade at any store whatsoever and the payment of all wages in cash; a day wage for laborers outside the pits of $4.75 a day.

To this program was affixed a comment, duly adopted:

"In drawing up these demands it was tried to fix it so that everybody would get about the same—not just the same, but so that a man getting a higher wage wouldn't refuse to fight alongside of him who gets less."

The growth of the National Miners Union has been amazing. As I write this a new strike call for this winter has been agreed to, under this leadership, by 8,000 of the 12,500 Harlan County miners and by 3,000 Bell County miners. The organization claims 40,000 adherents in the entire Kentucky field. The Lexington, Kentucky, *Herald* declares that papers and records seized by authorities indicate that there were more than 1,000 members of the Communist Party in Harlan County alone at the end of August of that year.

The causes for the success of the National Miners Union and the Communists in the Kentucky field are numerous. In the first place, as I suggested at the beginning of this article, is the character of the people themselves; but even more important is the character of the National Miners Union and the Communist approach. To this must be added a complete bankruptcy of faith in mine operators, the "law" [1] and conservative unionism. When the National Miners Union came into Harlan County it brought with it the Workers International Relief, which immediately organized five soup kitchens (one of which was later dynamited and another destroyed by rifle fire) and the International Labor Defense, which set about arranging the legal and public defense of the men and women held on murder and Criminal Syndicalism charges. On the left fork of Straight Creek, in Bell County, 500 miners organized themselves into a National Miners Union local and *then* notified headquarters. I asked one of the organizers how that came about.

"It's ourn, ain't hit?" he said.

Perhaps among the most successful of the National Miners Union and Communist tactics has been the organization of the women as well as the men. The United Mine Workers had

[1] A Harlan mine woman was asked what the "law" meant to her. "The law is a gun thug in a big automobile," she said.

many of the aspects of a secret lodge. Women were not supposed to be informed of impending strikes nor of the reason for them; and they resented it. In the National Miners Union conferences sit wives, daughters and sweethearts as well as miners.

Together with other invited guests I attended a mass meeting held at Straight Creek, under the auspices of the National Miners Union. The meeting place was a Baptist Church, bare to the rafters, floored with rough pine boards. Every seat was filled and so were the aisles. There were men and women, with their children in their arms. The place was lighted by a single electric bulb and the faces below it looked horribly thin. The chairman was a youth who had "never spoke to such a congregation as this here is, before. Never to so many folks."

An old woman got up to sing "a ballitt I have made myself and sung."

Another woman, whose husband was killed during the Harlan strike, rose. She said:

"My companion has darted in and out of his house; he daren't to take off his socks, nor to lie down in his house to rest. I hated for to give him up, but he died in a good cause. . . .

"The time was, when the men came off on strike and brought their dinner pail into the house we'd say: 'Now, John, take your dinner pail and get you back to work.' No, nor we wouldn't know the meanin' of the strike nor why. But now when our man comes in without a goin' through the driftmouth for demands we know that and tell him, 'John, lay down your dinner pail and the woman's section of the union will stand and fight with you until our kids is fed.' "

### 6

In Hazard County I talked to a group of miners and miners' wives, members of the National Miners Union who also professed a Communist allegiance. I asked them if, when they had won their wage increase and better living conditions, they would not be satisfied.

"No," a miner answered, "we won't. What we get we will have to fight for; and keep on fighting till there's no one left to fight against."

"But," I said, "the operators can show that they aren't making money either. In the office of this camp they told me that any wage increase must shut the mines and that no dividends will be paid this year in any case."

There was no answer for a long time. Then a woman spoke.

"If that's true," she said, "and I ain't saying it ain't, why then, by God, it's time for them to get out and leave us to take holt. We can't do worse than them and it may be we can do things a mite better. We'll try, sure enough."

# IV. ORGANIZING A UNION IN KENTUCKY

## by Charles Rumford Walker

THE unorganized coal areas of the south have always been strategic in the empire of coal—for both the miner and the operator. They are constantly throwing a monkey wrench of competitive uncertainty into the labor market and the coal market. Miners complain that as long as it is possible to ship non-union coal into a union market the union's wage scale is in jeopardy. The union operators point out that an uncertain wage scale means a chaotic price structure, cut throat competition and failures of mining companies, etc. The economists divide on the matter. Some say that the non-union mines keep wages and prices down to a reasonable level and so are desirable; others that they disorganize both wages and prices by underpaying and underselling. Whatever the views of others, Kentucky operators have with few exceptions been bitterly and successfully anti-union. Harlan County is the great coal county in Kentucky. In 1928, it produced 15,205,972 tons of coal or three times the amount of any other county. It has the reputation of being "the toughest spot to unionize" in the United States.

If the center of this committee's attention has been focussed on Harlan for obvious reasons, it is important to remember that the poverty-stricken condition of the Harlan miners is not unique. The wound has been opened, so to speak, in eastern Kentucky but the whole body of bituminous coal is sick. Wages in the industry as a whole have fallen to or below a subsistence level and living conditions as is inevitable have closely followed the degradation of pay. To quote Louis Stark, special investigator for the New York *Times:* "—in its broad essentials the plight of Harlan is the same as that of other coal areas with a few exceptions. . . . Change Harlan County to Hazard or Bell, and Kentucky to Virginia, or West Virginia, Alabama or Tennessee, and the general features of 'King Coal'—a very sick monarch indeed, will remain clear and visible."

It is instructive to examine the income of bituminous coal miners at the peak of American prosperity in 1929. Due to part-time operation so widely prevalent then, it was unexpectedly low. The average miner's income was $1,200 a year, or $23.00 per week. The Kentucky miner at the prosperity peak averaged $21.00 a week, and certain other states were even lower. Kansas was the worst. There at the peak of American prosperity, the Kansan miner earned $644.00 a year, or $12.38 a week. Since this boom era, the wages of bituminous miners have been repeatedly slashed, not only in tonnage rate but the number of days worked a year. Work time this year is 20 per cent lower than last, and last year's was 25 per cent lower than the year before. There are no recent figures available, but Louis Stark who collected data in several states reports a current wage of 80 cents to a dollar a day, and only a few days' work a month. In addition there are large numbers of entirely idle men living on union relief or starving. In Harlan County we found 3,000 blacklisted miners whose families were in complete destitution. This in general is the economic background for the history of the union in Kentucky.

The bitter illegal battle fought by the operators in Harlan which has received recent publicity is not a new tactic in Kentucky history. It is merely the intensification of traditional practices. Repeatedly the union has been rooted out of various counties and has never obtained more than a precarious foothold in any part of the state. This history is an interesting one and is important to an understanding of present-day Harlan.

Certainly as early as 1897 there was some trace of a miner's union in Kentucky, and between 1897 and January 1899 the men succeeded in organizing 18 locals with 2,000 members. By 1900, District 19 comprising Kentucky and Tennessee had been formed with 4,000 members and 36 locals. There were joint agreements with many operators, but the union met determined opposition in Hopkins County. Hopkins operators "paid whatever wages they chose and entered any market they desired." Peaceful overtures were refused and a strike called in November 1900 resulted in the importation of Negroes (as strike breakers) and the use of the injunction. The injunction in this case went so far as to *forbid the United Mine Workers of America to furnish strikers with food and supplies*. Not until 1908 did the organization consider the situation favorable enough to seek to gain a joint conference, but even then the efforts of the miners' leaders were not successful.[1]

It is interesting to note that Negroes as strike-breakers were again imported in the summer of 1931—in the modern instance under the protection of state troopers sent in by Governor Sampson of Kentucky. The injunction as a means of denying food to striking miners is a curious precedent to the newer method of using dynamite toward the same end. (See Committee's testimony on the destruction of the Evarts soup kitchen.)

From 1900 to 1920 the United Mine Workers of America grew vigorously in the rest of the country: from 250,000 in 1900 to the surprising total of 467,172 in 1920, at which figure it was the second largest labor union in the world. The organizing impetus which won this great strength made itself felt in Kentucky. For District 19 (Bell and Harlan counties and Tennessee) there were 5,957 unionists in 1920; for District 30 (Eastern Kentucky exclusive of Bell and Harlan) there were 1,280—note the small figures for Harlan—for District 23 (western Kentucky) 11,369. The total for Kentucky was 18,646. In the decade following 1920, the United Mine Workers in the county as a whole lost between 200,000 and 300,000 members. In Kentucky the union dwindled and became for all practical purposes extinct. Total figures for Kentucky on December 1, 1929, 1,501 out of a total of 62,195 miners in the state. I claim no precision for these figures. They are taken from the *Illinois Miner* for April 19, 1930, a paper published in opposition to the policies of President Lewis of the U. M. W. of A., and are designed to show the collapse

[1] Suffern, "Conciliation and Arbitration in the Coal Industry of America," p. 56.

of the union under his leadership. However both operators and unionists agree to the basic fact that the power of the union was broken in Kentucky in the decade from 1920 to 1930. The operators' story of the break is about as follows: "During boom times the men made so much money they forgot to pay their dues and so the union collapsed." When it was gone, the operators saw to it that it did not return. There seems to be good evidence, however, to show that union officials of the U. M. W. of A., in cahoots with the operators, or for financial reasons of their own, broke their own union. At the United Mine Workers' convention in 1920 a new Kentucky district was announced, District 30 (eastern Kentucky except Bell and Harlan counties). Samuel Pascoe was sent in by the union as "provisional president." [1] Pascoe promptly recalled all organizers from the field—against the wishes and repeated protests of his locals. In the end he revoked charters of the three locals which remained and made no further attempt to organize the field. [2]

These extraordinary tactics by a union president which appear mystifying to the outsider are easily explained by the coal miner. He asserts that either Pascoe himself was receiving a direct bribe from operators or that the national officials had previously made a deal with the coal owners. Indeed every old U. M. W. of A. man I talked with in Kentucky gave me a new story of a "sell out" by the officials of the miners' union. In the great coal strike of 1922 when the unorganized fields of Kentucky and other areas joined the union in a general walkout, Lewis left them out of the final settlement. The interests of nearly 100,000 men who had borne the hardships of the strike were "forgotten" at the council table. Certain direct

[1] John L. Lewis, President of the United Mine Workers of America, long ago initiated the "racket" of provisional Presidents for unorganized or semi-organized fields. These officials are not elected by miners but appointed by Lewis. They draw a handsome salary and are responsible solely to the President. Thus they furnish a convenient instrument for selling out the rank and file miner and insuring the power and affluence of the union's bureaucracy.

[2] Alonzo Walters, *Industrial Pioneer*, April, 1925.

testimony on the methods of U. M. W. of A. officials appears in a speech by the miner Donaldson at the Wallins Creek union meeting attended by our committee. The testimony is the more trustworthy in that Donaldson accuses himself of connivance with official corruption:

"The United Mine Workers in their day was a success but we got traitors in and they sold us out. I want to say that there is a delegate here that was in the Convention in 1927-28. At that time I was not a member of any union but I was sent down there to vote the Lewis issue, and they gave me $75.00. I took the money. The labor leader has led you into captivity. That's what they take the money for, and they have the money, and you have the beans and bread. . . . In that 1928 convention we voted a raise for Lewis from $8,000 to $10,000 and then he came back home and told the men that they would have to take a cut in wages!"

After 1920, the United Mine Workers made no real effort to organize a union in eastern Kentucky until the spring of 1931. The response was overwhelming. During the lean decade and especially in the preceding two years the condition of the miners had been degraded beyond description. Wages as we noted above had reached the starvation level of 80 cents to a dollar a day, and the time worked been reduced to a few days a month. Company cheating of tonnage weights and exorbitant prices for food at the company stores were prevalent. The unanimous conclusion reached by the miners was: "We starve while we work; we might as well strike while we starve."

On March 1, 1931, in Pineville, the county seat of Harlan, 2,000 miners attended a mass meeting called by the United Mine Workers of America. Miners tramped to the meeting from mining camps all over Harlan and from its adjoining counties. They came to hear Philip Murray, International Vice President of the United Mine Workers of America. He reminded them that their condition could not be more intolerable, and he told them that their sole hope lay in the union. As a result of this meeting held openly in Pineville, 200 men lost their jobs in the mines. The Black Star Coal Company fired 35 men for attendance, the Black Mountain Company, Insull and Peabody interests, cashiered 175.

A second mass meeting was held three weeks later at La Follette. The meeting was open, moderate and eminently respectable. The mayor introduced William Turnblazer, the President of the union District 19, and Turnblazer introduced Congressman J. Will Taylor who strongly urged the men to organize a union and fight for better living conditions. Turnblazer reported the inhuman hostility of the operators who had fired 200 men for attendance at the previous meeting. He added: "They did not stop with throwing them out of work. They made them vacate their homes during the worst weather of the season. They kicked out the entire families of any of the workers that went to that meeting." The United Mine Workers promised the miners support. They said: "If you will form a union with 10,000 dues paying members, we will give you food and money for a strike." In answer Harlan miners joined up in huge numbers. A man would pawn his rifle, I was told, or sell his overcoat if he had one, to get dues money. Then mine after mine through the spring months went on strike.

In April a meeting of miners was held on the lawn of the court house to protest against the wholesale evictions by companies of strikers and their families. "They starve us," said Bill Green, miner, "and then order us out of their houses. Do they expect us to live under brush heaps?"

On May 16th, a mass meeting of 800 was held in Bell County. Dwyer, International representative of the United Mine Workers, said the miners were not asking an increase in wages but merely the right to join the union, and to work without signing the "yellow dog contract."[1] He said if the mine guards were removed and the other terms met, peace would come to the coal fields in forty-eight hours. George Burchett of Harlan County urged the miners to quit and "not mine another ton of coal till the guards were called off." He asked

---

[1] In a "yellow dog contract" a miner is required to swear away his right to join a union as long as he remains in the company's employ.

for a vote of hands and most of those present held up their hands.

As no food came to them from the union they had just joined, stores and gardens were looted during this period by starving miners. The operators continued to fight the strike by evicting families of miners and by physical attacks by their deputies upon union men. On May 4th a union meeting was held and the delegates elected to go to Harlan to protest the tactics of the thugs and mine guards deputized by the companies. The delegates were instructed in particular to protest the actions of Deputy Jim Daniels and the threats of deputies "to shoot up the town of Evarts"; further, to ask Sheriff Blair to help in the avoidance of further shootings.

While this committee was interviewing Blair, the "battle of Evarts" occurred, in which several carloads of deputies near Evarts, armed with high powered rifles and machine guns, engaged in battle with a score of miners (the number is variously reported from 10 to 100). The battle lasted thirty minutes. One miner and three deputies were killed and wholesale arrests of miners followed. It is charged by the miners that the deputies at the time of the battle were bringing in scabs to work in the mines.

This episode brought Harlan into the limelight of national publicity. The Governor of Kentucky was called upon for troops, and promptly responded by sending 400 of the national guard into Harlan on May 6th. Before the troops came, William Turnblazer, union President of District 19 (Harlan and Tennessee) entered into an agreement with the Governor. He welcomed coming of the troops but insisted that "no transportation of outside or foreign labor be sent into Harlan and Bell counties while the troops are in the field." Food and relief were promised and it was agreed that all mine guards be disarmed and their commissions revoked. This agreement signed by two representatives of the Governor and by Turnblazer and two others representing the miners seems to have had little influence with the military command. During the stay of the militia, arrests of union leaders continued, outside scabs were brought into Harlan under guard, and deputies and mine guards continued their work as before.

On May 11th, five days after the arrival of troops, the Kentucky *News-Sentinel* reported that "nearly all of the mines in the county were idle because of a general protest strike in which the union seeks to have the mine guards removed." On the same day, Sheriff Blair was reported in an Associated Press dispatch as saying that he *knew of no agreement whereby state troops replaced mine guards.* He stated that he had no intention of relieving deputies in charge of guards at coal mines.

On May 16th, a new and valuable weapon fell into the hands of the operators. A raid by Sheriff Blair on the U. M. W. of A. union at Evarts revealed that the local had an I. W. W. membership and had applied for an I. W. W. charter. The "wobbly" membership was a sort of inner group which had been operating behind the regular local, using the latter as a screen. The Dreiser committee investigated the strength of I. W. W. membership in Harlan and found it to be about 200, but despite this small membership this discovery of a clandestine "red" organization put a weapon of great strength into the coal owners' hands. All union organization work in eastern Kentucky was promptly branded "red" and propaganda and action to root out the "red menace" begun. Tom Connors, representative for the I. W. W., was beaten up by Sheriff Blair personally in the Sheriff's office and "taken for a ride" across the border.

During these spring months over 11,000 miners had joined the United Mine Workers Union and paid dues to it. Most of them had gone out on strike. They were now told by the union officials to go back to work, that they could expect no food or money from the union, that they were out on a "wildcat" strike. To the miners it was clear that the Governor had "let them down" in the affair of the troops, and that the union had "sold them out."

At this point the National Miners Union entered the field. The miners were ready to welcome it. On June 19th, Dan Brooks, organizer for the N. M. U. entered Harlan, and on

June 30th, Jessie Wakefield for the International Labor Defense began relief and defense work for the families of the arrested miners. The National Miners Union spread through eastern Kentucky with extraordinary rapidity. Within a few weeks of the arrival of the first organizer there were 4,000 members. On July 2nd, the N. M. U. held its first general committee meeting under cover, with fifteen delegates present, representing groups in 10 mines. The committee voted to send delegates to the July convention of the N. M. U. in Pittsburgh, and from July 11th to 18th, 28 delegates from Harlan County attended the convention. The story of Harlan from that date to the present is the story of the concerted drive of the operators to break up the National Miners Union. By the use of successive regiments of deputized thugs, by firearms and dynamite, by the use of the courts, county officials and police, and by the suppression or intimidation of the press, the operators conducted their warfare on the union. In spite of this, however, the legal process of organizing the miners of Harlan County into the union of their choice continued.

The union formed women's auxiliaries to aid in organizing relief; soup kitchens were set up, and new N. M. U. locals formed. In many instances locals of the U. M. W. of A. came over intact. The operators opened their attack shortly after the Pittsburgh convention. On July 20th there was a raid on the home of Bill Duncan, Pittsburgh delegate. On July 23rd, Jessie Wakefield's car was dynamited during the night. On July 25th, twenty-eight additional thugs were imported, increasing the force to sixty-five. The operators were thoroughly aroused and ready to fight with every weapon at hand. A report went about that orders had been given to the new thug army to "shoot, kill and slay four red leaders" in Harlan County, and that they were to do this within two weeks *or it would be too late to stamp out the N. M. U.*

On July 26th, the union held a picnic attended by 2,000 miners, their wives and children, at which open speeches were made. Eleven heavily armed deputies came to the picnic but left. The miners had armed themselves.

Instances of brutality to union leaders, intimidation of newspaper men, etc., which was characteristic of this period have received attention in other portions of the committee's record. On the whole the operators' drive succeeded in putting the union underground, but did not prevent its rapid growth.

It is interesting that on July 30th Judge Howard in a labor case found occasion in court to condemn roundly the N. M. U. and to offer words of praise and defense for the United Mine Workers of America. Only a few months before this in the spring of the year he had condemned the U. M. W. of A. and warned the miners against it. This about-face we found characteristic of operators and officials in Harlan. Now that the U. M. W. of A. was dead in Harlan, the corpse came to be spoken of with touching respect by its old enemies.

From July 30th to August 3rd there were strong efforts on the part of the operators to prevent the holding of a state convention of the N. M. U. at Wallins Creek. Wholesale raids on miners' homes were accompanied by a great deal of illegal searching of automobiles. The convention was held however on August 2nd, in spite of the terror which had led up to it. Miners guarded the entrance to Wallins Creek and 500 negro and white elected delegates were present including women. Late at night after the convention two carloads of N. M. U. men were arrested and personal property taken from them. The arrest was without warrant or provocation.

On August 10th, the Evarts soup kitchen was dynamited. This was one of the seven maintained by the N. M. U. Shortly after the dynamiting, Finley and Caleb Powers who were guards at another soup kitchen were arrested on charges of "banding and confederating." They were unarmed and at the time of their arrest were fixing the fires for the next day's cooking. Other acts of terrorism committed against the union are to be found elsewhere in the committee's record. Their repetition here is unnecessary: they did not succeed in halting the spread of the union.

At this writing, December 16th, an N. M. U. convention

has just been held in Pineville and voted for a general strike in eastern Kentucky to be called for January 1.

The conclusion of this history may be briefly summarized as follows:

That since the beginning of coal mining in Kentucky operators and the government have ruthlessly resisted organization with every means in their power.

That the present terror is an intensification of traditional policies.

That the miners of eastern Kentucky organized themselves last spring into the United Mine Workers of America.

That every weapon legal and illegal was brought to bear against this union.

That the United Mine Workers of America "sold out" the miners in the spring of 1931.

That after the "sell out" the National Miners Union entered the field and organized the miners of Harlan and Bell counties.

That the operators fought the N. M. U. as they had fought the U. M. W. of A. with the courts and with illegal violence.

That in addition to the traditional means of intimidation the operators have adopted the "red menace" as a weapon to beat the union and starve the miners. That they use this as a shield for illegality and claim that they have always fought only the "red union" and not the U. M. W. of A. in contradiction of their acts of terror last spring.

That in the face of bitter opposition the N. M. U. has succeeded in organizing the coal fields of eastern Kentucky and proposed to fight against starvation for checkweighmen, a living wage, decent living conditions and a recognition of the union.

The attitude of the miners toward their new union we found to be one of intense loyalty. It was well summarized by the miner Donaldson in his speech at Wallins Creek. Speaking of the plight of the coal miners he said: "the National Miners Union is ready to handle it, to give you the same living conditions you had before the government put in these laws that were unjust. [He has in mind the Criminal Syndicalism statute which is the operators' easiest legal weapon against the formation of a union. See the chapter on legal terror.] The National Miners Union stands for the principles that our forefathers fought for us. . . . I know some time men will have to make a complete sacrifice; hundreds of men's lives will be sacrificed but nothing good ever came without somebody making a sacrifice. . . . The National Miners Union is the only thing that has not failed us."

# V. WHO OWNS THE MINES?

## by Anna Rochester

BIG capital had taken possession in the wild mountain valleys of eastern Kentucky before 1914. During the war and since the war it has strengthened its hold over a steadily increasing area. Today Wall Street and capitalists in Chicago, Detroit, Baltimore and Cincinnati dominate the coal fields of Harlan and adjacent counties. Morgan, Insull, Mellon and Ford are strongly entrenched in Harlan County; Rockefeller and Mellon companies are important producers in the mountains northeast of Harlan. The Morgan empire includes the railroads that carry out the coal. Morgan and Insull utilities between them supply the light and power for eastern Kentucky.

Things began to happen in 1910. Coal had been mined before then along the few railroad lines that were running through eastern Kentucky. But the Louisville and Nashville crossed Bell County to Pineville and, avoiding Harlan, went southeast into Virginia through Cumberland Gap. The Chesapeake and Ohio had been gathering coal cars along the track from Elkhorn City to Ashland, but the winding narrow valleys from which coal is now fed to that older line were still unexploited wilderness. The rich coal seams of Harlan and Hazard and most of the present Elkhorn field were undisturbed because there were no railroads to connect the coal beds with the outside world.

### MORGAN ENTERS HARLAN COUNTY

Before 1910 the long arm of big business had reached in to Harlan County. The Wisconsin Steel Co., a subsidiary of the Morgan-McCormick International Harvester Co., had bought up 22,500 acres in the remote northeastern corner. So in 1910 the Louisville and Nashville Railroad, which behind its Baltimore "control" had—and still has—the solid financial backing of the House of Morgan, was quite ready to take stock in a little company building an extension from the Louisville and Nashville line into Harlan County. It was certainly not by chance that the new line followed the Poor Fork valley most of the way and turned off from it just in time to touch the International Harvester properties—and stop there.

Only a few years later, during the war, Morgan's United States Steel Corporation through its subsidiary, United States Coal and Coke Co., Inc., began to buy up coal lands alongside the domain of International Harvester. Acres were added as the years went by, until this property in Harlan County and over the mountain in Letcher County has become an important part of the immense coal reserves and coal production of the United States Steel subsidiaries. On the Letcher County side the property is still undeveloped, but in 1930 over one-tenth of the steel corporation's coal came from its Harlan County mines at Lynch, and one-fifth of the Harlan County tonnage came from this domain of United States Steel.

Louisville and Nashville (having absorbed the little local railroad company in which it had always held stock) carried out over 3,160,000 tons of coal from these two Morgan strongholds at Benham and Lynch in 1930. From Harlan County as a whole it carried out over 13,000,000 tons.

Small by comparison with the operations at Lynch but still an important part of the Morgan hold on Harlan County is the Kentucky King mine at Wallins Creek. This was started by Kentucky capitalists during the war boom and was taken over in 1923 by the Utilities Coal Corp., as a "captive" mine to produce coal for public utilities. In 1929, these utilities and their "captive" coal property became part of the Morgan system in the section organized as Commonwealth and Southern.

## INSULL UTILITIES AND INSULL COAL

In Harlan County itself, light and power are sold not by a Morgan utility but by the Insull system, for the belt of Insull light and power companies which crosses the center of Kentucky ends with a flourish in the Harlan valleys. Incidentally it is worth noting that Insull utilities supply Mt. Sterling and Winchester, the towns to which mine strikers indicted on murder charges were transferred for a "fair" trial.

Black Mountain Corporation, one of the large coal companies in Harlan County, has been an Insull property ever since it began to produce just after the war. In 1928, when the Insull coal properties were reorganized, control was formally transferred to Peabody Coal Co. The Black Mountain mines in Harlan County and the Peabody Coal Co. mines in Pike County are part of a network of coal properties in Illinois, West Virginia, Indiana, and Oklahoma. While Insull and Morgan are battling for control over utility systems, the Insull-controlled Peabody Coal Co. is operating mines of the Morgan-controlled Erie Railroad in Pennsylvania. Against workers who protest against starvation wages, these two strong groups put up a united front.

## MELLON AND FORD

The Mellon family went into eastern Kentucky in 1913, when the Pittsburgh Coal Co. bought a few thousand acres. Pittsburgh Coal has in recent years been disposing of most of its Ohio properties and concentrating production in a few big mines in the Pittsburgh district. But the company keeps its foothold in Kentucky through a subsidiary, the Pike-Floyd Coal Co., which in 1930 produced a mere 340,000 tons in Floyd County.

Mellon coal mining interests outside of Pennsylvania have been developed chiefly through the Koppers Company, a holding company with many subsidiaries,—utilities, coke, tar, and coal. As one of its coal properties, Koppers bought the Elkhorn Piney Coal Mining Co., operating in West Virginia and in

Floyd County, Kentucky. Through another subsidiary, Koppers had acquired the big Kayu mine at Coxton in Harlan County, which was later transferred also to Elkhorn Piney Coal Mining Co. Even before the Mellon company acquired Elkhorn Piney, it had been a "captive" property, owned jointly by Milwaukee Gas and Coke Company and by Youngstown Sheet and Tube Company and mining coal for their use.

Another first-rank capitalist operating in Harlan County is Henry Ford who went into Kentucky and West Virginia coal after the war. In Harlan County he bought from local (Virginia) interests two large mines on Wallins Creek, but his main Kentucky coal properties are in Pike County, in the upper part of Pond Creek which is closer to bloody Mingo County, West Virginia, than to any other coal field in Kentucky.

PREPARING THE WAY FOR ROCKEFELLER

North of Harlan County also, 1910 was an important year, for Consolidation Coal Co. began some big buying at low prices in Letcher, Pike, and Knott counties. C. W. Watson, who was shortly afterwards sent to the Senate from West Virginia, and A. B. Fleming, an ex-governor and judge in West Virginia, and a group of their friends in that state and in Baltimore dominated Consolidation Coal Co. at that time. The company had a profitable history of 45 years and had won a place on the big board of the New York Stock Exchange. It had already expanded from the coal fields of western Maryland into the Fairmont field of West Virginia and Somerset County, Pennsylvania. In 1910, these gentlemen drove a sharp bargain for 100,000 acres in eastern Kentucky, paying one dollar an acre in cash and $44 an acre in new stock, issued against the profits to be made from the coal miners who would ultimately produce about 9,000 tons of coal from each acre of land.

Railroads stopped many miles short of the new Consolidation Coal territory. But the Jenkins family (who were heavily interested in Consolidation Coal) and their friend Henry Walters were important stockholders in Louisville and Nashville Railroad, and the Wall Street backers—Morgan and Belmont—were ready to oblige. For coal carrying is one of the most profitable railroad operations. So a Louisville and Nashville subsidiary built a 100-mile extension from Jackson, Kentucky, through Perry County (the Hazard field), to the western valley of the Consolidation Coal domain in Letcher County. Consolidation itself built a shorter new line from the eastern side of the mountains down to Shelby Junction which was taken over first by the Baltimore and Ohio and later by the (Morgan-controlled) Chesapeake and Ohio.

Senator Watson and his friends kept on buying coal lands in eastern Kentucky and West Virginia. In 1915 they set up the Elkhorn Coal Corporation to combine small companies they had organized outside of Consolidation Coal and to hold a big minority block of Consolidation Coal Co. stock. C. Bascom Slemp, a Virginia member of Congress at that time and later secretary to Calvin Coolidge, was in Watson's Elkhorn Coal group. So were—and are—J. C. Fenhagen, partner in the Baltimore banking house of Robert Garrett and Company, and J. N. Camden who was for a brief term a senator from Kentucky.

Just after the war, the Rockefeller family, well pleased with their coal and iron company in Colorado—where women and children of strikers' families were massacred at Ludlow in 1914 —secured an interest in Consolidation Coal. Gradually they acquired control. For some years the company has been cross linked with Standard Oil of New Jersey through Walter C. Teagle, and with the Equitable Life Assurance Society and Chase National Bank through Thomas I. Parkinson. A vice-president of (Morgan's) Bankers Trust Company and a Baltimore banker—Bladen Lowndes—also sit on the board of directors.

Elkhorn Coal Corporation still owns a minority block of Consolidation Coal stock. The two companies no longer have any directors in common, but both are linked with the Fidelity Trust Company of Baltimore.

Consolidation Coal Company is the largest producer of

eastern Kentucky coal, and in 1930 about one-third of the Consolidation Coal Company tonnage came from its Kentucky mines. It is the one large producer in Johnson County; Consolidation Coal and Elkhorn Coal Corporation dominate Letcher County (although the undeveloped reserves of U. S. Steel will be important there also as time goes on); and Elkhorn Coal Corporation mines, Mellon mines and Inland Steel Company mines produce more than half of the Floyd County tonnage. Consolidation Coal Company and Elkhorn Coal Corporation are even more important than appears from their own tonnage, as both lease coal properties for operation by other companies, but names of lessees and their Kentucky tonnage are not published.

## OTHER INTERESTS

These few companies do not complete the list of outside capital "interests" that have gone in to draw profits from the low-paid Kentucky miners and the fine quality of eastern Kentucky coal. King Harlan Company is linked with Detroit Edison Company; Utilities Elkhorn Coal Corporation (in Floyd and Pike counties) is owned by Utilities Power and Light Corporation, one of the smaller utility systems, close to the Byllesby group; Wheeling Steel Corporation has taken over the Portsmouth By-Product Coke Company in the eastern part of Pike County; General Refractories Company has a mine in Carter County.

In the Hazard field (Perry County) no outstanding powerful corporations are operating, but smaller outside capital controls nearly two-thirds of the tonnage. These outside companies include Blue Diamond Coal Company (Cincinnati) which produced over 900,000 tons from its Perry County mines in 1930, along with smaller output in Harlan County and in Tennessee. Columbus Mining Company and Daniel Boone Coal Corporation are owned by a Chicago group which has a small mining company in Indiana. Hatfield-Campbell Creek Coal Company and Lincoln Coal Company are headed up in Cincinnati, by a group active also in West Virginia mining. Kenmont Coal Company and Blue Grass Mining Company are controlled in Toledo, and Carrs Fork Coal Company in Portsmouth, Ohio.

McCreary County, west of Bell and Whitley counties, is the domain of Stearns Coal and Lumber Company, a Michigan concern.

But still the list of outside companies is incomplete. Broadly it can be stated that at least two-thirds, and probably more, of the eastern Kentucky tonnage is controlled outside the state. Most of the small properties and a few large companies are still controlled by Kentucky and Tennessee capitalists.

Among these "native" companies, the Mahan group is most important. No one of the Mahan companies came into the half-million ton class in 1930, but the eleven of them together produced over 2,000,000 tons in eastern Kentucky (apart from the tonnage of two or three others in Tennessee). As a group they ranked third in the eastern Kentucky list: with U. S. Coal and Coke Co. (U. S. Steel), second, and Consolidation Coal Co. at the top. Next larger of the local companies (by 1930 tonnage) was Ambassador Sackett's Black Star Coal Company in Harlan County. This together with his Pioneer Coal Company in Bell County produced over 900,000 tons in 1930. About the same size as Black Star is the Harlan-Wallins Coal Company, with its three mines near the Ford properties on Wallins Creek and one mine in Bell County. This is closely owned in Nashville, Tennessee. Of special importance to the miners is the Three-Point Coal Company controlled by the Hall family one of whom married Judge D. C. Jones, the bitter enemy of the miners.

## PROFITS DRAWN FROM KENTUCKY MINERS

That the capitalist class has had a "good thing" in eastern Kentucky coal is beyond question. Workers in Kentucky coal mines have been paid always less than mine workers in any northern state. Wage-cutting drives have pulled down the northern wages and reduced the difference, but eastern Kentucky wages have been pushed down also and kept below the northern figures.

Eastern Kentucky coal is of high quality and holds its market. Until 1929 production was on the upgrade in the Harlan and Elkhorn fields and in West Virginia,—their coals displacing more and more of the northern coals. This helped to create a crisis in the coal industry before the general crash of 1929, but it put money in the pockets of companies operating in Kentucky.

Exact profits from eastern Kentucky coal are hard to trace. The smaller companies publish no financial statements. In the statements of the larger companies, coal mining in Kentucky cannot be separated from coal mining elsewhere. And profits of "captive" mines usually disappear in the accounts of the owning corporations. When a steel making subsidiary of United States Steel Corporation buys coal from a coal-mining subsidiary, there may be no "profit" in the transaction, but the coal miners have nevertheless contributed to the profits of the United States Steel Corporation. Or a utility company may pay its subsidiary a maximum price for coal and cover this "expense" with high rates for electric current.

Reports of Consolidation Coal Company and Elkhorn Coal Corporation show a decline in "profits" on their stock in recent years. But these "profits" are complicated by bond issues, depletion reserves, and depreciation accounts,—all of which involve payments of millions for the immediate or ultimate advantage of the capitalist class. Going back of the "profits" or "net loss" on stock, we find that Consolidation Coal Company had an "operating profit" of $3,000,000 to $4,000,000 a year up to and including 1930. Peabody Coal Company has had a net "operating profit" of over $2,000,000 a year. Elkhorn Coal Corporation (which is now in receivership) did a $4,000,-000 business in 1930 and cleared an "operating profit" of $600,000. But these companies are attempting to squeeze from the labor of their miners a return for capital invested in immense reserves good for 100 to 300 years. Also, the recent decline in stockholders' profits has followed years of rich pickings for the capitalists. If Senator Watson, for example, held his block of stock in Consolidation Coal Company from 1905 to 1925, his holdings were almost doubled by stock dividends, and in the course of the 20 years he had drawn at least $173 in cash for each $100 share he had had in 1905.

Now when the operators talk of hard times, the eastern Kentucky miners can remember that they have always paid a heavy toll to the capitalist class while endangering their lives and earning a near-starvation wage in the coal mines. And in fighting against further wage cuts and unemployment, they are doing battle with outposts of the strongest forces in the capitalist world.

# VI. THE LAWLESSNESS OF THE LAW IN KENTUCKY

## by Arnold Johnson

HARLAN COUNTY stands with Sacco-Vanzetti, Mooney-Billings, Centralia, Imperial Valley, Patterson, Lawrence, Scottsboro, and innumerable historic cases, revealing the so-called due processes of law as tools turned against that portion of the working class which has revolted against the paternalistic dictatorship of the capitalists. This is evidenced in the personnel as well as in the activities of these so-called duly constituted authorities.

Immediately after the Evarts battle of May 5th, in which three deputies and one miner were killed, Judge D. C. Jones called a special grand jury to investigate the lawlessness in Harlan County. I am told that in the picking of this special grand jury the Judge deliberately passed up name after name from the jury wheel until he came to the man that he wanted. That man promptly went into the grand jury. And the result was a grand jury chosen to do just what it did do. The wife of Judge Jones has vast mining interests. His brother-in-law is one of the operators of Harlan County. The Judge himself was elected as an operators' man.

Near Evarts a crime had been committed. In Evarts were a number of union leaders. Combine the circumstances. Let the union leaders burn for the crime, not because they committed the crime, but because they were union leaders.

Thirty men were indicted on three charges of murder each; thirty indictments were made on a conspiracy law, "banding and confederating," and one for criminal syndicalism. Not a single indictment was made on the other side! Sacco-Vanzetti and Mooney-Billings on a wholesale scale!

Without hearing any testimony as to guilt or innocence or the amount of existing evidence, Judge Jones held without bond throughout the summer all the men indicted for murder. Exorbitant bail was demanded of the others. Keep the strike leaders in jail and break the strike!

The third act of the Judge was in the selection of the regular grand jury for the August term of court. The law of Kentucky provides that the jury wheel shall be kept in the office of the Circuit Court Clerk. The Clerk shall keep the key to the office and the judge the key to the wheel. The present Clerk is about the only Harlan official who is in sympathy with the miners. Accordingly, the wheel was taken from the Clerk's office to the Judge's private chambers and kept there all summer. The result was another operators' grand jury which brought scores of indictments against labor leaders, mostly for "criminal syndicalism," but also for "murder" and "banding and confederating." Scores of acts of violence were committed against miners. Yet all but one of the indictments were against them.

The Judge then refused to vacate the bench and to permit a special judge to be appointed to hear the cases. This he did in spite of affidavits signed by the defendants giving definite reasons why they believed Judge Jones to be unfair and prejudiced. Thus it was he who ruled on motions of the Commonwealth for the change of venue which transferred the murder cases of twenty-two men from Harlan to Clark and Montgomery counties, from the mountains to the blue grass area, whose farmers look upon mountaineers generally as little more than white trash and murderers. From the prejudiced farming group a jury was drawn. Was this transfer by Judge Jones in the interests of justice? Then too, the cases were transferred to a point 150 miles distant, and at the time of the transfer the miners were forced to pay for the transportation and expenses of all their defense witnesses. They were already penniless, their families already starving. Was that transfer just?

Again, the Judge called prisoners, some of whom had spent more than five months in jail without trial on trumped-up charges, and made in effect the proposition: "Quit this union and you can go at large." In other words he ordered the men to sell their brains as well as their bodies and labor to the bosses—or stay in jail and let their families starve. Judge D. C. Jones—operators' ace against the workers!

Sheriff John Henry Blair, familiarly called by his first two names, obtained his office by means of high-handed politics as an operators' man. For a period of time he lived entirely within his office, sleeping on a cot, having his meals served to him, with a bodyguard to watch over his safety. Both Judge Jones and Sheriff Blair maintain that the Evarts battle of May 5th was a trap for the sheriff.

However, the high sheriff is only a leader for a vast army of deputies, comparable to the Coal and Iron Police of Pennsylvania, an army not of his own creation, but built up over a period of years. According to one official, operators carefully watch the criminal dockets, pick out the crudest and most fearless murderers, and then do them some favor in court or after conviction. From then on these criminals are in debt to the operators and may be called upon in times of crisis. The official from whom this admission comes has also stated that two men were pardoned from the West Virginia Penitentiary in order that they might become "thugs" in Harlan County.

Deputy Bill Randolph provides a good example of the type of thug which makes up this army. Facing a fourth murder charge in another Kentucky county, Randolph was released by the operators on $25,000 bond to become a thug or "deputy" in Harlan. He killed his fifth man by shooting Chasteen, a union sympathizer, *in the back*. He was indicted by the regular grand jury—the only indictment brought against the operators' side. But he was cleared in the Harlan Court on a plea of self-defense.

Twenty-eight gunmen were imported into Harlan on July 25th. Most of them were from Breathitt County and bore the reputation of professional killers, being willing to work for $50 the job. They raised the total of deputies working in the open to 65. Some 150 to 200 are working under cover. This grapevine of spies is a difficult machine. A president of the U.

M. W. of A. local at Evarts was at the same time an undercover man for the sheriff. Another deputy carried credentials from Chicago as an I. W. W. organizer. Some place the number of armed deputies into the hundreds and as high as a thousand.

The joker in this army of deputies is a chap from Chicago, supposedly one of Al Capone's gang. In the earlier stages of open warfare, he came to Harlan as a munitions salesman. He sold the sheriff nine machine guns, a quantity of tear gas bombs, steel breast plates, and other implements of modern warfare. Later he was made a deputy—even though the law provides that one must be a resident of the State for one year before becoming a deputy—in order that he might show others how to use all this machinery for human destruction. And they used it!

Commonwealth Attorney Will Brock bears the reputation of "selling out." Affirming that he was elected by the miners and that he would remain loyal to their cause, he posed as a champion of their rights. Declaring that the special grand jury of May was an illegal operators' body, yet he signed the indictments it brought. Condemning the Judge with extreme vulgarity on the one hand, he himself still played the hand of the operators to the limit. His main concern was to keep his brother, Hiram Brock, in the office of State Senator. When the first of August arrived and his brother was elected by the crudest political robbery in the history of Harlan, Will Brock openly took his stand with the Judge on the operators' side. Earl Brock, son of the Commonwealth Attorney, is a deputy sheriff.

Previously Will Brock had announced that he would not consent to the scattering of miners' cases to the far parts of the State so as to make justice virtually impossible, but with the convening of the August term of court he became an ardent advocate of injustice by arguing for the change of venue, revealing thereby his boundless ignorance of facts and labor organizations. His was a plea which made the miners feel the cold chill of death. To him, as well as to other officials, the joining of a union, especially the National Miners Union, was an act of criminal syndicalism. To him, possession of a copy of the *Daily Worker* was not only criminal syndicalism, but also such a breach of peace as to warrant placing of a $5,000 peace bond against a miner to keep him in jail. To "keep up the hopes of the miners" and to seek adequate defense counsel was criminal syndicalism and disturbing the peace. For outside reporters to tell the facts of Harlan called for a threat of jail sentence in open court.

Not only was Brock a party, together with the Judge, in making propositions to release men illegally arrested upon their promise to leave the county or give up union activities, but also in bargaining with men to turn state's evidence. Thus eight men facing triple murder charges were offered the chance to sign an affidavit stating that Judge D. C. Jones was a fair and impartial man and that justice could be obtained through him, thus insuring their freedom upon being tried in Harlan Court. These eight men, with twenty-two others, had previously signed an affidavit declaring Judge Jones to be unfair and prejudiced. Six of the eight fell into the trap. The other two refused to sell out.

When Pless Thomas, one of these last two, reaffirmed his belief that Judge Jones was prejudiced and refused to sign the new affidavit, the prosecutor stated that they could not promise him a release. Thomas demanded to be taken back to jail. The courage of this small, frail miner who is suffering from asthma and at that time showed signs of rapidly developing tuberculosis, is deserving of admiration. His family of six starves and freezes. With his trial now postponed until next April, he is doomed to rot in jail for a year or more without trial.

But the men who sold out to the prosecution by signing the statement are caught fast in a trap. They are being used as weapons against other men. Those who signed are: J. W. Holdsclaw, with a family of eleven; Tom Hicks, a family of six; C. O. Chamblee, a family of eight; Charley Bradley, a family of nine; Lloyd Gilbert and Marion Hensley. Lloyd Gilbert, who is comparatively well off financially, was arrested and charged with murder when he came to the courthouse to provide bond for one of the other men. Starving families increase the desire for freedom. Marion Hensley was the first and most enthusiastic signer of the previous affidavit declaring Judge Jones to be unfair. Was it a mere coincidence that two others who turned state's evidence earlier, Hugh and John Lester, known as professional "lie swearers," were acquitted by the Harlan Court of another murder charge which had nothing to do with the labor case?

Fred Jones, special assistant to Will Brock in the prosecution, has gained the reputation of being the special frame-up man. When a comment to this effect appeared in one of the labor papers, he shouted out in court a threat to bring the "law" against reporters. It is not surprising to learn that Fred Jones is special assistant prosecuting attorney in all of the labor cases and at the same time defense attorney for Hugh and John Lester.

County Judge H. H. Howard, although occasionally forgetful, has almost consistently followed orders or taken his punishment. Early in the struggle he condemned the U. M. W. of A. Later, when the National Miners Union had come to the aid of the sold-out miners, he took occasion to reprimand two men for joining this organization, at the same time praising the U. M. W. of A. and reading at length from a "one-hundred per cent Americanism" letter from Bill Turnblazer of the U. M. W. of A. The letter was quoted as solemnly as if it were the law itself.

In one day Judge Howard made two mistakes. In the morning he allowed an attorney to provide bond for Jason Alford, who had just been arrested for criminal syndicalism, thus permitting the miner to remain at large. During the same afternoon Alford came to court as a spectator in the case of two miners charged with possessing ammunition. Deputy Mars, the sheriff's husky bodyguard, started to manhandle Alford in the courtroom while attempting to arrest him on another charge of criminal syndicalism. The improperly served warrant caused an argument between the deputy and Alford, who is about six feet three and also husky. Deputies had packed the small court-room. The defense attorney jumped up and told the miner to remain in his place until the trial was over. Deputy Mars wheeled on the attorney, declaring that no lawyer could inter-fere with him. Mars quickly thrust his hand into his jacket pocket, apparently for a gun. It looked like a battle with mass murder possibilities.

Judge "Hamp" Howard pounded on his desk, declaring that at least he would have law and order in his courtroom and calling upon the high sheriff to restore it. "John Henry" Blair took his stand by the Judge. The Judge rested and the case proceeded. Proper papers were made out and Jason Alford was arrested after the trial. At this trial, men who were form-erly officers in the National Guard, which recently had been removed from Harlan, appeared as deputies. For this indirect reprimand to Deputy Mars, and for failing to place exorbitant bail against Alford in the morning Judge Howard was, from that time, conveniently absent from the bench whenever labor cases came to trial.

Judge Whitehead, who is said to be a plumber by trade, had been appointed a special judge and he filled the judge's seat for labor cases until the return of Judge D. C. Jones, who was resting and regaining his health in a hospital. Whitehead is famous for his ability completely to disregard evidence and to give the miners the limit, especially by placing heavy "peace bonds" against any person who is active in behalf of the miners.

Legal authorities reveal themselves as tools against the working class more explicitly in the actions of the grand juries of May and August by failure to bring indictments.

No indictment was made for the shooting of Bill Burnett, a miner, in the battle of April 17th; nor for the killing of Carl Richmond, another miner, in the Evarts battle of May 5th; nor for the associates of Bill Randolph in the killing of Chasteen in June.

No indictment was brought in for shooting into homes of union leaders on May 1st; nor for illegal household evictions on thirty-minute notices in April; nor for brutalities of deputies, such as ordering strikers away from post-offices located in company stores, or jabbing miners in the ribs with guns.

There was no indictment for the conspiracy to starve out the striking miners. Some 3,000 were blacklisted. This meant that at least one-fourth of the people in Harlan County faced immediate starvation. The fate of the others was not much better. Persons who brought in aid or did relief work were intimidated or arrested on framed-up charges. Two men who were in Tennessee securing aid were indicted on May 5th on three charges of murder each. Two men who were making a fire and preparing food at a National Miners' soup kitchen were arrested for "banding and confederating." A minister and a miner, both active in relief work, were arrested on a charge of "obstructing justice." A merchant who gave a carload of flour to the strikers was charged with "criminal syndicalism."

An automobile of the International Labor Defense, which was used to carry food to the families of prisoners, was dynamited. Then a soup kitchen of the National Miners Union in Evarts, which had been feeding 420 persons a day, was dynamited. Threats were made to dynamite six other kitchens. As a trump card, Deputy Sheriff Lee Fleenor drove up to another soup kitchen near Harlan and in cold blood killed two unarmed miners and shot a third in front of the kitchen. This was all done to produce starvation and it did just that. Starvation resulted in a disease known as "flux," caused definitely by undernourishment. This has been causing on an average of one death a day in Harlan County. Company doctors refuse to attend such cases. Even the county doctor, supposedly employed for public welfare, refuses to attend such patients. That is murder. But there have been no indictments for any of these crimes against humanity.

During the week-end of July 30th through August 1st, practically every home in the town of Wallins Creek was raided. About a dozen usually, and at times as many as thirty, deputies would line up outside of those small houses, set up machine guns and enter without warrants. If the occupant was not at home they broke down the door. They ripped mattresses, destroyed furniture, and tore down window casings in an effort to find copies of the *Daily Worker*, National Miners Union membership cards or weapons. Personal property was in many cases either confiscated or destroyed. On one occasion Sheriff Blair smashed weapons belonging to miners on the concrete pavement outside of the courthouse as a threat to all workers. Automobiles were stopped on the highways at night. Men, women and children were subjected to illegal search. Some were illegally arrested and held for hours without cause. But there were no indictments for any of this!

On July 26th, a car being used by the National Miners Union was dynamited. During the night of July 29th, a charge of dynamite was set off in the yard of another union leader's home, smashing the windows.

No indictment was brought for breaking up a peaceful miners' meeting at the courthouse in June with tear gas, nor for the sheriff's blanket order against any meeting near the courthouse during trials, nor for use of terroristic threats of mass murder used to break up other union meetings.

Within Harlan County, censorship has been enforced with bullets. Bruce Crawford, an editor from Norton, Virginia, had written some articles favorable to the miners. One evening he paid a visit to Harlan. As he walked across a swinging bridge over the Cumberland River the next morning, shots were fired at him, one of which struck him in the leg. Boris Israel, a Federated Press reporter, was taken from the courthouse by deputy sheriffs one afternoon for a ride up the mountainside. He was told he had five minutes to live. He made his escape but was shot in the leg in the attempt. Mrs. Harvey O'Connor, who succeeded Boris Israel, received a threatening letter the day following her arrival, which ordered her out by sundown, and was signed: "One Hundred Per Cent Americans." Threats to dynamite the home of a local reporter made him an exile from his native town. Two writers for *Scribner's Magazine* were illegally searched, arrested and intimidated. Benton Stong, of the Scripps-Howard papers, wrote a series of embarrassing facts about Harlan. The Kiwanis Club, together with the operators, publicly urged a boycott against Knoxville business men in an attempt to force them to bring pressure against the Knoxville *News-Sentinel* to prevent the publication of the truth about Harlan. There were no indictments for any of this.

One Saturday night, deputies took Henry Thornton, better known as "Rabbit," a sixty-seven year old Negro union leader, and a Harlan County resident for twenty years, for a ride on a lonely mountain road, threatening him with death unless he would promise to either quit the union or to leave the county, both of which he consistently refused to do. Finally he was jerked out of the car, beaten with a blackjack or the butt of a gun, slugged every time he attempted to move. Bleeding from a large gash over his forehead, he was then taken to jail on a charge of intoxication. The next night, his brother-in-law, Mc-Kinley Baldwin, also a Negro union leader, was taken from the same house, strapped him to a tree, and literally beaten to a pulp. Afterward he was shown the way out of the county at the point of a gun. These beatings, attempts to intimidate the Negro miners and keep them out of the union, occurred at about the same time as the burning of two Ku Klux Klan crosses on the hillsides in Harlan. Beating up union leaders has been used in a number of other cases. But—no indictments!

The absurdity of grand jury indictments is shown in two cases. Deputy Lee Fleenor, who admitted killing two miners and shooting the third in front of a soup kitchen, with at least four available witnesses to the fact that it was cold-blooded murder, was cleared behind closed doors by the grand jury which failed to bring in an indictment. Fleenor, therefore, does not even have to go to court. On the other hand, Roy Taylor, an illiterate miner with a family of nine, gave a copy of the *Daily Worker* to a blind man. For this he was arrested, jailed and indicted on a charge of criminal syndicalism.

The tactics used by the operators and their henchmen include: bullets with accompanying murder, starvation, disease, propaganda, terror, intimidation, tear gas, dynamite, brutal beatings, imprisonment of leaders, and now, cold prison bars or the electric chair. Yet the miners march! They organize. They strike against the lawlessness of the law, the terror, starvation.

Aligned against these militant miners are operators, judges, sheriff, grand juries, commonwealth attorney, deputies, the National Guard, the Governor, the laws of the country, local churches, the American Legion, the Kiwanis Club, the capitalist press, the United Mine Workers of America, a revived Ku Klux Klan, and the vast economic power of Wall Street. Yet— blacklisted, behind prison bars, or slaving in the bowels of the earth, the miners fight for life, for a new society. Harlan County adds another chapter to class war!

## 2. DYNAMITE AND HARLAN COUNTY JAIL

### by Jessie Wakefield

FOR almost a quarter year I felt and observed Harlan terror at first hand. Five weeks of those three months I spent in Harlan County Jail.

Representing the International Labor Defense I went to Harlan in June to arrange defense for the almost 50 miners then in jail, and to get relief for their families.

Each prisoner's family that I visited represented a new story of hunger and suffering. Five was the average number of children of the men then in jail. In one family, living in a decrepit two-room shack, there were thirteen children. The cupboard was bare except for a handful of flour and a cup of lard—enough to make one more meal of bulldog gravy.

I lived with the Perkins family. Frank Perkins was under $3,000 bail because the sheriff's deputies had found a *Southern Worker* in his house when they searched it.

Mrs. Perkins was a frail, small woman, but she managed to support the family by spending two long days a week over a wash tub, for which she received $1.50. The rest of her time was spent in her garden, trying to raise food for the family. A 15-year-old daughter helped out with the 50 cents a week she earned by washing and ironing all the towels of a near-by barbershop. Luther, 10 years old, did his share by carrying a pail of water morning and evening to a family a quarter of a mile away, adding a dollar a *month* to the family income. The oldest lad was blacklisted because he had come out on strike with his daddy.

After my second visit to the men in jail, Judge Jones' 250-pound personal body-guard trailed me for the rest of the day. And later when I myself was in jail the jailer told me that he knew I was going to get myself arrested sooner or later—everybody did who visited the union miners in jail.

For one month, in spite of the trailing, I was able to go up and down the forks and valleys of Harlan County to the mining camps where the prisoners' families lived. I attended the miners' meetings, started the organization of a Harlan Miners Defense Committee, which was to have been a body of miners representing what there were of United Mine Workers and I. W. W.'s, as well as the arrested members of the National Miners Union. The I. W. W. nationally, however, in spite of the wishes of the local members, refused in a purely sectarian spirit to coöperate in any such united front of the rank and file. The United Mine Workers hired as its own attorney ex-Senator Robsion, professional "red-baiter," and leader of the Ku Klux Klan.

The coal operators were not slow in a further attempt to stop the organization of the Harlan miners' defense.

On the morning of July 22nd, Marion Allen, the toughest thug—and deputy sheriff—left after Jim Daniels was killed in the Evarts battle, followed me to the Perkins shack in Sunshine Camp. He stood off a bit, taking in the lay of the land, and concentrating his attention on my Ford parked in front of the house, and then left. He was seen in the camp that night after twelve o'clock—a peculiar incident in an area where people retire at nine.

At two-thirty A. M. the whole camp of Sunshine was shaken by an explosion. Windows were broken, kids tossed out of bed. The whole community was aroused to see what the thugs had done this time. Dynamite had been set off in the engine of my car and the only part remaining intact was the tail-light.

The city police came the next day to say that there was nothing they could do. No one from the sheriff's office showed up. There was no investigation, and no arrests were made.

The dynamiting had obviously been done to prevent food from getting to the prisoners' families, to cripple the miners' defense, and to scare another miners' sympathizer out of the field. But it only added one more grievance to the already militant miners, as they milled about the scrap heap of what was once a Ford.

The following Sunday the National Miners Union held such a successful picnic of 3,000 Negro and white miners, that when the fresh recruits of gun thugs arrived on the scene and looked about at the strength of the miners, they turned tail and left. But that night one of the new thugs stopped me on the street in Harlan town with "you better watch your step, girlie."

On August 6th, I was arrested on a charge of Criminal Syndicalism. I was released on bail the following day in spite of the fact that Sheriff Blair told Mrs. Perkins that "that woman is going to stay in jail until she rots." When my examining trial came up a few days later the judge was embarrassed by the lack of even a single witness against me and was forced to let me go.

I spent the following week quietly in Pineville, coming to Harlan only with the lawyer and other defense representatives to witness the hearings of the scores of N. M. U. men then being arrested. While there, however, in the court house, on the street, or in a restaurant, the deputies stayed no more than 10 feet behind us. But other deputies were busy gathering witnesses and cooking up evidence against the miners and sympathizers.

Upon arriving in town with the attorney one morning the deputies came forward with two new warrants, one for Arnold

Johnson of the American Civil Liberties Union and a student of Union Theological Seminary, and the other for myself. We were both charged with criminal syndicalism: Mr. Johnson for having "inflammatory literature" in his possession and I for making a speech. I was again released on $5,000 bail. The story of that is told in George V. Middleton's testimony before Governor Sampson's investigating committee:

"One day in court Captain Golden asked me to make bond for a lady named Wakefield. I did so. In less than ten minutes a friend warned me I had better leave town. I went to Middlesboro. That night my house was burned. No investigation was made."

Our hearings were held shortly after. To both Johnson's and my $5,000 bail was added a $5,000 peace bond. (If a person is released on a peace bond and then convicted of breaking the peace, the total amount of the bond is forfeited.) Johnson's crime was possessing a free speech pamphlet, the *Survey Graphic*, and a copy of the *League for Industrial Democracy Monthly*.

Against me they had two witnesses to say that I had made a speech uncomplimentary to Sheriff Blair and Judge Jones. The speech, incidentally, had been made the day I was in jail the first time, by Caroline Drew, who was organizing women's auxiliaries of the union. But that made no difference to the judge. Court was adjourned long enough for the prosecution to offer us our freedom if we would agree to leave the county —otherwise back to jail.

The next five weeks spent in jail gave me a feeling of what the miners had been suffering behind those bars all during the long, hot summer months.

The jail is on the top floor of the court house, where the sun beats in and only a patch of sky can be seen from the windows. No exercise at all except for the prisoners held on liquor and similar charges, who were taken downstairs regularly to be questioned on any "dope" they might have picked up in conversations with the union prisoners.

Because of the "labor trouble" the jail was packed to the

rafters. Prisoners slept on the concrete floor, many without blankets. Of vermin, however, there was no lack.

Also there were meals: For breakfast—bulldog gravy, a slab of fatback, and a few biscuits oozing with the gravy they had been dropped into—all served on rusty tin pans.

For dinner—pinto beans and potatoes. And for supper the menu was changed from potatoes to cabbage and beans.

A sympathetic paper published the information that the Harlan jailer received $1.00 a day for each prisoner and that he spent a total of 12 cents. The jailer was infuriated by this attack. His answer to it, made to me, was: "I only get 75 cents a day for some of these prisoners."

While I remained in jail Harlan was becoming a major issue, not only in the South, but throughout the country. The authorities discovered that instead of the union falling to pieces when the scores of its leaders were jailed or driven from the county, it was spreading.

After a month in jail the jailer came to me and said, "Aren't you getting tired of staying here? This ain't no place for a lady. These here newspapers is writing too much about you-all, and I'm getting too many threats from the miners. If you won't leave—and Johnson too—we're going to take you to a place where you won't cause *us* any more trouble anyway. There's a little jail up at Hyden that's 27 miles from a railroad, and I guess no newspaper reporters can git to you there. If they did they'd have to go by mule because there's no road over Pine Mountain. And you won't find the people so friendly there because they never heard of a union. As long as you stay in Kentucky you will stay in jail." I told him that the International Labor Defense, of which I am a member, is a legal organization and has a membership throughout the United States. His reply was, "I don't care what they do other places. It ain't legal here and we don't intend to have anything to do with it."

The miners held a meeting in the bull-pen that day and it was decided that we should not go to Hyden. They asked us to see what we could do for them on the outside.

A few days later I saw Judge Jones and Prosecuting Attorney Brock, asked them if it were true that I was to be moved to Hyden. When they said it was, I told them that under the circumstances I would accept their offer to leave. They spent some time giving me advice against the "reds," and quoting at length from the Fish Committee report, and telling me I should go back to housekeeping.

The indictment against me declared that I was guilty of "advising, counseling, and suggesting that divers persons free the miners who was (*sic*) then in jail, and to wipe J. H. Blair, the duly elected, qualified, and acting Sheriff of Harlan County, and Judge D. C. Jones, the duly elected, qualified, and acting Judge of Harlan County, from off the map, and to not leave a sign of them."

The duly elected and qualified authorities had now taken it upon themselves to release this vicious criminal, undoubtedly dangerous to the community at large, merely on a promise to leave their own territory.

# VII. HARLAN COUNTY AND THE PRESS

## by Bruce Crawford

ASSOCIATED PRESS writers excepted, newspaper men are anathema in the coalfields of Kentucky. Unless a reporter seeks information from the secretary of the coal operators' association, the commonwealth attorney or the sheriff, he is regarded pretty much as a spy is regarded in war time and often he is treated as badly.

Terrorizing press correspondents, forbidding the sale of Scripps-Howard papers, threatening to boycott advertisers of one that exposed the Harlan terror, playing down of news by the local newspaperman, who reports for the Associated Press—these and many other methods of news concealment have been used to prolong mine-owner tyranny and mine-guard thuggery.

While the class war began early in 1931, war on representatives of the press did not start until the middle of the summer. On August 17, Boris Israel, a Federated Press writer, was "taken for a ride" from the steps of the Harlan courthouse, thrown out at the county line, and shot through the leg. This incident took place two weeks after a bullet hole occurred in my own leg as I was crossing a bridge in the town of Harlan. I had gone there to investigate for my own newspaper. While I did not get to talk with the sheriff, I believe I got his point of view.

Another writer, Mrs. Harvey O'Connor, was sent to Harlan by the Federated Press. While dining at a hotel on the day of her arrival, Mrs. O'Connor received the following note by special delivery through the mails: "Madam: You have been here to long already and remember to other red neck reporters got what was coming to them so don't let the sun go down on you here. If you do it will be just to bad. We got your number and we don't mean maybe.—Hundred percent americans."

75

Just previous to the mistreatment of these three writers, the Knoxville *News-Sentinel*, a Scripps-Howard daily, had sent its staff correspondent, Benton J. Stong, to Harlan. Stong succeeded in getting interviews with miners as well as company and county officials. The material he gathered appeared in six daily articles in the United Press.

Naturally Harlan resented the Stong articles. The Kiwanis club voted a resolution of protest to the business interests of Knoxville against the *News-Sentinel* "misrepresentations." Knoxville wholesalers, who sell to commissaries and independent stores in Harlan County, were threatened with a boycott. Among the outraged Kiwanians were officials of the American Legion, the Harlan school superintendent, and a convulsively patriotic Methodist minister.

A committee of Knoxville business men called on the editor, Edward J. Meeman, and received assurance that the *News-Sentinel* would gladly publish articles from Harlan citizens giving "the other side" of the situation in the coalfields. A goodwill tour to Harlan followed. But no articles giving "the other side" were forthcoming. In two or three mining towns the *News-Sentinel* and the Cincinnati *Post*, another Scripps-Howard paper, were forbidden.

A New York *Times* writer managed to get into Harlan, take some pictures, and get out without running afoul the "law." It is doubtful that he obtained any interviews. His series of articles, written from Chicago, seemed to be worked-over material that had already been in print. Still, it was publicity of a kind that the Harlan coal barons did not relish.

Kentucky authorities have the least patience with publications that are avowedly radical. Not only do they forbid distribution of radical papers, but they forbid *possession* of radical papers. Miners have been arrested for possessing copies of the *Daily Worker*, after having received it through the United States mails. "Radical papers like that may be admitted as legal by the post office department," said Commonwealth Attorney W. A. Brock, "but they are a violation of our Kentucky criminal syndicalism law."

Taken as a whole, the Kentucky press has gagged at red and swallowed all the yellowness of company trickery, U. M. W. of A. betrayal and official corruption in Harlan County. And this, of course, is not surprising. Kentucky newspapers, like newspapers everywhere else, may circulate among the masses, but they are sensitive to the bosses.

While the large city dailies deplored, with some urbanity, the disorders of the coalfields, the smaller newspapers shelled off their veneer and said exactly what they felt about strikers and agitators. The Mt. Sterling *Gazette-Courier*, which proclaims from its masthead that it stands for "the republicanism of Abraham Lincoln, the democracy of Thomas Jefferson and the Americanism of Theodore Roosevelt," editorialized the Harlan situation as follows:

"There has been altogether too much leniency shown agitators of the type of men and women in jail in Harlan, and the sooner such culprits are shot at sunrise the better off the United States will be. . . . They should be deported, if possible, and if not, should be made to face a firing squad for the protection of society. . . . It is useless to send men and women of the stripe of the Harlan agitators to the penitentiary. . . . They would be much safer in a pine box six feet under ground."

The Louisville *Courier-Journal* and *The Times*, both owned by Robert W. Bingham, were savagely hostile to the Dreiser committee from the time the investigation was announced to the day of its departure from Kentucky soil. "Theodore the Terrible" was the title of an editorial intended to prejudice the public, coal miners especially, against the committee before it had undertaken its task. "Judge Dreiser" was a follow-up editorial ridiculing the public hearings conducted by the committee. The Bingham papers based their criticisms on dispatches of the Associated Press, which assumed a phony air of impartiality. It is significant that the owner of the *Courier-Journal* and *The Times* is connected with Louisville banks and trust companies, whose depositors include many of the large coal companies. Mr. Bingham is also chairman of the Louisville and Nashville Railway, which hauls coal from Harlan and Bell counties. Hence the antipathy of the Louisville dailies to the "self-appointed" investigating committee and their steadfastness for the status quo.

By the time the Dreiser committee had arrived, its un-Americanism was already a household word—except among the harried and starving miners. Its "traitorious philosophies" were subjects for patriotic editorials. The fact that Dreiser had been "blessed by Moscow" on his sixtieth birthday was all that the little editor, who did job printing for the coal companies, needed to load his guns for the committee. The investigation was called "one-sided," notwithstanding the fact that Judge D. C. Jones had been invited to give testimony and to examine witnesses or the committee itself in the open hearings. The Harlan *Enterprise*, always friendly to the coal operators, declared that "it is the radical, un-American views as preached by Dreiser and his motley followers that have caused conditions in these hills to reach the breaking point." The Pineville *Sun*, whose editor prefers charity to Dreiser's equity and contributes to the Red Cross—which denied relief to striking miners—remarked: "Now for another Scopes trial and all the attendant monkey business." The Middlesboro *Daily News*, agreeing with Judge Jones, denounced the committee as "publicity seekers," although it was plain that what annoyed them was publicity givers. "The Dreisers with their twisted and distorted patriotism," the Middlesboro daily continued, "must be met with firmness and patience, and their traitorous philosophies must be overwhelmed in a tidal wave of new and exalted dedication to our free America . . . so that the next generation will receive from our hands unimpaired the liberties and opportunities which we have enjoyed." Of course "we" includes the terrorized and impoverished coal diggers and their children!

An instance of deliberate news suppression was afforded by the Harlan *Enterprise* on the afternoon of the committee's open hearing in that town. The town was excited about two things—the investigation and a football game. The football game was of greater importance. Judge Jones chose to attend the game instead of the hearing. And the *Enterprise* spread an eight-column headline over a vast waste of space about Harlan's football victory, but gave only two inches at the bottom of the page to a story of epochal significance. On another page it reprinted the editorial, "Theodore the Terrible."

The committee felt that it was not getting an even break in the Associated Press stories. Unimportant matters were played up, significant things slurred over, and deliberate misrepresentations crept in. For instance, a coal miner was testifying to conditions in more prosperous times. He stated that he made as high as $500 some months. This was not clear money, however. He was a contractor, employing two other miners whose wages were deducted from the $500. But the Associated Press story left the impression that the miner *cleared* $500 a month.

The Associated Press man occasionally asked questions of witnesses to bring out testimony favorable to the operators. And once, when Aunt Molly Jackson, who works among her fellow-sufferers of Straight Creek, ministering to the sick and delivering babies, was testifying that seventeen babies had died of flux during the summer, the Associated Press man skeptically inquired: "Can we see the graves?" It was plain why Associated Press writers enjoyed immunity in the Kentucky coalfields.

Contrasted with the attitude of the Associated Press was the decent policy of Edward B. Smith, Knoxville representative of the United Press and correspondent of the Knoxville *News-Sentinel*. This paper published full accounts, devoting columns to the testimony taken down by the committee's stenographer. This despite the fact that Smith expressed himself privately as having little sympathy for "these radical organizations." Smith simply reported the facts as revealed by the investigation, the chips falling where they would.

But one thing stood out, regardless of the sort of publicity given the investigation. The contention of the National Miners Union, to the effect that the operators controlled courts, government and churches, was abundantly proved. The authorities themselves had proved it. Then they punished "agitators" for stating what they themselves had demonstrated! One did not have to read between the lines to see this.

The biggest story connected with the investigation, if one may judge by the eagerness of the press to get it, was the indictment of Dreiser on a misconduct charge a few hours after his departure. Here was a story after a bourgeois reporter's own heart. For a few days this story was played up to the exclusion of anything concerning the crimes against the miners. The Kentucky press joined the authorities in meeting the grave social challenge of the coalfield with a bit of personal scandal.

A few newspapers in other parts of the country, however, referred to the misconduct charge as a screen to hide the ruthless dictatorship of the coalfields, and persisted in calling for the truth. "Dreiser is not on trial," said one. "Kentucky is on trial. It is on trial before the unofficial court of humanity, decency, and honor." Another declared that the situation is "now a national scandal" and that it "must be handled as such."

The story of Harlan and the Press is not wholly unique. It is the story of every other class struggle, for the prostitution of the press is commonplace. If the Harlan story is different at all, it is different because Harlan has over-reached itself in its efforts to intimidate reporters and buffalo the press and thus maintain a Chinese wall of insularity wherein to exploit native minerals and native people. The shooting of press representatives, together with attempted boycotts, has constituted a challenge to the American press—a challenge which the radical papers would not permit the capitalist papers to ignore.

## 2. REPRESENTING THE PRESS

### by Boris Israel

I WENT into Harlan for Federated Press. The second day I was there some one told me that I'd be in jail within a week.

The first day I had been shadowed by deputies. That lasted all the time I was there.

The day court opened Judge Jones spoke, telling the assembled courtroom that members of the National Miners Union, the International Labor Defense, etc., were radicals and had "no right to look to this court or to any other court in this country for justice." Later, downstairs in the courthouse, a deputy told me that I hadn't better let the sun set on me in Harlan County. I didn't care about leaving, I wanted to get the news.

The day before, I had been tc a meeting miners held in the woods. I had been introduced to one of the fellows who said he could tell me some things. He was told that I was "all right," that he could talk to me. That night a shot was fired as I walked across a swinging bridge at one end of Harlan. Just as a warning. We found out later that the fellow I had spoken to in the woods was a stool pigeon.

In a war you're either on one side or the other. If you're "all right" for the miners in eastern Kentucky, you're not all right for the bosses or the sheriff. I was standing there in the courthouse the day court opened when several of the deputies gathered about. "How do you like the air down here?" one of them asked me. I said it was all right. I wasn't anxious to talk to them. "How do you like the mountain air?" this deputy asked. They all had forty-fives on their hips. I didn't have a revolver. They had searched every one who entered the courthouse to make sure of that. I told him that I'd never been up in the mountains. "Come on, then," he said, "we'll give you some mountain air."

We drove up the mountain silently. I had tried to back out on the invitation but they had grabbed my elbows and helped me along to the car. Three of them went with me. I started to talk once or twice but they told me to shut up. When we got a few miles out of town they stopped and two of them got out of the car. I was left with Marion Allen. He questioned me and made me turn out my pockets while the others had a little target practice behind the car. Then Allen told me to get off down the road and out of the county. I started. There wasn't anything else to do, that I could see. When I was a little way off, Allen started firing at me. After the first shot whined past I turned and saw him there in the middle of the road with his legs spread and a sneer on his face. He fired twice more and one of the bullets almost knocked my leg from under me. I got around the bend in the road as quickly as possible and turned off down the mountain side. A fellow who was up the mountain that day and saw it told me later that they had come after me down the road but that they hadn't seen me in the underbrush on the mountain side.

I saw Governor Flem B. Sampson in Frankfort. I told him about the gunman rule in Harlan County and told him that Marion Allen, a deputy sheriff, had shot me. He mumbled something about an investigation but said he didn't know what he could do about Harlan, he didn't think he had any authority. He didn't do anything, of course. Marion Allen is now personal bodyguard for Judge D. C. Jones.

# VIII. LIVING CONDITIONS IN THE COAL FIELDS

## by Adelaide Walker

IN 1922 and 1923 a voluminous report was issued by the United States Coal Commission. Owing to the depression, conditions in the coal fields have on the whole grown worse since that time, but as this is the last set of exhaustive statistics available, certain of them are valuable as giving a background to the findings of the present committee in Kentucky.

Of the 71,000 company-owned houses investigated in approximately 713 communities chosen from among all the coal producing states, 2.4% had bath tubs, 3% had inside flush toilets, 13.8% had running water (though 61% of the towns had water systems) and 66.3% had gas or electricity. Over a fourth of the communities did not reach a rating of 50 on water supply and only two communities out of the 713 reaches the very modest decency minimum established by the commission on both water supply and sewage disposal.

It may seem at first glance that bad as it is, at least Kentucky is no worse than any of the coal producing states. But there is some justification for centering with particular emphasis on conditions in Kentucky. The commission lists the 66 best communities, the ones which rated 75 or over and of these 6 or 11% were in Kentucky. It also lists the 82 worst ones with ratings below 50, and 21 of these or one-quarter were Kentucky coal camps.

For the investigation conducted by this committee there are no statistics; the committee lacked both time and resources. They chose instead to get the personal stories in a number of typical camps; to present these together with the committee's own observations to the American public.

The houses are built in close-set, even rows in the valleys or perched precariously and irregularly over the mountain side. In a few of the so-called captive mines (mines which keep their output for use in their own industry, such as railroads and steel companies) conditions and houses are slightly better; some of the houses are sturdily built and a few are even painted. In most of the others however, they are tumble-down and decaying shacks in various states of decrepitude and disrepair. Built of one thickness of flimsy board raised on tottering posts, without paint, the best of them papered with newspapers or patched with cardboard and the worst of them full of gaping holes in ceiling, floor and walls through which the rain pours and the wind blows, they are criminally unfit for habitation by man or beasts. The company managers concur in this statement in deeds if not in words and they do not risk the lives of their horses and mules by letting them live in similar buildings. In one of the worst camps the committee saw, Fox Ridge, Straight Creek, there were just two weatherproof and livable buildings in the town, first the miner's shack where the manager's mistress, a miner's wife, lived, and secondly, the manager's barn, which had not only well-built walls and a sturdy roof but even the unique luxury of paint.

This town was so appalling in every respect that it seems useful to describe it at length. The "sanitary" arrangements were non-existent. In other communities the committee found very primitive privies and sewage disposal, here they found for the most part none at all. The water was supplied by three springs, all of them outside the town, and a little stream running down the center of the village which completely dried up in summer and which was not deep enough for the dipping of more than a cupful of water at a time. All the springs were polluted, and many cases of typhoid had resulted during the summer. The enormous importance of water in coal camps is obvious. Miners come home every day with their clothes and themselves covered with grime and dirt, the coal dust blows into the houses all day long and the added burden on the overworked housewife of walking many blocks each day with water buckets is enormous.

What do miners eat? Beans—everywhere beans—corn bread made without milk, "bulldog gravy," being flour, water and a little grease, and in summer when they can manage to find a small patch to cultivate or a kind hearted farmer, a few pumpkins. The old American habit of "three square meals" has vanished, the lucky miners have only two. There is no milk, not even canned milk for the children. In one camp we found a few cows, gone dry from lack of fodder. Milk was regarded as medicine; when children were sick they tried to borrow a few cents to buy a little. The result of this diet is the prevalence everywhere of flux, a peculiarly terrible form of starvation dysentery. In nearly every family we spoke to more than one member had suffered from it in the last few months; in many all the children had had it, and in one home the whole family had had it and the youngest of five children died after the fourth attack. Pellagra, another starvation disease, is also common, and of course susceptibility to tuberculosis and other diseases is greatly increased by malnutrition.

We found the miners' wages averaged about a dollar a day when they worked. As they are paid every two weeks, or once a month and must have something to live on in the meantime, the company issues "scrip" good only at the company store or convertible—sometimes—into cash at a large discount. But first, before a man is allowed any scrip, come the company's "cuts." The mine operator deducts money for rent, light, coal, and various so-called "services" such as doctor, hospital, burial fund and sometimes schools and church. Also, before the miner or his family can get scrip for food his "mine expense" is deducted. This is the cost of the light by which he works and the powder he uses to blow out the coal. Our testimony shows that often these expenses take all the miner has made in ten or twelve hours' hard labor and when his wife goes to buy food, she is told, "You have nothing due you today, your husband only earned enough to pay for his coal light and carbide." One woman wept as she told me how for three days, while her children cried for food and her husband went hungry to work, she had been allowed no scrip because she was told her husband had only made enough to pay the coal company the expense of mining their coal!

To return to the cuts or "deducts" as the miners call them, there is the doctor to whom the miner pays $2 of his meager $27 or $30 a month. Complaint as to company doctors is almost universal. The miners have no power to hire and fire these doctors and the doctors being quite independent of their clients and paid by the coal companies, do as they like and as they find convenient about coming when they are called. And if a lone doctor happens to be humane and kind-hearted and able to overcome the taken-for-granted prejudices of his class, what a ghastly business it must be to be called day after day for diseases and illnesses, the only cure for which would be the sufficient food and decent living conditions that it would be a mockery to prescribe.

The burial fund also is a cause of much irritation and it is significant that in several strikes one of the chief demands has been administration of their own burial fund. Everywhere one hears bitter and macabre stories of mismanagement and graft in its administration.

After the cuts what is left? Let us examine a typical statement. Rent and light, $8, Doctor, $2, Burial fund, $1, Coal, $3; the rest of the $15 or $16 in scrip (remember we are now dealing with the exceptionally lucky man who has worked all month—only a few of them are so fortunate). This $15 or $16 has usually been taken in scrip and traded at the company store for food and coal light and carbide, if the latter have not already been deducted. Thus statements at the end of the month are usually *statements* and not pay checks. Again and again we saw statements in which the miner had been paid 38 cents or 12 cents in cash or sometimes was left in debt to the company. The advantage of this system to the companies is clear; it enables them to operate with almost no actual cash outlay in wages, which is the largest item of the mine's expense. Operating expenses are thus reduced to a minimum. The shacks used for housing have cost little to build in the first place, or may even have been moved over from an abandoned camp.[1] In any case once the original outlay is over the expense of up-keep is reduced to zero in many of the camps. Little pretense is made of keeping them in repair.

The provision of food is somewhat less satisfactory from the viewpoint of operator's economies, than the supply of shacks for homes, or the racket of deducting "mine expense." Food of a sort must be provided from week to week. The company store is the company's means of doing this with the absolute minimum of outlay. Here we found prices were considerably higher than at near-by independent stores but the miners cannot go to these for two reasons; first, because they have no money—only scrip, and if they can persuade the independent store to take it, they must do so at a discount which usually eats up what has been saved on prices. Secondly, there is pressure, more subtle of late but quite definite, in many camps, to trade at the company stores if a man wishes to keep his job. Another way in which the worker's purchasing power is further limited is in a habit we found in some company stores, of selling in 25 cent packages only and not permitting purchases in smaller amounts. If a housewife has only a dollar to spend and is prohibited from buying less than 25 cents' worth of sugar, 25 cents' worth of bacon or lard or other foodstuffs, she is still further hampered in her efforts to stretch her husband's meager pay into convincing meals for the family.

Where do the miners get clothes when their last penny is spent in an effort to get sufficient food? The answer is they do not. I visited one village where not a single child I saw had shoes, and this in November when it was already cold. Most of them had no underwear and few of them had sufficient

[1] It is interesting to note that though the excuse often made for the flimsiness of the houses is that a coal camp is an impermanent settlement and the houses only a temporary makeshift, the Coal Commission found that of the eighty-two communities at the bottom of the list scoring less than 50 points, there were 31, nearly 38%, for which the probably remaining life was estimated by company officials at from 30 to 100 years.

clothing to go to school. One mother told me of her little seven-year-old boy who had that morning gone barefoot over the white frost because he insisted on getting to school anyhow. He had no books though the county is supposed to provide free school books.

When we asked the women where they got the clothes they were wearing, we found that most of them were gifts from some relative in another part of the country, slightly better off, or bought five or six years ago, and mended and patched ever since.

Many of the men go to work without underclothes. The effect of a long hard day in the cold and damp underground without sufficient clothing is partly seen in the frequency of flu, pneumonia, and similar diseases among the miners. By its nature, coal mining promotes other diseases such as rheumatism, tuberculosis, asthma, and other pulmonary maladies. These arise from bad air in mines, coal dust and noxious gases. It is important to remember in considering the smallness of wages and inadequacy of living conditions, that coal mining has the highest accident rate of any industry. Every week in the United States, 40 men on an average are killed, and 2,000 injured.

The question arises: Has no effort been made to feed and clothe these people by any of the charitable organizations in this richest of countries where "nobody is allowed to starve"? What of the Red Cross? We found that in the last months before the strike the situation had become so undeniably appalling that the Red Cross had been forced to help a little though it is repeatedly alleged that a family's chances of help were very much better if the father was the underpaid employee of some coal company than if he were unemployed or sick or dead and the family destitute. This apparently illogical and strange conduct can only be explained if it is admitted that the persons in charge of the Red Cross were definitely and personally interested in preventing industrial unrest, not in feeding starving babies. With the advent of the union this attitude became completely frank and no effort was made to disguise the rôle of the Red Cross as a strike-breaking agent.

From the minute men joined the union even before the strike, the Red Cross withdrew all aid. After the strike the Red Cross undertook the work of a scab-hiring agency. A man coming for help was given an employment card to the nearest mine stamped with the seal of the Red Cross. When he protested that the mine was on strike he was insulted by the Red Cross representative and asked what he meant by daring to ask for aid if he was too lazy to work. Again and again they were told, "Go back to work. If you can't make enough to live on, then we'll help you." In other words, the money collected from the American people and American workers could not be used to help Americans fighting for a living wage and an "American" standard of living—that would be taking sides in an industrial dispute—but it could be used as a subsidy to the rich corporations and coal operators to help them get away with continuing to pay less than a living wage and force the workers to charity and starvation.

The miners all claim that when times were good the miners had contributed generously to the Red Cross, giving a day's pay during drives and that more money had gone to the Red Cross from the miners than from any other group in Kentucky. Certain it is that the Red Cross has never refused the dollars or pennies of the workers and that as it claims to be an organization of "mercy" and "service to humanity" and an organization belonging to the American people as a whole, the people have a right to ask how their money has been spent and to object to its expenditure to enforce starvation against men exercising their constitutional rights to organize a union or to strike.

The Red Cross, however, is only one of the more subtle weapons which the operators wield to break the strike by enforcing starvation and misery. One of the first means always used to "bring the strikers to their senses" is that of eviction. In the spring, after the first U. M. W. of A. meeting, 200 miners were fired, blacklisted and evicted from their homes.

I talked to one woman who, at the time of the evictions, had also lost all her furniture. The sheriff who evicted her had taken the trouble to notify the furniture company to whom she still owed payments to come for the furniture. She and her family lived in a garage all summer without any household possessions but a borrowed stove and a bed with no mattress in which four of them slept, and no means of getting food except from neighbors almost as poor as themselves. In spite of this, her husband continued active in the union and when the National Miners Union opened its first soup kitchen in Harlan she went to cook for them and her husband helped gather supplies. They lived and ate at the kitchen. The last thing, however, the operators were willing to do, was to risk the success of the strike by allowing a union soup kitchen to function. Early in the summer the one in Evarts was dynamited. In July deputy Lee Fleenor shot and killed two men and wounded a third in the Harlan soup kitchen. The effort to break the strike through starvation did not stop there. In the Black Mountain Coal camp near Evarts, pigs were shot by deputies to prevent the hungry strikers using them for food. All summer there were from thirty to sixty miners in jail which meant that their families were left in complete destitution. Three thousand miners in Harlan and Bell counties are now blacklisted, unable to get a job of any kind. They have no possible means of getting away, no place to go if they could and their only help comes from the union soup kitchens which are the constant center of attack by company gun thugs.

The extraordinary fact about Harlan is that, faced by this starvation and destitution enforced by all the power of law and of gunman terror, the miners of Kentucky are uncowed. With a magnificent courage and absolute loyalty to each other, they are continuing their fight for a union, men and women fighting side by side. It is neither pity for their sufferings nor fear for their future that one takes out of Kentucky, but a conviction of the miners' ultimate victory.

# IX. THE MINERS SPEAK FOR THEMSELVES

EXPLANATORY PARAGRAPHS BY JOHN DOS PASSOS

## I

## THE WRITERS' COMMITTEE

THE National Committee for the Defense of Political Prisoners had sent letters to a long list of politicians, educators, writers, and publicists suggesting that a public investigation of conditions in the Harlan coalfields might do some good. Later, as Mr. Dreiser has explained, telegrams were sent to a selected list of men, eighteen of them, who might have been expected to interest themselves in this matter. The purpose of sending a delegation to Harlan would be to call the attention of the press and the country to the terrorist methods by which the Harlan County Coal Operators Association, with the help of Circuit Judge D. C. Jones and Sheriff Blair, was trying to stamp out the attempt of the National Miners Union to unionize the mines, under the pretext that the N. M. U. was a communist organization.

Unable to enlist help from these eighteen men, Mr. Dreiser, as Committee Chairman, asked for volunteers. In the end, only Theodore Dreiser, Charles Rumford Walker and his wife Adelaide Walker, Melvin P. Levy, Sam Ornitz, Lester Cohen, Bruce Crawford of *Crawford's Weekly*, and myself were able to go. We were joined in Pineville by George Maurer of the International Labor Defense, Harry Gannes of the *Daily Worker*, and Celia Kuhn, stenographer, who took down most of the statements published in this record. Newspaper men and several people from surrounding states who happened to be interested sat in on the hearings and traveled around with the committee.

There was one thing that contributed a lot to Mr. Dreiser's interest in Harlan and that helped induce him to aid in forming a committee. This was a talk he had with Jim Grace and Debs Moreland, who had been working to build up the National Miners Union in Harlan County and who, as a result, had been taken for a ride, beat up, shot at, and left for dead by the coal operators' gunmen. The following two affidavits, sworn by Jim Grace and Debs Moreland, give the story.

## 2

STATE OF NEW YORK ⎫
COUNTY OF NEW YORK ⎬ SS:
CITY OF NEW YORK ⎭

JIM GRACE, *being duly sworn, says:*

I was born in Virginia, where I remained until 1904. I came to West Virginia in 1904, where I became a miner, and worked in the mines until 1924. I left West Virginia and came to Kentucky, Harlan County, and secured employment with the Creech Coal Company as trackman in the coal mines. I worked for this company until 1927. Since then, I have not been working in the mines, although a member of the United Mine Workers of America and active for that organization until July 1931, after this strike had been in progress since April. I then joined the National Miners Union and became active in that organization.

I was chosen as a delegate to the Pittsburgh Convention of the National Miners Union in July of this year, along with twenty-six other delegates from Kentucky, and made the report of the Kentucky situation. I returned to Kentucky and was still active in the National Miners Union as a member of the General Committee.

On account of my activities in this union, my house was raided on July 27th by twelve deputies armed with machine guns. I happened to see them before they reached the house and escaped through the back way. I heard them inquire for me. They rifled the house looking for radical literature, as they said. I made my escape to the house of a sympathizer and remained in the County for a few days under cover. After a few days I went to Caryville, Tennessee, and remained there for two weeks, then returned to Bell County, Kentucky. I stayed at the home of a friend for some ten days or two weeks. From there I went, in company with Tom Myerscough, to Neon, Letcher County, Kentucky. As I was coming out of a boarding house in Neon, I was accosted by four or five men, some wearing uniforms. They said I was under arrest. In their conversation, one of them was referred to as Sheriff.

I was hustled into a car, and one of the men in the car said to the man in the uniform, "I thank you, Sheriff, for helping me make this arrest." This was on September 25th at about 8 P.M. I was taken to Jenkins, Kentucky, a distance of five or six miles, where there are coal operations belonging to the Consolidated Coal Company. There I was placed in the Company jail, and on entering the cell I found Tom Myerscough was already in the cell. The man who had the key said, "Hello, Tom, here's Jim." We did not know him but he knew us. Tom and I remained in jail that night until about midnight. We were asleep, when I heard the jail door open. The same man that placed us in jail called us to get up and dress. We dressed and an officer who seemed to be an officer of the Jenkins Operations, escorted us out of the jail. We were ushered into a car occupied by three armed men—large men, who were well armed. They had Tom's and my suitcases and brief-cases in the car. After we were placed in the car, the driver and some uniformed officer held a short consultation. Tom and I were both placed in the back seat, by the side of an armed deputy, with two deputies in the front seat (one the driver), well armed, all husky. On the way from the jail, I asked the man in the back seat if he was from Harlan. He said no. One of the deputies asked us if we were I. W. W.'s. We said no, we had no connection with that organization. He said, "What are you then, Red necks?" We said no, we were organizers for the National Miners Union. "Are you having much success?" they said. We said we hadn't been there long enough to find out. They said, "Don't you fellows know you are ruining the country, causing men to desert their families and causing trouble in Harlan County?" We said no. There was no further conversation.

In the meantime, I thought they were taking us to the Harlan jail because I had understood I had been previously indicted in Harlan Circuit Court for Criminal Syndicalism and perhaps other charges. We went on until we came to Cumberland. I was well acquainted with the territory, but Tom was not. Instead of taking us toward Harlan, they turned to the left and went to Lynch. I said to Tom in an undertone, "They're not taking us to Harlan, but to the Big Black Mountain. They're taking us up there to kill us." Tom answered, "If they are, it's all up with us."

They stopped in Lynch in front of the Police Station and the driver went into the Police Station. He returned in about fifteen minutes and took his place in the car. Then, instead of going to Harlan, they proceeded in the opposite direction, towords Virginia, until they reached the top of Big Black Mountain, at the Virginia line, on the Virginia side. There they stopped the car suddenly. It was about 2 o'clock in the morning. They all three got out and held a conversation in low tones for about a minute. Then they told us to get out. I heard one say, "That old big one ought to come first." (Meaning Tom.) They came back to us and said, "What have you in your hand-bags?" Tom said, "Some papers relative to the union." They said, "What's in the big suitcase?" I said, "My clothes." That was the last we ever saw of our belongings. They robbed us of them, and had searched our pockets several times during the evening.

Then two of them stood guard, while the largest one, weighing more than 200 pounds, came around to us and said, "Do you fellows ever fight any?" We said, "We haven't practiced that very much." He said, "How would you like to take me on for a few rounds?" Tom said, "We do not care to fight under the circumstances. We are unarmed. Those men are well armed." At that moment the large man struck Tom and glanced him on the jaw. Tom acted as though he had been skilled in maneuvering and kept out of his way until he backed close to the precipice on the right of the road looking towards Virginia. He attempted to turn around and jump over. The big man said, "Don't you run, I'll kill you." He reached down and picked up a rock weighing about two pounds and threw it at Tom as he turned to go over the embankment, and hit him on the shoulder but did not knock him out. Tom went over the hill anyway, through rocks, stubs, briars, grape-vines, and other entanglements, and disappeared in the darkness. Meantime the thug fired at least twenty shots at Tom. They called Tom and cursed him but got no response. They kept shooting in his direction.

When they got no response, they turned on me. He struck me on the back of the head with something and knocked me to the ground and kicked me on the other side of the head. When I tried to rise they struck me with something else and broke my right cheek-bone. With difficulty I rose again—but that time I was close to the edge of the darkness where the light from the car did not shine. I made an escape into the darkness amid a hail of stones and bullets. I went down the road a few jumps, then over the embankment into the wilderness. After that, I heard perhaps twelve shots more. By then, I was bleeding so at the nose and my eyes were so bruised I could hardly see. In fact, I was only semi-conscious. I lay there about an hour before I was able to stand up. I was uneasy about Tom. I felt sure they had killed him. They seemed to shoot so straight in his direction.

After the car disappeared, I crawled up the bank and went to look for Tom. I could see where he had gone over the bank. I called him several times but got no response. I started to go down to look for him but it was so dark and the place was so rough I was afraid I could not return to the road on account of being so weak. So I started to walk to Appalachia, Virginia.

The rain poured down. I reached Appalachia (about six or seven miles), and there I hoped to get some trace of Tom. I thought perhaps he had stopped at the Western Union to report by wire. But when I reached Appalachia I found that the Western Union was located in the Appalachian Hotel, a hangout for the Operators Association. I felt it would be unsafe to enter, and decided to walk to Big Stone Gap (about five miles). When I reached Big Stone Gap, I found I had $2 in the watch pocket of my pants, barely enough to buy a ticket to Middlesboro. I reached Middlesboro the same day, and went to the house of a sympathizer.

I was so weak, and my face so swollen, they did not recognize me and did not even invite me into the house because they didn't know who I was. Even after I told him, they doubted it. Then they looked at my hat and knew it, and so recognized me. Of course I was taken care of, bathed my wound and washed off the blood in a bath prepared with water and salts.

In the meantime, my wife had heard of the kidnaping and was on the hunt for some one to report to, and unexpectedly came into the house where I was. She said to the lady of the house, "They caught Jim and Tom in Neon and I suppose have them in jail somewhere but we can't find out where." The lady said, "No, they haven't got Jim. He's here."

We hadn't heard yet from Tom, and I knew nothing of his whereabouts until a day or two later, when his whereabouts were reported by Bruce Crawford in Norton, Virginia. I remained at this house for perhaps ten days, then was sent to N. Y. Since then I have been on Relief Work in New York City and New York State.

(*signed*)   JIM GRACE.

*Sworn to before me this fourth day*
*of November, 1931*
(*signed*)   HERMAN CERBERT.

STATE OF NEW YORK        ⎫
COUNTY OF NEW YORK    ⎬ SS:
CITY OF NEW YORK         ⎭

DEBS MORELAND, *being duly sworn, says:*

I am a resident of the town of Panzy, Harlan County, Kentucky. I was born in Birmingham, Alabama, and lived there until 1925 when I came to Panzy where I have since resided, being employed during such time by the Perkin Harlan Coal Company, in the capacity of miner.

On April 7, 1931, the employees of the Perkin Harlan Coal Company went out on strike. I was among them. From that date until the present time, although the mine has resumed periodic operation I have not been reëmployed there, or elsewhere. On or about the beginning of August I was placed in charge of the Panzy Relief Kitchen which was being operated by the National Miners Union: This Relief Kitchen furnished food for about 100 families of striking miners. Food was furnished at the Kitchen and was also provided for families of miners who were unable to come to the Kitchen.

I was arrested on or about August 24th and placed in jail where I was held on a trumped-up charge of Criminal Syndicalism until September 26th, when I was released without having been brought to trial. Judge D. C. Jones called me into his office that night about 6 P.M. and asked me to leave the State of Kentucky. He said, "I will release you on condition you do not go back and resume work which you have been doing." He asked me whether I belonged to the National Miners Union. I replied in the affirmative. He said he proposed to do away with the National Miners Union on the ground that it was a Communist organization and inquired whether I was aware of the fact that the National Miners Union was a branch of the Communist Party's affiliated bodies. I replied that I had not been aware of it, but that if conditions in Harlan County would be improved by the Communists or any one else, I would throw my lot in with them. At that point, he showed me the door and as I emerged from his office he told the Deputy Sheriff in the anteroom to turn me loose. During this conversation, Judge Jones also stated there would not be a chance of my getting work in Harlan County, intimating that I was to be black-listed. I returned home and on or about the first of October, I resumed work at the Relief Kitchen.

On October 15th, at about 11 P.M., four of John Henry Blair's imported deputy sheriffs knocked on my door, called me by my name, and when I opened the door rushed by me into the house. I recognized these as the same men who had come to my house time and again and searched it, claiming to have search warrants. They organized raiding parties which went through house after house on regular trips and which broke up meetings whenever the miners attempted to hold them. These were a part of a group who were lodged in the Harlan Hotel and were not local police officials but were strangers to Harlan County but working hand in hand with the officials and the mine owners. They said they wanted to know if I lived there. I said, "Yes." They said, "We have a warrant against you for banding and confederating." I asked to see the warrant. One of them held out a paper. I reached for it. Another one grabbed it and said, "You don't have to see this. You are the man we want." I said, "It's mighty funny you have a warrant for me for banding and confederating. I have not been in any trouble." They said, "You know how it is. We have to do our duty. We have the warrant and we have to take you in. You can tell that to the judge."

I was hustled into their auto. They drove through Harlan (where the jail was located), through Cumberland, through Lynch, into Virginia, up at the top of Big Black Mountain, altogether a distance of about 60 miles. When we reached a point about a half mile beyond the top of Big Black Mountain, in a section uninhabited for miles about, in the midst of a thick forest, the car stopped. On one side of the road was a steep embankment, almost perpendicular, which fell to a depth of about 40 feet; on the other side was a sheer precipice at the top of which was an impenetrable forest. It was then about 1:30 in the morning, and a dark, moonless night. Three of these hired thugs got out of the car. The fourth sought to obtain information from me as to the number of organizers there were for the National Miners Union in the county, how many guns we had, and where our guns were. I said I had no knowledge of these matters. He said, "You are nothing but a thoroughbred red, and we haven't any use for you. And we intend to break it up." At that point he said, "Unload." And followed me out of the car.

I emerged from the car and they formed a circle about me. I asked what they intended to do, beat me up? One answered, "No, you son of a bitch, we are not going to beat you up. We are going to kill you. We are damned tired of being bothered with you reds." At that time I was given a terrific blow from behind on the back of my neck which felled me. When I arose, another one hit me on the cheek and knocked me down again. They pulled me to my feet, tearing at my clothes. I saw that my only hope was to make a dash, so I tore loose and made a lunge over the embankment. I slid and rolled down the embankment about 30 feet, tearing my clothes more and being bruised by the stones and shrubs until I was stopped by a large rock. I lay there half stunned, just conscious of their flash lights playing about and the whiz of bullets flying all around me. About 25 shots were fired. Then I heard them say, "That's one red son of a bitch we are rid of." I saw the reflection of the head lights of their car rounding the curve as they drove away.

I was unable to move and lay there until about 5:30 A.M. Then after numerous attempts I succeeded in reaching the top of the bank. At about six o'clock a car came along and at my request consented to take me along to Big Stone Gap, a town about 10 miles further into Virginia. At the moment I left this car at Big Stone Gap, two cars crowded with Harlan thugs drove by, probably coming from the place where my death had been planned to see whether the job had been satisfactorily done. I darted into a hallway when I saw them, and in this way probably saved my life for the second time. I got a lift in a truck out of Big Stone Gap and slept on the side of the road that night. In the morning I got another ride in Middleboro. From there, I made my way to Chattanooga, Tenn., then to Lexington, Ky., then to New York.

It was not until a week after I had been kidnaped from my home for the purpose of murder that I was able to communicate with my wife and child in Panzy. I received a letter from my wife thereafter that Blair denies having issued any warrant for me at any time.

(signed)    D<small>EBS</small> M<small>ORELAND</small>.

*Sworn to before me this fourth day*
*of November, 1931*
(*signed*)    H<small>ERMAN</small> C<small>ERBERT</small>.

Commissioner of Deeds New York
County Clerk's no. 1925
New York Co. Reg. No. 76 C2
Commission Expires Oct. 7, 1932

# 3

## ARRIVAL IN PINEVILLE

BREAKFAST in the station at Cincinnati. After that the train crosses the Ohio River and starts winding through the shallow valleys of the rolling section of central Kentucky. At lunch time to get to the dining car we have to walk through a federal prison car on its way to Atlanta. Change at Corbin onto a local train for Pineville. The Louisville papers say Governor Sampson is sending a detachment of militia into Harlan County. As we get near Pineville the valleys deepen. Steep hills burnished with autumn cut out the sky on either side. There's the feeling of a train getting near the war zone in the old days.

At the station is a group of miners and their wives come to welcome the writers' committee: they stand around a little shyly, dressed in clean ragged clothes. A little coaldust left in men's eyebrows and lashes adds to the pallor of scrubbed faces, makes you think at once what a miserable job it must be keeping clean if you work in coal. At the Hotel Continental Dreiser is met by newspaper men, by the mayor and town clerk of Pineville, who offer their services "without taking sides." Everybody is very polite. A reporter says that Judge D. C. Jones is in the building. A tall man in his thirties, built like a halfback, strides into the lobby. There's something stiff and set about the eyes and the upper part of his face; the look of strain and bullying of a man who feels he's under criticism. When he comes up to us he draws himself up to his full six feet five or six. "Well, they grow 'em big down here anyway," says Dreiser. "Yes, sir, we grow tall down here in these mountains." They go on talking guardedly. Somehow the Judge comes around to the Harlan County jail, says it's a fine new jail, resents how it's been spoken of, says the food was so good Mrs. Wakefield gained three pounds in the month she spent there.

He says the trouble is all over now, never was anything except a few outside agitators trying to make money out of the poor shiftless miners. Judge Jones says he's willing to answer any questions put to him about the situation in Harlan County. Mr. Dreiser and Judge Jones are photographed together on the steps of the hotel. Mrs. Grace of Wallins Creek, the wife of Jim Grace, a union organizer who was beaten up and run out of the county, comes up and asks Judge Jones why the sheriff's deputies raided her house and ransacked her things and her boarders' rooms. The interview comes abruptly to an end.

When the members of the committee settle down at a long table in a room off the lobby to decide on a plan of procedure, stories start pouring in.

Dreiser did most of the questioning. Mrs. Grace, who had met us at the train, started the ball rolling. John R. Neil of Tennessee, of Scopes Trial fame, sat in on the first session.

# TESTIMONY TAKEN IN PINEVILLE

*Pineville, Kentucky, November 6,* 1931

TESTIMONY *taken at the Continental Hotel, Pineville, Kentucky, before the National Committee for the Defense of Political Prisoners, Theodore Dreiser, Chairman, and others.*

## VIOLA GRACE

Q 1   What is your name?
A   Viola Grace?
Q 2   Where do you live?
A   At Wallins Creek.
Q 3   You are the wife of a miner?
A   I am the wife of Jim Grace.
Q 4   Is he a miner?

A      It has been some years since he worked in the mines.

Q 5    What has he been doing? Has he been connected with the mines?

A      Well, he has been round and about with the miners. He was the general manager at Ed Hoskins' store for about three to four years.

Q 6    This is a grocery store?

A      Yes. He has also worked for the Baldwin Piano Co. for about a year and with the Singer Sewing Mach. Co. about 3-4 months, and he has been with this Ohio W. Va. miners committee.

Q 7    Has be been injured in any way?

A      Yes.

Q 8    When?

A      About six weeks ago.

Q 9    How was he arrested?

A      I was not with him but he was arrested in Letcher County. Leon, him and Tom Myerscough were together.

Q 10   What were they doing?

A      They were trying to get the union organized. They were organizing against starvation. They were establishing a union for better conditions.

Q 11   What happened to him?

A      After they came to the house looking for him, he went away and stayed at a friend's house and then he and Tom went to Neon, Letcher County. There he was arrested and they took him to the jail in Neon. Then he was turned over to the Jenkins bunch of gunmen.

Q 12   Who is this Jenkins bunch?

A      This bunch is from Letcher County.

Q 13   Well, what did they do?

A      They didn't do anything.

Q 14   Whom does this bunch work for?

A      For the Sheriff of Letcher County.

Q 15   Well, what happened then?

A      Him and Myerscough were turned over to the Harlan County bunch and they takes them over to the Big Black

Mountains of Virginia. They bust him in the face and broke his cheek bone, they kicked him in the back. He ran into the woods and they fired at him

Q 16   How many shots did they fire?

A   About fifty, I guess.

Q 17   Did they hit him?

A   Well, he was grazed at the elbow.

Q 18   What did he do?

A   He went on to Middlesboro and stayed at a friend's house. But I didn't know. When I first got word that Grace and Tom was held in jail, I didn't know whether he was in Harlan, Jenkins or Neon. I goes out and went to get some one to find them. We thought they were killed. I started to get hold of the I. L. D. and I just happened in where Mr. Grace was and I asked the lady whether her husband was there and then I found out that Jim was there. His face and eyes were swollen and black and blue. He was crazy as a loon.

Q 19   What did they say to him when they picked him up?

A   I don't know.

Q 20   What did they do to you?

A   They came down in July along about the 18th. He was sittin' on the running board and he saw them come in and he dodged them.

Q 21   Did they come again?

A   Oh, yes, sir. They came around the 30th of July.

Q 22   How many were there?

A   I don't know exactly.

Q 23   About how many?

A   No less than fifty of them.

Q 24   Who were they?

A   Blair says they are County Patrol men. They carry a gun and claimed to be deputy sheriffs. Judge Howard says they are deputy sheriffs.

Q 25   What did they do when they came in?

A   They came and turned over the house; they looked in every dishpan; they looked in every one of the pots and in every hole and corner they could find and they took all the papers. They raided my home and others. They said they were looking for home brew and for I. W. W. stuff.

Q 26 Did they find any?

A They said they got this I. W. W. stuff in my house.

Q 27 Did they?

A I don't know whether I had any I. W. W. stuff. I had some U. M. W. of A. papers but they said they didn't want that, they belong to that themselves.

Q 28 Did you have any I. W. W. papers in your house?

A If there was any, I didn't see it.

Q 29 Did you have any other kind of papers?

A Yes, I had a copy of the *Daily Worker*, that is I. W. W., that is what they say. They got that.

Q 30 Did they come again?

A Yes, many times.

Q 31 How many times?

A About five times.

Q 32 Tell us about it.

A They came and ransacked my house about five times while I was there. They busted the locks on the door. They turned up the bed. They made a complete rough search looking for documents. They did this every time except the last time.

Q 33 What happened then?

A Why then I just said, "Come right in, boys," and I invited them in. They had a machine gun tripod settin' up the railroad. It was settin' over there. They had one great big husky fellow. He stands there with this tripod. Then here comes another little smart alecky with a Browning automatic.

Q 34 Did they have a search warrant?

A No, sir, I never saw any. They just come in and said they were raiding for home brew and literature.

Q 35 Communism or home brew. Well, go ahead.

A Then one of our neighbormen came out and one of the

gun men, George Lee said, "God damn him, shoot him."
They were after Mr. Grace. He said, "Next time shoot
him, God damn him." They cursed me all right.

Q 36  Who is George Lee?

A     He is a deputy sheriff. Lee says so. He is paid by the
Black Mountain Coal Co.

Mr. Smith of the Knoxville *News-Sentinel* questioned.

Q 37  Did you say George Lee is paid by the Black Mountain
Coal Co.?

A     Yes.

James Price stated: I am a representative of the General Defense Committee and I know Lee is paid by the Black
Mountain Coal Co.


## RICHARD WOLFE

Q 1   What is your name?

A     Richard Wolfe.

Q 2   How old are you?

A     Thirty.

Q 3   What kind of worker are you?

A     I am a coal miner.

Q 4   How long?

A     Since 1915.

Q 5   Are you working at present?

A     No, sir.

Q 6   How long since you worked?

A     I have not worked since March.

Q 7   Where did you work?

A     I worked for the Star Coal Co.

Q 8   Why did you stop working?

A     I was fired.

Q 9   Why were you fired?

A     I attended a mass meeting on March 1st and I was fired
the next day.

Q 10 Did you work in the union?

A Well, I enrolled members into the U. M. W. of A. among the miners until the strike was called.

Q 11 When was this?

A This was about May 11th.

Q 12 Have you done anything since then?

A I have been working in the National Miners Union.

Q 13 What have you been doing?

A I have been soliciting members to this day for the N. M. U.

Q 14 What has happened to you, that has been injurious, since you were fired?

A My home has been raided.

Q 15 How many times?

A Several times.

Q 16 When did they raid your house for the first time?

A About two months ago was the first time they came.

Q 17 What did they do? How many were there?

A The first time they came there was 14 of them.

Q 18 Who were they?

A Harlan County gunmen.

Q 19 Do you know any by name?

A Bob Blair is one, but I don't know the others.

Q 20 Who is he?

A He is a deputy sheriff.

Q 21 Were they armed?

A Yes, they were armed. They had machine guns.

Q 22 How many?

A Three of them.

Q 23 How do you know?

A I saw them.

Q 24 What time was this?

A About 10 A.M.

Q 25 Tell us about it.

A I was sittin' on the porch and they came into the house and all around the house and they said they had a search warrant.

Q 26 Did they show the warrant?

A I asked him to show me the warrant, but he didn't. Then he says to me, "What is this I. W. W. literature around here?"

Q 27 Did you have any?

A I never had any I. W. W. literature.

Q 28 Did you have any other kind of literature?

A No, sir, I had no other literature there.

Q 29 Did you have any guns there?

A My father had an old gun which he has had about 24 years, .22 rifle which they took and a .38 special which I had. They took a pistol and two guns.

Q 30 Did they destroy any of the property?

A No, they did not.

Q 31 Did they come again?

A Yes, they came again in a week. They asked me what I was doing with those high powered rifles, but I never had any, and the I. W. W. literature. They called me a red neck.

Q 32 Is that a Communist?

A Yes.

Q 33 Did they threaten you?

A They said there would be trouble if I mixed with those reds.

Q 34 Did they come again?

A Yes, after that they came several times, and surrounded the house, but I was not there. My mother was there.

Q 35 Did they find anything there?

A They found U. M. W. of A. literature there and leaflets but they said that was all right.

Q 36 What was the nature of the circular?

A It called upon the miners to stand by the United Mine Workers. It was against the National Miners Union and the I. W. W. and the Communists and called us to stand by the U. M. W. of A.

*Questions answered by John R. Neil:*

Q 37 Is it against the law to have a gun?

A    No, there is no reason why they cannot have guns as well as bullets.

Q 38 Is it illegal to have literature of this kind in the house?

A    No, it is not.

Q 39 Then they are outside the law in confiscating the gun and searching the house for this kind of literature?

A    Under the laws you are allowed high powered guns.

Q 40 Is there a C. S. law in Kentucky?

A    No.

(Note: Mr. Neil later told us that he was mistaken. That a Criminal Syndicalism law was on the statute books in Kentucky.)

*Questions answered by Mrs. Grace:*

Q 41 Do they take the trouble to swear out any warrants in these cases?

A    They never showed no warrants.
     They accuse you of being from Pennsylvania, if you work for the N. M. U. They call you agitators from Pennsylvania. They call you a red neck.

Q 42 Do you feel insulted when they call you a red neck?

A    No, I don't care.

*Lawyer Neil questioning:*

Q 43 You never had those guns restored?

A    No, they never have.

The next witness called was


# JEFF BALDWIN


who was questioned as follows

*By Theodore Dreiser:*

Q 1   What is your name?

A    Jeff Baldwin.
Q 2    Where do you live?
A    Whitley County.
Q 3    Do you live in any town, or just in the county?
A    In Jellico, Tennessee.
Q 4    How old are you?
A    32 years old.
Q 5    What is your business?
A    I have been a miner for the last fourteen years. I haven't worked at it lately.
Q 6    How long has it been since you were actually mining?
A    The 25th of last May is two years ago.
Q 7    You mean it was two years the 25th of last May since you have worked at mining?
A    Yes, sir.
Q 8    Why haven't you been mining since?
A    I got hurt in an automobile wreck and the Company wouldn't give me no work afterwards.
Q 9    Are you a Union man?
A    I was at that time; belonged to the United Mine Workers of America.
Q 10    When was that that you belonged?
A    In 1917, when they first came into the 19th District.
Q 11    What has happened between the last time you worked as a miner and now that brings you into this case? Did somebody say that you were shot or injured in some way?
A    Yes, sir, I was shot.
Q 12    When?
A    The 30th day of last August.
Q 13    Why?
A    I don't know why. The only thing I could figure out is that I belonged to the National Miners Union and had tried to help out at the kitchen.
Q 14    What kitchen? The soup kitchen?
A    Yes, the soup kitchen.
Q 15    Who got you to do that?
A    My brother, for one, and others that I knew.

Q 16 The miners came to you and wanted you to help organize the soup kitchen, did they?

A   They had already organized the soup kitchen but I had a car and they wanted me to help with the car and do work for them.

Q 17 How long had you started doing this work before you were injured?

A   I started one Thursday night in August and I was shot on Sunday, the 30th day of August, and I had started the Thursday night before that.

Q 18 And you were shot on Sunday?

A   Yes, sir.

Q 19 And the Thursday night before that you started to work for the soup kitchen?

A   Yes, sir.

Q 20 How were you injured?

A   I was shot through the left shoulder; right through the joint.

Q 21 Were you in the hospital long, or were you in any hospital at all after that?

A   I was in the hospital from Sunday night until Wednesday evening.

Q 22 Do you know who shot you?

A   I don't know the man that shot me except from a statement that he made himself. He made a statement in regard to it. His name was Lee Fleenor.

Q 23 Who is Lee Fleenor?

A   One of the gunmen that John Henry Blair has got up there.

Q 24 Who is John Henry Blair?

A   He is High Sheriff of Harlan County.

Q 25 Was Lee Fleenor working for the High Sheriff of Harlan County?

A   Yes, sir.

Q 26 What did Mr. Fleenor say about your being shot?

A   He asked me what it was—what time it was, and I said I didn't know.

Q 27 Was that before you were shot that he asked you that?

A    Yes, sir.

Q 28 Where was that?

A    At the swimming pool, at the soup kitchen in Harlan County.

Q 29 Where was the soup kitchen in Harlan County?

A    They called it Clovertown. It was about a mile beyond Harlan Town from here.

Q 30 You were near there?

A    Yes, I was at the soup kitchen.

Q 31 Were you in your car?

A    No, I was standing something like ten steps from the car at the corner of the soup kitchen.

Q 32 Were you using the car?

A    No, I had stepped out to see if anything was around the car before I went to bed.

Q 33 And you were then shot?

A    Yes, sir.

Q 34 Was it before this you say that this man spoke to you and asked you what time it was?

A    Yes.

Q 35 What makes you think that he had anything to do with this shooting?

A    I saw him while he was doing the shooting.

Q 36 You saw him shoot you?

A    No, I saw him in a shooting position and I saw him with the gun in his hand.

Q 37 But you didn't see him shoot you?

A    No.

Q 38 Why not?

A    I had my back to him whenever he shot me. I had started in the house, and I felt the shot.

Q 39 When you felt the wound you turned around and saw him with a gun in his hand?

A    No, when I felt the shot I turned around to give my brother a chance to come in the house. I gave him a chance to get in the door and I was waiting for him to come in.

Q 40  Was your brother with you at the car?

A     Yes, sir.

Q 41  Was he shot?

A     He was killed.

Q 42  Was he killed before you were shot or afterward?

A     He was killed after I was shot.

Q 43  You were shot and you turned around, and then what
      did you do? Did you do anything at all after you were
      shot?

A     I never done anything except wait for my brother to
      come in at the door. He was outside standing at the
      corner of the building near the car.

Q 44  And you felt this shot and then you looked around for
      your brother?

A     Yes, sir.

Q 45  Did you see your brother?

A     I saw him fall across the door. There was about three
      shots fired from the time I was shot until my brother
      was hit. There was eight shots altogether.

Q 46  And after you were shot you turned and saw your brother
      fall?

A     Yes, sir.

Q 47  And then you turned and saw Mr. Fleenor?

A     I saw Fleenor whenever he first shot at me.

Q 48  Then you saw your brother fall after you saw him shoot?

A     Yes.

Q 49  Did you see him shoot your brother?

A     I didn't see him shoot my brother, but I saw my brother
      fall.

Q 50  You saw him fire a gun?

A     Yes.

Q 51  And then your brother fell and you assumed that he
      killed your brother?

A     Yes, and he shot Joe Moore and killed him. Joe Moore
      was sitting in the door of the soup kitchen by the side of
      his wife.

Q 52 Did anybody go over and beat him up or fight him after he did this shooting?

A    No, sir; nobody spoke to him.

Q 53 You mean that you saw two people killed and didn't do anything?

A    We didn't have anything to do nothing with. I turned the lights on in the house, there wasn't no lights on, and I found out there wasn't nobody in the building except Moore's wife and my brother's wife and she was in the bed asleep.

Q 54 What time was this?

A    About 8:30 in the evening. I woke my brother's wife up and told her that my brother was killed and I went out to where he was and I came back and got a dipper of water.

Q 55 When you went out again, did he take another shot at you?

A    No, as soon as they shot their pistols empty they had the engine of the car running and he got in the car and they drove off. There was three of them. Crip Niclerk and Lawrence Howard was with him.

Q 56 Did Crip do any firing?

A    Yes. Oh, I don't know.

Q 57 Did Lawrence Howard do any firing?

A    Yes, I saw him.

Q 58 Do you think he shot you or that Lee Fleenor shot you?

A    I think Lee Fleenor shot me and also my brother and Joe Moore.

Q 59 You don't think Lawrence Howard killed any one?

A    No, sir, I don't think he hit any one but he shot eight times.

Q 60 And they had the car running and jumped in and ran away?

A    Lawrence Howard never got out of the car.

Q 61 Did you make a complaint against Fleenor for killing anybody?

A    No, sir.

Q 62 Why not?

A    Because I figured there wasn't any use of it. He came clear in the examining trial whenever I was at my brother's burying in Whitley County. We took him to Whitley County to bury him and Fleenor come clear in his examining trial whenever I was there burying my brother.

Q 63 Somebody arrested him then?

A    The paper stated he was arrested and was given $5,000.00 bond.

Q 64 By whom?

A    Sheriff Blair, I suppose.

Q 65 How soon after the killing was he arrested?

A    The paper stated on Monday morning he was under bond after the killing.

Q 66 He went off then and gave himself up and furnished $5,000 bond and was ready to kill somebody else?

A    I reckon so. He came back to the kitchen about 25 or 30 minutes after he done the killing and had eight or ten car-loads of gun-thugs of John Blair's in the bunch and they raided the kitchen for literature and guns and they found a shotgun or two in the kitchen and they talked about blowing the kitchen up.

Q 67 That was 30 minutes after the killing and you had told your brother's wife that your brother was killed; then what did you do after that between the time they went away and came back?

A    As soon as the first man came in the kitchen I asked him if he would help carry my brother inside.

Q 68 This was a man that came in for something to eat?

A    He was there and had had supper a short while before that, and I asked him if he would help carry my brother in and we carried him in and laid him down and by that time four or five more men and women had come in.

Q 69 They had come to get something to eat, had they?

A    They was neighbors and wasn't working and they stayed

around there a right smart bit, and they came inside after the shooting.

Q 70 Where were they before the shooting or at the time the shooting was done?

A    Part of them was there; six or seven men besides the three that was shot. Just around there.

Q 71 Did you call these people and ask them to help you?

A    I just asked the first one I saw to help me carry the man in the building, to help carry my brother in where we could see what was wrong with him and how bad he was shot and after we carried him in the building I asked them to call a doctor. I didn't know whether there was any phones around there and some of them said there wasn't any phones and then somebody said they would go and call a doctor and then I happened to think about my car and I turned to this fellow and asked him if he would help me put my brother in the car and take him to the hospital, and when I drove around to the front with the car they had my brother out there and I took him to the hospital and he died Tuesday evening, and I wasn't back out to the soup kitchen any more. I stayed in the hospital until Wednesday evening.

Q 72 Were you afraid to go back out there?

A    I would have been afraid to have went back if I had been able.

Q 73 If you went away at that time, how do you know what happened 25 or 30 minutes after the shooting?

A    Just as I was leaving the soup kitchen for the hospital they drove up and was going in.

Q 74 How many of them were there?

A    There was eight or ten cars of people. I don't know how many men.

Q 75 And the High Sheriff?

A    Yes, sir.

Q 76 And they found a couple of shotguns and some papers?

A    No, they didn't find any literature concerning the National Miners Union.

Q 77 Nothing in the way of *Daily Workers?*
A    No, no *Daily Workers.*
Q 78 Nobody filed a charge against this man and on Monday he was out on bond?
A    Yes, sir.
Q 79 Was he ever tried?
A    They claimed he was tried.
Q 80 Before whom?
A    Judge Hamp Howard.
Q 81 Is he at Harlan?
A    Yes, sir, he is the County Judge of Harlan County.
Q 82 Are you willing to swear to this?
A    Yes, sir.

The witness was then sworn by the Notary Public who signs this testimony that what he has told here is true and that the remaining part of his testimony is also true.

*Questioned by John R. Neil:*

Q 1  They made no effort to get you at the preliminary hearing that you know of?
A    No, sir, none of the eye witnesses were called.

*Questioned by Mrs. J. M. Grace, of Wallins Creek, Kentucky, (Harlan Co.):*

Q 1  Hasn't Lee Fleenor killed another man since he killed Baldwin?
A    Well, I don't know.

*Further questioning by Theodore Dreiser:*

Q 83 Did you see Lee Fleenor?
A    Yes, I saw him in the position of shooting, the way he shot at me, but he shot at me whenever my back was turned.
Q 84 Who is Lawrence Howard?
A    Lawrence Howard is the County Judge's boy, and Lawrence Howard and Lee Fleenor is the two that done the shooting out there and Lee Fleenor had his examining

trial before Judge Howard at the time I had gone to
bury my brother.

Q 85 And you say his son did part of the shooting?

A    Yes, sir.

Q 86 But you don't know whether he killed any one?

A    His son didn't. He was in the back seat of the car at the
time Lee Fleenor was doing the shooting.

Q 87 Was there any particular reason why you and your brother,
other than helping these people out at the soup kitchen,
—could there have been any other reason why these
people wanted to open fire on you and your brother, or
either of you?

A    No, sir, I didn't even know the man.

Q 88 You knew Lee Fleenor?

A    No.

Q 89 You knew of him?

A    Yes.

Q 90 And you knew this fellow, Lawrence Howard?

A    No, I didn't know him.

Q 91 When did you find out he was the Judge's son?

A    He made a statement with Lee Fleenor in the newspaper
that Fleenor and Lawrence Howard,—I mean the paper
stated that it was Lee Fleenor and Lawrence Howard.

Q 92 Then you really didn't know that this fellow in the back
seat was Lawrence Howard, of your own knowledge?

A    No sir, I didn't know it was Lawrence Howard. I saw
him and the papers said it was this man Lawrence Howard—Lee Fleenor and Lawrence Howard, and both of
them made the statement to the papers that they were
in the car and did the shooting.

*John Dos Passos:*

Q 1 Did you say it was about dusk when this happened?

A    It was about 8:30.

Q 2 Were they sober or drunk?

A    Lee Fleenor was the only one that spoke to my brother

and me and he asked what time it was and he spoke like a man that was under the influence of liquor.

*Mrs. Grace* (the same one mentioned above from Wallins Creek):

Q 1    What was it he said about blowing up the kitchen? Joe Myers told his sister-in-law that it wouldn't take him but a minute to blow the kitchen up and every G—— damned woman there was in it.

*Theodore Dreiser:*

Q 1    He works for the county, does he, the man that made that statement?

A    John Henry Blair says he works for the county and the county says he works for John Henry.

Q 2    He works for one of them?

A    Yes, he carries three or four guns and that's all I know. But he said this about the soup kitchen and he was in Harlan at the time this was done. This talk was handled when they came back to investigate the shooting. They were talking awful mean around the two women whose husbands were killed and they talked awful mean to them.

(The last two answers were made by Mrs. Grace.)

*Mr. Dos Passos:*

Q 1    How did you first know that this car had driven up? Did you hear the man and come out of the house?

A    My brother and me was standing there and we had come out of the building and my car was parked at the corner of the building and we came out there to the corner of the building.

Q 2    Did you hear that car before you came out?

A    No, we came out before it came up. We were standing at the corner of the building facing up the road and the car came down the road and drove to the side of us and stopped.

Q 3    You could see the headlights of the car?

A    It was coming down the road to the soup kitchen and

whenever it came down the road—I mean whenever it drove up to the corner where we were standing it stopped and then they asked what time it was.

Q 4   And you couldn't see who was in the car when they asked you that?

A      Yes, I could see there was three men in the car but I couldn't see to recognize them if I had known them.

Q 5   The lights were in your eyes?

A      No, there wasn't any lights in the house and the car was by the side of us, and we could see that there was three men in the car, you see, and this fellow at the right side of the driver leaned over and asked my brother and me both, "Hey, fellows, what time is it?" and it happened that I spoke and said, "I can't tell you for I have not got any watch, and I don't know," and there was an alley that went to some houses around there and when he drove up and stopped he was heading down this alley to these houses, and then my brother said, "Let's go in the house" and we turned and Joe Moore and his wife was sitting in the door and Joe was next to the car that done the shooting and about the time we started in the door I heard the shot from the car that I thought was going down this alley.

Q 6   They had started off, had they?

A      They was backing up and they had their lights so that if we had had guns and started to fire, we couldn't do nothing because the lights would be in our eyes, and when the first shot fired I turned around to see where it came from and this fellow that made the statement that he done the shooting, he had the right front door there with the glass down and his arms over the glass like that and about the time I looked around he fired the second shot and I seen that he was shooting at my brother and me.

Q 7   What kind of a car was it?

A      It was a Plymouth sedan. They stated it was Lawrence Howard in the back seat. After I got to the door this shot hit me in the shoulder and I turned to the left to give my brother a chance to come in and about three shots were fired from the time they hit me until my brother fell across the door, and the car pulled out, and this fellow in the back seat was shooting over the glass rolled down and he shot three shots—we could see the dirt fly by the side of my brother, and then he shot the rest in the building as he passes.

*By Theodore Dreiser:*

Q 93   Was there any particular reason they should shoot at him?

A      He was Secretary of the National Miners Union—the Local, and he was living there at the soup kitchen and feeding the starving wives and children of the miners.

Q 94   What was his full name?

A      Julius Baldwin.

Q 95   Was he a miner also before this?

A      Yes, sir.

Q 96   How old was he?

A      29 years old.


## BRUCE CRAWFORD

who, having been first duly sworn, testified as follows under questioning by

*Theodore Dreiser:*

Q 1    How old are you?

A      37.

Q 2    Where do you live?

A      Norton, Virginia.

Q 3    What is your business?

A      Editor and publisher of the weekly newspaper at Norton.

Q 4    You were shot?

A      Yes, sir.

Q 5  In what connection? Where were you when you were shot?

A    In Harlan.

Q 6  When was it?

A    July 28th.

Q 7  Morning or afternoon or evening?

A    In the morning at nine o'clock.

Q 8  Do you know why you were shot?

A    I don't know exactly why, but I think I do.

Q 9  Where were you shot?

A    In the right leg.

Q 10  Seriously?

A    Seriously.

Q 11  Have you any idea why you were shot?

A    Yes.

Q 12  Let's hear it.

A    I had been to Harlan in April of this year.

Q 13  What caused you to go to Harlan at that time?

A    Interest in the strike situation and sympathy with the miners. I had been writing things in my paper about the situation and had criticized the Sheriff after that first trip.

Q 14  How long had you been watching the situation and writing about it before you decided to go over there?

A    After the first trip in April I started writing and then I went back in July.

Q 15  What was the nature of the material that you had written about this strike and anything else about which you may have written?

A    I had written of the strike and had written criticism of the Sheriff and I had written of the mis-treatment of the defense workers and miners, the defense attorneys.

Q 16  Was there any particular thing or any particular treatment that aroused your sense of injustice and brought you over there?

A    One thing that I published that aroused the Sheriff was a letter from Tess Huff in Harlan.

Q 17 Who is Tess Tuff?

A    He is the son of lawyer Huff, a lawyer there in Harlan.
     Capt. B. B. Golden:
     Attorney for the Miners:
     (Or some of them.) Some of these outside representatives
     of institutions that were helping the miners boarded at
     Tess Huff's house.

Q 18 Well, go ahead.

A    He was in sympathy with the miners and he wrote a
     piece for my paper, an article describing the alleged mis-
     treatment of a man named Connors at Harlan. This
     article described the alleged treatment that Connors re-
     ceived from Sheriff Blair and his deputy. He was taken
     to the State line as I understood and beaten up some and
     driven out of Harlan County. That was the substance of
     his letter which I published and Sheriff Blair came over
     to see me about it.

Q 19 When was this?

A    Probably in May of this year.

Q 20 What did he say?

A    He said the letter was a bunch of falsehoods and said he
     was going to sue Tess Huff for libel and that he would
     sue my paper if he could get service on it. Then he sub-
     scribed for the paper for three months and left. On July
     27th, E. S. Fraley, a Norton hardware merchant, and I
     went to Harlan to see a young preacher held in jail up
     there.

Q 21 Who was this preacher?

A    A Congregational minister at Evarts, Allen Keady.

Q 22 Why did they have him in jail?

A    He said it was a frame-up. They had him charged with
     intimidating witnesses in connection with the murder cases
     at Evarts and he claimed that all he was doing was taking
     contributions to help the families, and he wrote us to
     come to see him. When we got there we found that he
     had been released.

Q 23 Who had released him?

A    I don't know what authorities did it but he was released and warned to leave. Soon after I got to Harlan Sheriff Blair recognized me from his office window. I saw him looking out of his window and recognized him and he thumbed at me and called the attention of some one else in his office to me on the street, and I suppose it was 15 or 20 minutes after that that I found I was being followed.

Q 24  Did you know by whom?

A    I didn't know that. I saw two or three men following us to different places, to the drug store and the restaurant and the depot and the hotel, and we came back around the street, Fraley and I, and we got in our car to drive out of town and we saw a man taking our car number on a pad and he turned and walked away. We didn't know him. We put our car in a garage then and went across the foot-bridge to the other side of town to the home of Tess Huff, intending to come back to the hotel for the night. When we got to Huff's home a friend of his was there to warn us not to come back across the foot-bridge. He said that a car-load of deputies was running up and down the street evidently looking for us and seemed to have lost sight of us and he didn't think it would be wise for us to come back across the foot-bridge. The bridge is high over the river and exposes one up there clearly against the sky. The next morning about nine o'clock, Fraley and I were coming across the bridge and we heard two shots, but didn't pay any attention because a car had been running up and down the railroad and some boys had put some torpedoes on the track, but I felt the third shot at the same time I heard it. I stopped and looked at my white sock and saw blood stains. It felt like a barrel-hoop or something had flipped up and hit me on the shin, and I called to Fraley and said that I was shot and he turned to come back, and the fourth shot splintered up the boards between us, and we realized then that we were targets and we looked at each other and started to run. We were about 200 feet from the end of the bridge on the Harlan side. The shooting seemed to come from back that way on Huff's side of the river, but it turned out that it came from the side we were running toward and it was the echoes from the other side that made us think the shots were coming from there. There must have been seven or eight more shots fired, and we ran over the end of the bridge into a residential section and people were all along the street, and we passed two or three men at the end of the bridge who seemed to be cool and unconcerned about the noise, but people were scattered around on the other side of the river and there was a good deal of excitement there. I didn't know who these men were, but we went to town and hunted out a sympathetic doctor and had my leg swabbed and dressed, and we went around to the front of the courthouse and saw Sheriff Blair looking out. He knew me but I don't know whether he knew what had happened or not. I took it for granted that he did and I didn't appeal to him, but went in to listen to a hearing that was going on.

Q 25  You say you didn't tell him what had happened?

A  No. As far as I know, neither the Sheriff nor the Commonwealth's Attorney made any attempt to investigate the shooting although the whole town was astir about it.

Q 26  Did he ever say anything to you about it?

A  No, sir.

Q 27  Did anybody communicate with you?

A  Not any official.

Q 28  Did any one make any ironic comment on what had happened?

A  No, sir.

Q 29  And made no taunting remarks?

A  No, sir. We went to the office of the Chief of Police, Pearl Noe and found that he was in the courthouse with two or three of his policemen and they went down to the bridge and made a little survey and investigation and he told us that the shooting came from Ivy Hill on the Harlan side of the river, opposite from the side where we thought the shots were coming from, and we were running in the direction of the men who were doing the shooting. They were off kind of diagonally to the left but the shots echoed from the other side of the river. The Chief said that the shots came from Ivy Hill and they found two or three shots near the center of the bridge, and he advised us not to come out in our own car but to come out in a bus or a train, as there was danger of them firing at us from out in the mountains and it was 25 or 30 miles to the State line. He seemed rather friendly and there was confusion between the police and the county officers. He seemed to have the same idea that we had, that it was because we were sympathetically interested in the miners' predicament. We stayed around town until three o'clock in the afternoon deliberating on how to come out and talked with a good many people and we finally decided to brave coming out in our own car. We turned the tags up so that they couldn't read the number and took our hats off and came out a back street. I don't guess if they had been trying to hit us we could have got out, but we came out safely, and when we got home the Associated Press reporters were calling about it. The Harlan papers had reported it and there was some confusion in the reports. Some one had reported that I thought the miners had shot me, thinking I was a strikebreaker.

Q 30   Is that all of the story?

A   There is a good deal more.

Q 31   Did you take any steps of any kind to find out who prompted this thing?

A   Not while we were in Harlan except to talk to people who seemed sympathetic, a lawyer or two and some politicians.

Q 32   Did you find anything definite from that time to this to show that this Sheriff did anything about this?

A    Nothing definite except rumors and reports and warnings.

Q 33  What kind of warnings?

A    I got warnings indirectly through friends of the operators who were also friends of my friends.

Q 34  Friends of the operators?

A    Yes, friends of the operators who had friends in my section who were also my friends warned me not to come back.

Q 35  That was communicated to you?

A    Yes, and I believed it. The Sheriff made some remarks about it afterwards I saw in print.

Q 36  To what effect?

A    That I was visiting Communist headquarters on the other side of town where some Communist literature was found.

Q 37  What have you to say about the conditions since that time? Have they been as bad, or worse, or better, as you see it?

A    Conditions after that grew worse and worse, according to all reports.

Q 38  Does that mean right up to now?

A    Up to two or three weeks ago. A number of labor leaders and representatives came out of the Harlan section, forced out, some of them, and stopped at Norton to see us and made some reports, and a soup kitchen was blown up, that was reported on this evening, and the trials, most of them, were held since then. And Arnold Johnson, of the Civil Liberties, was arrested.

Q 39  Who was he?

A    A student of the Theological Seminary who was arrested a month ago, and Jessie Wakefield was arrested and jailed.

Q 40  And there was no improvement until about three weeks ago?

A    Conditions grew worse.

Q 41  Where does the improvement lie at this moment?

A    I can't say there was an improvement except there was just a cessation. I saw in today's paper that the Governor was sending troops in there to preserve order. Tom

Myerscough, of the National Miners Union, came to Norton about six weeks ago, I think, with his clothes torn and his face and neck and hands scratched and bruised telling a story of his having been mistreated by the Harlan officers.

Q 42  Does that mean the Police Department or the county officers?

A  County officers, he said they were. He was taken to the Virginia State line and told to get out and fight. He said to them that it was not fair for him to try to fight because he was not armed and the three officers were armed, but one officer told him to come around in front of the car and fight anyway, and when Myerscough stepped around in front of the car this officer struck him a blow on the chin and Myerscough kind of jumped back and fell over the road bank and slid through underbrush and over rocks and logs for a distance of about 200 feet down the mountain on the Virginia side and he said as he was sliding down the mountain he could hear shots fired. He had with him a man named J. M. Grace, I believe, and he never knew until probably two weeks later what became of Grace, and Grace turned up in Corbin, and he said he went down to the foot of the mountain next morning near a Virginia coal mine and came out on to the road and was promptly picked up by Virginia officers and they seemed to have been running up and down the road looking for him. He told them his story, exactly what had happened the night before, and they took him back to the Kentucky side to verify the story. I am not sure whether they verified the story or not but they brought him back to Appalachia, Virginia, and told him to get away and not come back. He had heard about my being shot and knew Norton was on up there from Appalachia and he came on to Norton and stayed with me and Ed Fraley three or four days and told us a good deal about the situation,—the situation at Harlan, and we got various reports from others who came out of Harlan by way of Norton that showed that it seemed the terror was so great the unionization was being driven underground.

*Questioned by John R. Neil:*

Q 1  You have not been back there since the shooting?

A    No.

Q 2  Naturally you would have wanted to go back there to try to locate the man that shot you, or the men, wouldn't you?

A    I haven't been back there.

Q 3  You haven't been back there because you thought you wouldn't be properly protected?

A    No. The reason I didn't tell the Sheriff or the Commonwealth's Attorney what had happened was because I thought their side did the shooting and I thought it was useless to say anything to them about it.

Q 4  The officers of the law, in your opinion, were the ones who did it or incited it?

A    Yes, it seemed to be their side.

Q 5  We would like for you to send us the articles which were published in your paper.

A    I have got them at home and the letter of Tess Huff that I published.

Q 6  Is is dangerous around this district here for you?

A    I don't think so. If I were here by myself and they thought I was trying to get into Harlan it might be dangerous.

Q 7  Why are you here now?

A    To go with your Committee to Harlan.

# 4

## HARLAN TOWN

NEXT day the committee and attendant newspaper men, accompanied by three officers of the state militia sent as "observers" by Governor Sampson, drove up the fine valley of the Cumberland River to Harlan. It was a smoky fall day, the woods still flared with reds and yellows, hunting weather, mountain climbing weather; you felt what great country this must have seemed to the pioneers who first came over the gaps from Virginia. About half way up we passed the swimming pool where the soup kitchen was shot up, where Jeff Baldwin's brother had been killed.

Harlan is a lively little town; stores and bank buildings attest to the slightly flimsy prosperity of the boom period; the handsome courthouse takes away a little from the gimcrack air of a Southern industrial town. That Friday was a big day. There was going to be a football game between the Pineville and Harlan high schools. In the afternoon a parade with a band and boy scouts, automobiles decorated with green and white streamers and pretty high-school girls, went through the streets taking the home team to the ball field.

Perhaps it was on account of the football game and perhaps on account of the newspaper men and militia officers, but the "gun thugs" we have been told about were nowhere to be seen. There was no particular feeling of terror in the air. Everybody seemed in good spirits, out for a day off, sniffing with pleasure the winey fall day.

In all the bustle only the group of white-faced miners and their wives, waiting in their shabby clean clothes to tell their stories in the lobby of the hotel, were still, didn't seem to appreciate the football game or the fine afternoon. The townspeople wouldn't look at them as they ran in and out of the lobby. Finally, at the request of the management the whole business was moved upstairs to a large room in the front of the house. In a small bedroom next door a group of young men who looked strangely like company guards, kept watch on what went on.

Somebody said they had a dictaphone in there, though I can't imagine what they could have done with it, as the door was open all through the hearings and everybody who wanted was invited to come in and listen or ask questions.

TESTIMONY *taken at the Lewallen Hotel, in Harlan, Kentucky, before Theodore Dreiser, Chairman, and other members of the National Committee for the Defense of Political Prisoners.*

## CALEB POWERS

*Questioned by Theodore Dreiser:*

Q 1  How old are you?
A    42.
Q 2  Are you a native of this State?
A    Yes, sir.
Q 3  Where do you live?
A.   Here in Harlan.
Q 4  How long have you lived here in Harlan?
A    Ever since 1917.
Q 5  Where did you live before then?
A    In Whitley County.
Q 6  What has been your profession or your trade?
A    Miner.
Q 7  For how many years have you been a miner?
A    From 20 to 25 years.
Q 8  Have you done most of your mining here in Harlan County?
A    Since 1917.

Q 9    Are you a member of a Union?

A      Yes, sir.

Q 10   What Union?

A      I first belonged to the United Mine Workers and then I joined the National Union.

Q 11   When did you first belong to the United Mine?

A      In March, I believe.

Q 12   When?

A      This last year.

Q 13   Did you ever belong to a Union before that time?

A      Yes, sir.

Q 14   Which one?

A      The United Mine Workers.

Q 15   When did you join them?

A      In 1917.

Q 16   You had been a miner before that?

A      Yes, sir.

Q 17   Did you belong to any organization before that?

A      No, sir.

Q 18   How did you come to be a United Mine Worker at that time?

A      It started in here and built up an organization in 1917 and I joined it.

Q 19   Was there any trouble around here about that time?

A      Yes, there was a strike.

Q 20   And they came in here at that time?

A      Yes.

Q 21   Were you in good standing with the United Mine Workers from that time on?

A      No, sir, they died down here and I wasn't in good standing until it started again last year.

Q 22   The Union died down?

A      Yes, sir.

Q 23   And you just quit?

A      There just wasn't no Union here then.

Q 24   When did it die out?

A      I believe about 1927.

Q 25 Was there a Union here after that of any kind?

A     There might have been in some places. I think maybe one Local held up.

Q 26 When you were in good standing with this Union, how much did you make a day?

A     Before 1927?

Q 27 When you were a member of the National Mine Workers, how much did you make a day? When you were a Union man?

A     When we had the Union here I could make $4.00 to $5.00 and $6.00 a day.

Q 28 Regularly?

A     No, sometimes we would make more and sometimes less.

Q 29 How much did you make a month?

A     Anywhere maybe from $80 to $100.

Q 30 Regularly?

A     Yes, when we had the Union. Since the Union went away we haven't made it.

Q 31 Were you married at that time?

A     Yes, sir.

Q 32 Have you any children?

A     Six.

Q 33 Did you have them at that time?

A     I had two at that time.

Q 34 Is your wife still living?

A     Yes, sir.

Q 35 Are your children alive?

A     Yes, sir.

Q 36 Do you have to support them?

A     Yes, I have four to support now. I have two grown boys.

Q 37 When did the Union break up?

A     About 1927.

Q 38 Did you work then?

A     Yes, up until they fired me.

Q 39 How much did you work after the Union broke up?

A     They kept cutting wages down until you couldn't make hardly anything at all.

Q 40 Tell me after that time how much did you make either by the day or the month or the year? After 1927?

A   I done mighty well to make $40.00 or $50.00 a month.

Q 41 Did you work for the same Company all this time?

A   No, sir, for different Companies.

Q 42 At this time when the strike was on and the Union built things up, what Company were you working for?

A   I was working at Verda, known as the Wallins Creek Company.

Q 43 Is that around here?

A   It is five or six miles from here.

Q 44 Have you been working for that Company since?

A   Until they fired me last February.

Q 45 And at that time you were making about $50.00 a month?

A   Sometimes it went as low as $30.00.

Q 46 When you were making $30.00 a month, did any of your family make any money on the side?

A   No, sir, just myself.

Q 47 Did you live in the Company town?

A   No, not at that time I didn't. I have lived in the Company houses.

Q 48 What did you pay for rent?

A   All the way from $12.00 to $15.00 and $20.00 a month.

Q 49 When you were getting $30.00 to $40.00 a month, what did you pay for rent?

A   $12.00 to $15.00.

Q 50 That left you from $18.00 to $15.00 a month to live, or about that?

A   Yes, and your cuts came out of that, for hospital and for burial and for insurance, $1.50 for insurance.

Q 51 What is this insurance?

A   Sick and accident cuts they call it, but if there is anything the compensation covers, they don't cover it.

Q 52 You paid so much insurance a week or a month?

A   $1.50 insurance a month.

Q 53 Was that all the insurance you paid?

A    Yes.

Q 54  Were you ever sick?

A    No, I have been lucky all my life.

Q 55  Was this money paid back to you?

A    No, sir.

Q 56  You paid $1.50 a month for how many years?

A    I don't know.

Q 57  Don't you have any idea? One year, or two years or three years?

A    Five or six years.

Q 58  That money has never been paid back to you?

A    No, sir.

Q 59  Do you think they would give it to you if you asked for it?

A    Some of them did ask for it and they didn't give it back to them. I didn't ask.

Q 60  This $30.00 that you would get, was it in scrip or in cash?

A    No, sir, you hardly ever drew any money on that. You traded your scrip in at the store, the Company store, and part of the time they had you in debt.

Q 61  Did you buy clothing at the Company store or food?

A    Food. I couldn't get enough to buy clothing.

Q 62  How did you get clothing?

A    I generally sent out to beg, and did the best I could.

Q 63  The prices you paid for this stuff at the Company store— could you buy them there as cheap as you could at other stores?

A    No, they were higher.

Q 64  How much?

A    I don't know.

Q 65  10% to 20%?

A    I guess 20% higher.

Q 66  You worked on until when?

A    Along the last of February they fired me.

Q 67  Why?

A    They didn't give no reason but they just fired me.

Q 68  Had you done anything in any way that you knew of to make them fire you?

A    Well, no, I hadn't.

Q 69  Had you done anything to deserve being discharged?

A    No, sir.

Q 70  You hadn't attended any of these Mine Workers meetings?

A    Not at that time. The paper was passed about going to the meeting in Pineville.

Q 71  What do you mean by the paper?

A    The handbills were scattered around, and the next morning I went in to my working-place and that evening at four o'clock, it was supposed to be quitting time, and the boss came around to the place and we had just one trip of four cars in our place that day, and we had a full place cut, but four cars is all that we had had that day.

Q 72  What does a car mean in paper or scrip?

A    I guess from 50 to 75 cents a car.

Q 73  That would mean $2.00 that day at 50 cents a car?

A    Yes. And the foreman came around and said: "Are you going to clean up today?" and I said, "I can't. I haven't had but four cars all day and it is quitting time and I am fixing to go home," and he said, "So you are not going to clean it up," and I said, "I have got 16 or 18 cars in here and I can't load that tonight," and he said, "If you don't clean up, I have got orders to fire you," and I said, "All right."

Q 74  You had not attended any meeting at that time?

A    No, sir.

Q 75  How many cars a day did you expect to have?

A    We would load six to eight of them cars a day when we would get the cars.

Q 76  Are you talking about railroad cars?

A    No, bank cars. We would load six to eight.

Q 77  That would mean $4.00 a day?

A    Yes, or $3.00.

Q 78 Why didn't you clean up?

A From the lack of them getting cars to us in the proper time.

Q 79 What do you mean by cleaning up?

A If a man didn't clean up they discharged him, you see.

Q 80 What does it mean? How long does it take and what do you do?

A It would take maybe two days sometimes to clean up a place.

Q 81 Well, a man couldn't come in and ask you to do two days' work at the end of a day, could he?

A It didn't look like they could, but they did sometimes.

Q 82 What time did he come to you?

A Four o'clock.

Q 83 If you had said all right, that you would clean up, how long would it have taken you?

A To something like daylight the next morning.

Q 84 What did he actually expect—that you would stay an hour or so and do something?

A No, from the way he explained himself he must have meant to fire me.

Q 85 How long would it take to load 16 or 18 of those cars?

A It would take all night to load them.

Q 86 With what?

A Coal.

Q 87 Would they have paid you?

A Yes, they would have paid you the price they were paying.

Q 88 50 cents a car?

A Yes, sir.

Q 89 Wouldn't that have been worth doing?

A Yes, if a man hadn't stayed his day out, you see.

Q 90 Do you suppose he would have expected you to stay three or four more hours? How long would it have taken you to fill one car?

A Something near an hour.

Q 91 If you had stayed two more hours, you would have loaded two more cars?

A    Yes, and I had loaded four cars out of the place, and the place cut 24 cars.

Q 92  Were you angry for the reason that up to four o'clock you had only had four cars and there you were waiting for cars?

A    I had too much coal in there to clean up. The place cut 20 to 24 cars.

Q 93  Why hadn't you filled more cars that day?

A    Because of the lack of the Company getting them to me. I didn't have no cars and at four o'clock he came and wanted me to clean up, and he fired me.

Q 94  Since then, what have you been doing?

A    Since I were fired there I stayed around here a couple of weeks looking for work and then I came to another place known as Black Joe.

Q 95  Another mine?

A    Yes, sir.

Q 96  What did they pay you?

A    I believe 35 cents a ton.

Q 97  How much could you make there?

A    It was smaller coal and harder to get.

Q 98  How much did you make a day?

A    $2.00 to $2.50.

Q 99  At 35 cents an hour?

A    Yes.

Q 100  How many hours did you work in the week? How many days?

A    I suppose we got eight hours a day.

Q 101  Did you work that many hours a day?

A    Yes, I stayed the full time.

Q 102  You would work eight hours a day?

A    We would stay in there eight hours. Sometimes there would be a lay off of cars.

Q 103  How much did you make a month?

A    I couldn't have possibly made over $20.00 to $25.00 a month.

Q 104  As long as you worked there, did you make that?

A     I worked there a few days and then they discharged me.
Q 105 Where did you go then and what have you been doing?
A     I haven't been able to do anything.
Q 106 How have you managed to live?
A     Through the mercy of the people and organizations.
Q 107 What people?
A     The public.
Q 108 What public? Charity organizations?
A     On the charitable organizations sent in from different localities.
Q 109 Are you talking about such things as soup kitchens?
A     Yes, sir.
Q 110 Have you gone to soup kitchens?
A     Yes, sir.
Q 111 How long have you been going to soup kitchens?
A     I haven't been to one of them for a while because they wouldn't let them run.
Q 112 Since you cannot go to the soup kitchens, where do you go?
A     I can't go anywhere.
Q 113 What do you do? Do you beg?
A     Yes, we ask people for food. I went and worked a few days on the farm.
Q 114 Whose farm?
A     My mother's. My brother is down there.
Q 115 What does your wife do? Where does she stay?
A     She stays here.
Q 116 And the children also?
A     Yes, sir.
Q 117 What do they do? Do they beg?
A     Yes, sir.
Q 118 Do you pay rent for the house you live in?
A     The place I now live in I own it if I could just get the taxes paid. I am behind two years in taxes.
Q 119 How much?
A     I guess it amounts to about $50.00 or $75.00.
Q 120 How much do you think this house is worth?

A    I couldn't get at the present time, the way conditions are now, over $600.00 or $700.00.

Q 121  On that house you have to pay $75.00 a year taxes?

A    That is two years' taxes.

Q 122  Then it amounts to about $30.00 a year or a little more?

A    Yes, sir.

Q 123  How do you manage to pay those taxes?

A    I haven't paid them.

Q 124  What do you do for coal?

A    Pick it up on the railroad tracks, what spills off the cars.

Q 125  Do you eat regularly?

A    No, sir, just when we can get it.

Q 126  Do you go for days without anything to eat at all?

A    I have.

Q 127  How long ago?

A    Not so very long.

Q 128  How long?

A    Just a few days ago, and there is mighty precious little more than that now.

Q 129  Have you eaten today?

A    A little bit.

Q 130  What?

A    We got some corn and had it ground and I got in a little meat.

Q 131  Do you get an occasional job in the mine now?

A    No, sir, you can't get nothing around here now.

Q 132  Why can't you?

A    I don't know.

Q 133  Has anybody told you that you can't get any work around here at all?

A    Yes, sir.

Q 134  Who?

A    Different ones.

Q 135  Would you be afraid to say who told you that? Would it do you any harm to tell that?

A    It possibly might for people have told me I needn't expect to get any work and they have also sent me word that I don't need to never try to work any more in Harlan County.

Q 136  Have you joined the Union?

A      Yes, sir, the National Union.

Q 137  When?

A      I don't know; in August, I believe.

Q 138  After you joined that, did you do any work for this organization?

A      Whatever they asked me to do.

Q 139  What could you do?

A      They asked me to get all the boys on the inside to join the organization.

Q 140  People out of work, etc.?

A      Yes, sir.

Q 141  Have you attended to this?

A      Yes, sir.

Q 142  Did the National Mine Workers help you to live or give you any money?

A      They never gave it to me directly. Other fellows handled the money.

Q 143  Did they give you money or food to live on?

A      They furnished these soup kitchens, I suppose.

Q 144  Did anybody come and tell you anything about belonging to this organization?

A      I was arrested.

Q·145  When?

A      The first time was along about the primary election; I believe it was in August.

Q 146  What were you arrested for?

A      They claimed it was a charge of criminal syndicalism.

Q 147  What does criminal syndicalism mean to you?

A      The best I can give it is going against your country but that is something I never did do. I never thought about such a thing.

Q 148  When they said that you were going against your country, what do you think they meant?

A      I don't know.

Q 149 You haven't done anything that you think could be taken as going against your country?

A    No, sir.

Q 150 But you think that is what those words mean?

A    Yes, my family has always fought for the country and I have always been for it. I registered in the World War.

Q 151 Were you in the World War?

A    No, I was placed in the fourth class because of dependents.

Q 152 Did you ever serve in the Army?

A    No, sir, but all my people have, my great uncles on down.

Q 153 Where did your people come from?

A    I can't tell you where exactly.

Q 154 Was that the charge—that you were going against your country?

A    The charge was criminal syndicalism.

Q 155 And you say that you think they meant by that, going against your country?

A    Yes, that was my understanding.

Q 156 Where were you when you were arrested?

A    I said they arrested me, but I came over and gave up to them.

Q 157 Did they tell you to come?

A    They had been after me, raiding the house and I happened to be away and they searched the house and tore up everything.

Q 158 What did they take from your house?

A    A paper or two.

Q 159 What paper?

A    One little pamphlet, I believe, asking the miners and the coal diggers to be in Harlan on the days of the trials of the miners from Evarts during that trouble up there. There was one of them there. I don't know how it came to be in the house. I believe my wife said somebody passed by and had it and one of the kids brought it in the house. And there was a *Daily Worker* there.

Q 160 Did you subscribe for it?

A No, sir, somebody had just brought it there and they got that paper and called it an I. W. W. paper.

Q 161 Did they show your wife a warrant?

A No, sir, they didn't have a proper warrant.

Q 162 Did they search it anyway?

A Yes, sir, they tore the beds upside down and broke the window lights out and kicked the whole window sash out.

Q 163 Did they take anything that belonged to you?

A No, sir, nothing but the papers.

Q 164 When you went to give yourself up, what did they do?

A I knew I hadn't done nothing and I didn't want them to tear up the house again and I wanted to be turned loose because I have always tried to be a law-abiding man and I had never been in the courts before and so I went to the Sheriff to give up.

Q 165 Why?

A He was the proper authority.

Q 166 Were these men Deputy Sheriffs who came there to search your house?

A Yes, sir.

Q 167 You knew them?

A Yes, sir. They was supposed to have been Deputy Sheriffs.

Q 168 What did he say to you?

A He said, "Go on upstairs, they are on trial now," and I went up and I thought I would get my trial that evening and the county judge said it would not be held until the next Monday, and that was on Tuesday.

Q 169 Who was that?

A He was the pro tem judge, Mr. Whitehead, and he said, "I will set your appearance bond at $5,000.00 and your peace bond at $5,000.00.

Q 170 Did you furnish that?

A No, not that time. I went on to jail.

Q 171 How many days were you in jail?

A   Four days at that time. I was in jail twice. They said I was indicted for criminal syndicalism and they put me in again for thirty days.

Q 172   When you went to the Sheriff they put you in four days?

A   Yes, sir.

Q 173   Why did they let you out?

A   On account of it was unlegal.

Q 174   Then you did come in front of some judge and he said it was not legal and turned you loose.

A   Yes, sir.

Q 175   How long after that until they came and got you again?

A   Something near a month.

Q 176   Did they come again and search your house and take you and put you in jail?

A   No, after they put me in jail the last time they searched it again.

Q 177   You were in for four days and then they let you out?

A   Yes, sir.

Q 178   After that, did you do anything?

A   Nothing only helped to feed the little starving children and I was distributing food and taking it to the soup house and trying to feed the children.

Q 179   Did any one tell you not to assist?

A   Different ones told me I was aiding the violation of the law.

Q 180   What was the violation of the law?

A   Running the soup house.

Q 181   Did any Deputy Sheriff tell you it was a violation and that if you didn't stop, they would arrest you?

A   I don't know whether they was Deputy Sheriffs or not.

Q 182   Did he come to you and tell you it was a violation of the law?

A   Yes, sir.

Q 183   What did you say?

A   I said I couldn't see any violation for a man to try to feed the starving children.

Q 184 Was this one man or two men or ten men that said this to you?

A    One man, I believe it was.

Q 185 Can you tell us who that man was or what his job was? Was he an officer?

A    I can't say.

Q 186 Is he a man of some means or position around here? Is he connected with the Sheriff's office?

A    I noticed him around with the Deputy Sheriffs.

Q 187 And he told you it was a violation of the law?

A    Yes, sir.

Q 188 But you didn't stop?

A    No.

Q 189 After that, did they search your house before they arrested you?

A    No. I was afraid to let this here force get hold of me.

Q 190 Whose force? What force? What do you mean by that?

A    This law here. They had been taking men out and beating them up.

*Mrs. J. M. Grace* (of Wallins Creek): They are these men around here and Judge Howard says they are Deputy Sheriffs and the Sheriff says they belong to the county and are not Deputy Sheriffs and all we know is that they carry two or three pistols and sawed-off shotguns and machine guns.

Q 191 Why were you afraid?

A    Because they actually had done things like that around here.

Q 192 To people that you know?

A    Yes, sir.

Q 193 What particular man or men?

A    This here colored fellow that was in here a while ago and his brother-in-law and Debs Moreland and her husband, and they had killed a couple of fellows at the swimming pool.

Q 194 And all of this had happened before they arrested you?

A    Yes, before I gave up.

Q 195  After that, what did you do after you got so afraid? Did you go down to the Sheriff's office?

A    Yes, sir.

Q 196  What did you say when you went down there?

A    I just went and asked what charge they had against me and he said they had a-plenty to put me in jail on.

Q 197  What did he do to you?

A    He put me in jail.

Q 198  Did you say he put you in for thirty days?

A    Yes, sir.

Q 199  How did you get out at that time?

A    Judge Jones sent the jailer up there after me and called four of us down there and we went down there and I didn't see nobody and the jailer said, "Take seats there," and we sat down and the Judge called us out in a room, one at the time, and he said to us, "Well, Mr. Powers, I have had several conversations concerning you for the last week" and he said, "You have the reputation of a good man, a mighty good man and we don't want to see a good man in jail," and I said, "Judge, I have always tried to conduct myself that way," and he said, "We will turn you loose if you will leave the county," and he said, "This here is an unlawful organization."

Q 200  Was he referring to the National Miners Union?

A    Yes, and I said, "I didn't know that, Judge," and I said, "I have always been a law-abiding citizen and I ain't done nothing," and I said, "I am paying taxes over here and I have got children in school and maybe I can't leave the county," and he said, "Of course it is bad to take the kids out of school," and he says, "I will turn you loose, but if I turn you loose, will you go out to stirring up soup kitchens again and doing all you can to aid this organization around here?" and I says, "Judge, knowing the way you have got me here, you have got me, and I will promise until the charges come up and the trial is over and I am set free I will promise you I won't take no active part until that time," and he says, "All right, go on back in the room," and he called the rest of them out and he turned four out that evening and he turned more out the next day, and he told the jailer to go up and get the boys' clothes and send them home, and he did and sent us home.

Q 201 What happened after that to you? Were you arrested any more?

A No.

Q 202 Have you been molested any more?

A No, but I was scared for they come and taken one of the fellows off that they had taken at the same time they got me before.

Q 203 Have you been helping the starving children or doing anything else since then?

A No, sir, I have just been trying to help my own children.

Q 204 Do you believe that they would put you back in jail if you collected food for these children?

A I guess they would.

Q 205 Do you think they would slap you back in jail?

A I guess they would.

Q 206 Have you had your trial yet?

A No, I am waiting. It comes on the 22nd or 23rd.

Q 207 Do you know anything about a man being hung on Ivy Hill?

A I didn't see him but I heard some of the fellows that taken him down.

Q 208 Was he a miner?

A Yes, sir.

Q 209 Was he connected with the National Mine Workers?

A Yes, sir.

Q 210 Did he collect food for the starving children?

A Yes, sir.

Q 211 Did he help run a soup kitchen?

A Yes, sir.

Q 212 Had he done anything outside of that to be hung for?

A      No, sir, not as I know of.

Q 213   They hung him for that? Is that your idea?

A      I don't know.

Q 214   When was that?

A      Last July.

Q 215   What was his name?

A      Miller, I believe was his name.

Q 216   You don't know his first name?

A      No.

Q 217   Do you know how they hung this man—whether with a rope or how?

A      They said it was a barbed wire.

Q 218   That is just hearsay with you?

A      Yes, they said there was a barbed wire around his neck.

Q 219   After he was hung, was there any investigation made by anybody?

A      I never did hear of anything.

Q 220   Even when you are out of work and haven't anything to do, do you still intend to stick here?

A      I don't see no other chance. I can't locate no place I can get employment.

Q 221   But if you know they won't give you anything to do here?

A      I just have to do the best I can until I can get away.

*Questioned by Mr. Ornitz:*

Q 1   Have you any money to get away with?

A      No, sir.

Q 2   So far as you know, the only crime you committed was helping the starving children and you were given your liberty by Judge Jones on your promise that you would stop collecting food for the hungry children?

A      Yes, sir.

Q 3   And you didn't have to sign a bond to get your liberty?

A      No, sir.

Q 4   You were freed on that promise?

A      Yes, sir.

*Questioned by Mr. Maurer:*

Q 1    They speak of a "black list" around here—do you know what that is, and do you consider yourself black listed?

A    Yes, sir, I know they have a black list of men around here that can't get work. I have seen them run to the books and look when a man asked about work and come back and say, "You can't get work."

Q 2    Then they do have a black list?

A    Yes, sir.

Q 3    Are you on that black list?

A    I know in reason that I am.

Q 4    Whose books were these that they would go and look at?

A    The Company books at the mines, at the mine offices.

Q 5    Of any particular Company that you can think of?

A    I reckon they have all got them.

Q 6    For instance, this Company you last worked for, did they have a book with these names in it?

A    Yes, sir.

Q 7    What was the name of that Company?

A    Black Joe.

Q 8    And they had a book?

A    Yes, sir.

*Questioned by Mr. Ornitz:*

Q 1    Did you ever see a check-weighman at the mines?

A    There might have been at one or two of the mines.

Q 2    Do you know whether the law requires them to have a check-weighman?

A    Yes, sir.

Q 3    Then it is up to the Company to say how much coal there is?

A    They won't allow the men to have a check-weighman.

Q 4    Have you heard there is a law like that?

A    Yes, sir, but you can't enforce it here. If a man will mention having a check-weighman, he ain't got no job.

*Questioned by Theodore Dreiser:*

Q 1   Did you ever go back on the property of this Company that laid you off?

A   No, sir.

Q 2   Did you ever go to anybody's property and injure it in any way?

A   No, sir. After they discharged me I knew they was taking some of the men back on and I went back with a couple of them that they had discharged at the same time and they taken the other two men back and they said that I hadn't been off long enough.

Q 3   Did they go back at the same wages they had had before?

A   Yes, sir.

*Questioned by Bruce Crawford:*

Q 1   Did you ever sign a "Yellow Dog" contract?

A   I guess I have signed several of them.

Q 2   What is stated in a Yellow Dog contract?

A   I don't know hardly: I was so anxious to get a job that I don't know.

*Miss Cowden:* It is an agreement or statement that the corporation will not employ a man that is a member of the Union and the miner will not join the Union while he is in their employ.

*Mr. Ornitz:*

Q 1   You say you signed that contract because it was the only way to get a job? You knew it was the only way you could get a job?

A   Yes, sir.

*Courier-Journal Reporter:*

Q 1   Have you ever been connected with any shooting case up here?

A   No, sir.

*Associated Press Representative:*

Q 1   To get back to this original trouble, the first time you fell out with your Company, you fell out with them because you didn't clean up at the end of the day's work?

A     Yes, that's what they said.

Q 2   You say that they had that system all through the mine?

A     Yes, sir.

Q 3   You knew that before he came in there, didn't you? That you were supposed to clean up or get fired? They didn't single you out to make a goat of you?

A     They had fired several for it.

Q 4   You said you were making $30.00 or $40.00 and they paid in scrip?

A     Yes. Probably I would draw a dollar at the end of the month.

Q 5   How did you pay $15.00 a month rent?

A     I didn't. I own my own property over here.

*H. J. Evans:*

Q 1   That insurance—was that compensation insurance or does that simply cover burials?

A     That was a different insurance the Company carried from the compensation or the burial fund, either one.

*Mr. Ornitz:*

Q 1   How many cuts were made in your pay?

A     There was several, hospital and insurance and—

Q 2   What insurance?

A     They carry an insurance there of $1.50 a month that they call a sick and accident insurance, but the Company said it didn't cover anything that the compensation covered. It was a good health insurance. If you got hurt in the mine, the compensation covered that.

*H. J. Evans:*

Q 1   Did you have to take that insurance?

A     They cut it through the office.

*Bruce Crawford:*

Q 1   Did they cut for school?
A     Yes.
Q 2   For church?
A     No, sir.
Q 3   Did they cut for coal and lights? And houses?
A     The people that rented the houses paid rent for them.

---

The next witness, a woman, was then called.

*Mr. Ornitz:* You can't swear this witness. She can't give her name because if she does her husband will lose his job.

*Questioned by Theodore Dreiser:*

Q 1   Are you a native of Kentucky?
A     I have been here about ten years, I reckon. I came here from the north. My husband is a native Kentuckian and was born and raised in this State.
Q 2   Is he a miner?
A     Yes, sir.
Q 3   Has he always been?
A     Yes, sir.
Q 4   Have you any children?
A     I have got two.
Q 5   Are they young?
A     Yes, sir.
Q 6   They don't contribute to your support?
A     No.
Q 7   Do you live in a Company town?
A     Yes, sir.
Q 8   How much rent do you pay for this house you occupy?
A     $8.00 a month, without lights.
Q 9   How much does your husband average a month?
A     He has been working about three weeks but he hasn't averaged a dollar a day since he started there.
Q 10  When did he start there?

A    I reckon about three weeks ago.

Q 11  There was a time in the ten years that he did pretty well, didn't he?

A    Yes, there has been times.

Q 12  Did he do well up to 1927?

A    Yes, but in the last few years he hasn't done much.

Q 13  Why not?

A    Because the wages is small and he can't make it.

Q 14  Is he a strong man?

A    Yes, indeed, my man is a big, strong man and a good coal man. Anybody around any of the mines where he has been will tell you that he is a good coal man.

Q 15  Since 1927, would you say that you have had as much as $50.00 a month to live on?

A    No, sir, I wouldn't.

Q 16  You say he is working now?

A    Yes, but he had to go to work in order to get a house, a Company house. He didn't have no money to rent an outside house and he had to take a job at the mine to get a house.

Q 17  Has he received any money since he went there two or three weeks ago?

A    Just scrip.

Q 18  How do you manage to live?

A    We have just managed to exist. I will tell you that I have had one dollar in the last three days to live on, my husband and myself and two children.

Q 19  I wonder how you distribute that money around?

A    We live on beans and bread. We don't get no dinner.

Q 20  What do you call dinner? At noon or night?

A    We always have breakfast and then we have dinner at noon and that is what you call lunch, and we call supper at night what you call dinner. We have breakfast and I put up a lunch for him to take to work and he works hard. There don't none of you know how hard a man works that works in the mines, and I'll tell you what I had to put in his bucket this morning for him to eat and work hard all day, there was a little cooked pumpkin and what you folks call white meat, just fat white bacon, and that's what he took in the mines to eat and work on and he had water gravy for breakfast and black coffee.

Q 21  Water gravy—what is that?

A   Water and grease and a little flour in it, and he had black coffee.

Q 22  What do you give to the children?

A   They had the same breakfast and they don't get no dinner.

Q 23  Where do you get clothes?

A   We don't get none.

Q 24  Where did you get those you have on?

A   This dress was give to me and the shoes I have on was give to me—

Q 25  Recently?

A   Yes, recently, and this coat I have on I bought six years ago and my children is naked.

Q 26  They probably don't go to school?

A   They are not in any situation to go to school because they have no shoes on their feet and no underwear on them and the few clothes they have they are through them.

Q 27  Is there an organization in this city to help cases of this kind?

A   They say there is a welfare here but I have never had no help from them.

Q 28  Have you ever applied?

A   They say that the man that don't need help is the one that gets it and I am not right in the town and I never have asked them for help.

Q 29  In this life you have lived for the past four or five years, what do you do about entertainment? Do you ever go to a motion picture?

A   My children don't know nothing about a show or nothing like that.

Q 30  You have never had a Victrola, I suppose?

A   You see, I have a grown son in Detroit and he had a

bicycle and he traded for this Victrola when he was at home but it is old and the records are old and broke and the children plays with it sometimes.

Q 31 You haven't got such a thing as a radio?

A Oh, no, don't know nothing about such a thing.

Q 32 What do you do about heat in the winter time?

A We have a fireplace in the house.

Q 33 Where do you get the coal?

A Off the Company.

Q 34 Do they give it to you?

A No, sir, we have to pay for it.

Q 35 What do you pay for it?

A $2.00 or $2.50, I guess; I don't know.

Q 36 When sickness happens, what do you do for a doctor?

A The Company has a doctor and you pay for him but you can't always get him and if you get him maybe he will do something for you and maybe he won't.

Q 37 Do you carry insurance?

A No, sir, I did until this depression came on and we got so hard up we couldn't carry no insurance.

Q 38 Did you get any benefit out of it?

A I had myself and the two children insured in the Prudential and my husband belonged to the K. P.'s and he had insurance with them and we had to drop it and we have got no insurance of no kind.

Q 39 If your husband got injured in the mines or some of you got sick, you would have to go on public charity?

A Yes, sir, absolutely.

Q 40 Why doesn't your husband leave here and go to work somewhere else?

A He couldn't get enough to leave here on unless we walk out and you can't take a couple of children and walk out, and I ain't strong enough to walk.

Q 41 Before he got this job, did you and your children go to the soup kitchen for food?

A Yes, sir.

Q 42 Did you get any other help from any of these Union organizations?

A   No, sir.

Q 43 Is your husband a member of any Union?

A   Yes, of the National Miners Union.

*Questioned by Mr. Ornitz:*

Q 1 You say your husband is earning about a dollar a day?

A   Yes, sir.

Q 2 And that what you get, you get at the Company store?

| SIGN YOUR NAME to Receipt Below Before You Come to Office for Money | | |
|---|---|---|
| No. *6* | Cary, Ky., *9/8* | 193 |

## Old Straight Creek Coal Corporation
### Incorporated
### IN ACCOUNT WITH

Name *Fred Brady*

| CHARGES | | | CREDIT | | |
|---|---|---|---|---|---|
| Store | *6* | *00* | Tons at | | |
| Lights | | | Tons at | | |
| Rent | *2* | *50* | *797* Tons at *04* | *31* | *84* |
| Coal | | | Hours at | | |
| Smithing | | | Hours at | | |
| Doctor | *1* | *00* | Hours at | | |
| Hospital | | | Yards at | | |
| Insurance | | | Yards at | | |
| Car Checks | | | Yards at | | |
| Transfers | *22* | *00* | Car Checks Returned | | |
| Prev. Overdraft | | | Transfers | | |
| Burial Fund | | | Cash Retained | | |
| Paid first pay day | | | | | |
| Cash Advanced | | | | | |
| | *31* | *50* | | | |
| Bal. Due Workman | | *38* | Balance Due Company | | |
| Total | *31* | *88* | Total | *31* | *88* |

RETAIN THIS STATEMENT

A    Yes, sir, you get it in scrip and have to trade it out at the Company store.

Q 3   What do you get for that dollar? What is that dollar worth to you in that Company scrip?

A    I will say between 30 and 40 cents, I reckon.

Q 4   In other words, your husband is earning 40 cents a day so long as he is paid in scrip?

A    Yes, sir.

*Questioned by Theodore Dreiser:*

Q 1   You have worked that out yourself by judging what you get in the Company store and in another store?

A    Yes, sir.

*Mr. Ornitz:*

Q 1   You know what the Piggly Wiggly is doing and what your store is doing and what other stores are doing and selling for?

A    Yes. I know it is worth about 40 cents.

Q 2   They won't let you trade anywhere else?

A    No, sir.

Q 3   Is there a notice in the clerk's office telling you that you must trade there?

A    I haven't noticed any. I am not much of a hand to go to the store myself. I send the children.

Q 4   Do you know when your husband took this job whether he signed some sort of an agreement with the Company?

A    No, sir, not where he is at. It is a small place.

*Questioned by Mrs. Walker:*

Q 1   You say you have only had one dollar in the last three days?

A    Yes.

Q 2   But your husband has been working there?

A    Yes, sir, but when he went for money they said he didn't have it in there. They have to have their house rent and coal bill and doctor bill before we get anything.

Q 3    How much is your doctor bill?
A      $1.75 a month.
Q 4    How often do you have a doctor?
A      Whenever we need him, if we can get him.
Q 5    What about a burial fund?
A      I don't know whether they have a burial cut up there or not. I think they have.

*Theodore Dreiser:*

Q 1    Since this trouble started up here, has your husband been in any trouble of any kind?
A      No, sir.
Q 2    Has your husband ever been arrested?
A      No, sir. They came pretty hot after him one time and he had to leave Harlan and go to Tennessee.
Q 3    When was that?
A      After that *massacre* at the swimming pool.
Q 4    I don't know about that—what was it?
A      I can't tell you exactly about it but there was some people killed there.
Q 5    Did they think he had something to do with it?
A      No, but one of these men that was killed stayed at my house nearly all summer and what I think they thought was that my husband and this man was some connection and they were afraid that my old man would take the drop on some of these men that done the killing so they came after him.

*Mrs. Walker:*

Q 1    Before your husband went to work for this Company, who was he working for?
A      The Harlan Gas.
Q 2    What happened after he went to the Union meeting?
A      They just fired him and put us out.
Q 3    Put you out of your house?
A      Yes, they gave me three house notices and said if I didn't get out on a certain day they would put me out and

when I was packing up there was a car-load of the law sitting down here waiting to put me out and my furniture and I had $100. paid on it to the Green Furniture Company here in Harlan and when this law came and gave me my house notice I told them to be careful of the furniture for it didn't belong to me, it belonged to the Green Furniture Company and they busied themselves to notify the Green Furniture Company to come and get their furniture.

Q 4   What kind of furniture have you now?

A   I haven't got none. I am sleeping on a bed that was lent to me and wired up on a box and a pair of springs on that and no mattress and four of us is sleeping on it.

Q 5   Have you any chairs?

A   Not a one.

Q 6   How many children have you?

A   Two.

*Theodore Dreiser:*

Q 1   What Union did your husband join?

A   The United Mine Workers.

Q 2   He was fired for joining that Union?

A   Yes, sir.

*Mr. Dreiser:* I hope Mr. Evans is here to hear that.

*A. P. Man:* No, he is not in just now.

————————

TESTIMONY *taken at the Lewallen Hotel, in the City of Harlan, Harlan County, Kentucky, on the 6th of November, before members of the National Committee for the Defense of Political Prisoners. Theodore Dreiser, Chairman.*

Also the testimony of Mrs. Nannie Powers, given at the same time and place and for the same purpose. The witness after first being duly sworn testified as follows:

*Questioned by Theodore Dreiser:*

Q I   Are you the wife of the witness who just testified?

A     Yes, sir.

Q 2   How long have you been married?

A     Fifteen years.

Q 3   Have you resided in this town all this time?

A     No. Not all the time.

Q 4   In the country?

A     No.

Q 5   Well, just how long have you been living here?

A     We left and went to Gayliff, Kentucky, and stayed about two years and then we came back and I reckon we have been here about 12 years.

Q 6   Up to the beginning of 12 years ago, how did you get along? I mean, have you done pretty well for the past 12 years, how much money have you had during that time, did you live a comfortable life?

A     We always lived pretty well as long as he worked. We had a little house that we lived in.

Q 7   Up to 1927 did you live pretty well, comfortably?

A     Yes, sir.

Q 8   When did you get this house you speak of?

A     It has been about ten years ago that we bought it, I reckon.

Q 9   And now then, how many children do you and your husband have living with you that you have to support and look after now?

A     We got four at home now that we have to look after and feed and clothe.

Q 10  Up to 1927, tell us roughly just what did happen, can't you tell how you got along?

A     Well, I just can't exactly tell, not all of it, anyway. But I can tell you that we lived pretty bad.

Q 11  Did it get worse and worse all the time since 1927?

A     Yes, worse all the time.

Q 12  Were you getting along pretty well up until last August?

A    Yes, sir.

Q 13 What started all this trouble in your family as you recall?

A    What they call this here Union, I reckon, altho I don't know exactly, or I don't know very much about it.

Q 14 Your husband getting interested in this Union, was that what caused all the trouble?

A    As long as he had a job we got along pretty well, but since he ain't had no job, it has been pretty bad and we been up against it.

Q 15 Do you approve of his joining this Union, I mean did you want him to do it, or did you tell him he ought to do it? What did you say about it?

A    I don't know. It is all right as long as it is carried out right, but when times is hard they don't do much. I told him when this one died out, there used to be another one here in this county before this one was organized, I told him that when this one died out I never wanted him to join any more.

Q 16 You have lived pretty badly since this trouble came up, have you?

A    Yes.

Q 17 About the time your house was raided, can you tell us about that? Describe the raid.

A    Well, there was six of John Henry's "thugs," we call them, came down to my house and came right on in, they were drunk.

Q 18 What do you mean by John Henry's "thugs"? Who are they? And what are they?

A    Them is the Deputy Sheriffs, we call them "thugs."

Q 19 When was this?

A    I do not remember the date, I was all nervous and nearly wrecked that I don't remember the date nor the time, all I know is that they just came there and said they were going to search my house, that they heard I had some one there, or that they wanted my husband, I just can't remember all they did say, but anyway they came there to get my husband, and I asked them if they had a search warrant, and I told them if they didn't have no search warrant they sure couldn't search my home. It was about three o'clock in the afternoon, the best I remember. They came right on in my house and tore up everything, looked in all the drawers, tore up the mattresses, opened trunks, and messed up everything. And then one of them that was a-cussing around there said, "By God, we are going to take you to jail," and I asked him what I had done to go to jail and he said I never had to do nothing to go to jail.

Q 20  What did they find in your house, or what did they take away with them?

A    They got some *Daily Worker* papers and blanks.

Q 21  Did they break anything?

A    No.

Q 22  Did they find any guns or pistols?

A    No. But they found his National Union card.

Q 23  What did they do to you, did they take you to jail?

A    No.

Q 24  How come them not to take you to jail?

A    My mother came up there, she just lived about three doors from me, and when she came in she said she thought I was a-going to faint, and she sent me out on the porch to sit down, I was so mad and scared I didn't know what to do, and they was there spitting on in my house and drunk, why one of them was so drunk that he could not hardly get in the car, and I was excited and my kids was all a-crying and my mother she went in there and talked to them, and she told them if she knowed what was best they could get going from there.

Q 25  How long was it until they came back a second time?

A    I don't know, but them came after Caleb.

Q 26  Did they get him?

A    No. He warn't there and I have left home, too. I had gone down to my mother's who just lives a few doors away from me and I was a-watching for them, so when I seed that car that was a-bringing them up there, I went out on the porch, and when they got up there to my house and saw there warn't any one at home they pulled the screen off the window and kicked the window light out.

Q 27 Did they go in your house that time?

A No. My door neighbor told them I was out to my mother's.

Q 28 What did they do then?

A Well, they came on down to my mother's and she was a-talking with them, and then Abe Hensley came up and he spoke to one of them and asked him what they wanted, and he said, "Trouble, I guess," and Abe said that if that was what they wanted they could sure get it. Then he said that they was good buddies and they wasn't going to get mad about nothing, and then they asked Ma if they might come in to look and search for Caleb. She said, "Yes, sir. If you have a search warrant, and if you don't, well, you can't search my house without it," and they never showed no search warrant.

Q 29 Did you see them again?

A There was some clothing came out to my house, well, I believe there 725 pounds of clothes sent to the Union for the little, poor, starving children, and grown-ups that never had nothing, and they found it there.

Q 30 Who were the clothes for?

A For the people out of work. Some of them had been wore before and some of them had never been wore, some were brand new.

Q 31 Was that the last time?

A Well, Ma and Pa told us another time they had been in our things.

Q 32 Did they take the clothing?

A Part of it had already been given out and part of it was still there to be given out to all these people that was out of work.

Q 33 Well, did they take this clothing?

A No. They left that.

Q 34 Well, was that the last time they visited you?

A Last time I remember.

Q 35 Tell me, just how do you manage to live, how do you make your living?

A    I borrow most of it.

Q 36 What do you borrow, things to eat, or money, clothes, or just what do you borrow?

A    I borrow things to eat, coffee, flour, meal and things like that.

Q 37 Do you borrow this from your neighbors?

A    Yes, sir.

*Questioned by Mr. Ornitz:*

Q 1 When these men came to search your house the first time, what made you think they were drunk?

A    They spit on my floor and cussed and one of them staggered. And the way they tore up my house and my things, went through my trunks, drawers, beds, and everything I had.

Q 2 Were your children there?

A    Yes, sir.

Q 3 How old are they?

A    I have one boy that is ten years, then the twins are eight, and the baby is six.

Q 4 Are you certain they were drunk?

A    Yes, sir.

Q 5 And you saw one of them stagger?

A    Yes, sir.

*Questioned by United Press:*

Q 1 What is your brother's name that you spoke of as coming into your mother's home there and talking with these deputy sheriffs?

A    Matt Bryant.

Q 2 You said they were going to take you to jail, well, did they do that?

A    No, but they nearly scared me to death.

Q 3 Why do you suppose they didn't take you on to jail as they said they were going to?

A    I don't know.

*Questioned by Theodore Dreiser:*

Q 1    Did you go before the Judge or any one to try to get your husband out of jail while he was there?

A      Yes, sir. I tried to get them to let him make bond, or let me make bond for him, but I couldn't do anything for him.

Q 2    Did you make bond?

A      No.

Q 3    When you went down to try to get your husband out, what did the Judge say to you about your husband?

A      I went to "Baby" Jones, and he would send me over to Brock, and then I would go to "Baby" again, and he would send me right back to Brock.

Q 4    Did you ask him to let your husband out?

A      Yes, and he said, "No, we couldn't afford to let a man like that out."

Q 5    Did the Judge say that to you?

A      No, I believe it was Brock that said that.

Q 6    Well, who is this Brock?

A      He is the prosecuting attorney.

Q 7    Are you sure he said that?

A      Yes, he said they couldn't let them out with guys like that cause they would kill some other men just like those that had already been killed.

Q 8    What other men?

A      Those men that were killed at the swimming pool.

Q 9    And they said such men as your husband caused this to be done?

A      Yes, sir.

FURTHER THE WITNESS SAYETH NOT.

Signature waived.

Also the testimony of "JACK" SCALF, taken at the same time and place as stated above.

The witness after first being duly sworn deposes as follows:

*Questioned by Theodore Dreiser:*

Q 1    What is your full name?

A       Charlie Sever Scalf.

Q 2    Are you a resident of this county?

A       Yes, sir.

Q 3    Of this town?

A       Well, not exactly right in this town. I live over in Sunshine. I reckon it is this town.

Q 4    Are you a native of Kentucky?

A       Yes, sir.

Q 5    Were you born here?

A       Yes, sir.

Q 6    Lived here all your life?

A       No. This has been my home and I have been here most of the time, but I do a lot of traveling around.

Q 7    How old are you, Mr. Scalf?

A       I am 26 years old.

Q 8    What is your work, or what is your occupation?

A       Mining.

Q 9    How long have you been a miner?

A       I have been a miner ever since I was nine years old, that is, off and on.

Q 10   Where have you worked?

A       Lots of places.

Q 11   How many years have you been working?

A       Put it all together, I don't reckon I have worked as a miner more than six years. I used to go off and work at the factories, and then in the summer I would work in the mines and go to school in the winter.

Q 12   Have you worked continuously during the past five years?

A       Do you mean as a miner?

Q 13   Yes, as a miner.

A       Don't reckon I have.

Q 14   How long have you been working this time?

A       I don't know, I can't say.

Q 15 Well, one year?

A    Don't know.

Q 16 Two or three or four years, just about how many?

A    About three years, I would say, off hand.

Q 17 That is, steadily?

A    Yes, sir.

Q 18 Before that what did you do?

A    Well . . .

Q 19 I mean what other kinds of work did you do?

A    Well, sometimes I would work and sometimes I wouldn't.
     I went out west and worked out there some. I had one
     job with the D. & R. W. R. R. Company, and from there
     I went over into the harvest fields in Kansas, and then
     I come back up to this here country and went to work
     up at Golden Ash.

Q 20 When did you come back?

A    I don't know.

Q 21 When were you away?

A    I don't know.

Q 22 How long were you away?

A    About four years.

Q 23 Did you work the two years before that?

A    No. Not all the time, not that length of time. I would
     just get me a job and work six months or so and then I
     would light out on a spree.

Q 24 Before you went away were you married?

A    Yes, sir.

Q 25 When you first went to work were you a member of the
     union?

A    No.

Q 26 Was there one here?

A    No.

Q 27 And wasn't there a union at one time here?

A    Yes, sir. But they got to making plenty of money and
     wouldn't pay their dues.

Q 28 Did you join the union as soon as you could?

A    Yes, sir.

Q 29 Before the union came in here, how much did you make a day?

A    Fifty cents.

Q 30 What were you doing at that time?

A    I was tracking.

Q 31 What is that?

A    I open and close the doors for the mules. That was back when they used mules in the mines to work, you see, they don't use them much any more. And I was there to just open and close the doors for the mules to pass through.

Q 32 How long did you get fifty cents a day?

A    I don't know.

Q 33 When did you begin getting a reasonable wage?

A    I don't know.

Q 34 Was it when the Union came in here?

A    No.

Q 35 You say you started to work when you were nine years of age?

A    Yes, sir. I didn't work steady all the time. I worked in the summer and went to school in the winter.

Q 36 How old were you in 1917?

A    About thirteen years old.

Q 37 When did you begin making regular wages?

A    Not until about 1918.

Q 38 Then you were a full-fledged miner?

A    Yes, sir.

Q 39 How much did you then make a day, or how much per month?

A    Some months I would make $400.00 per month, and some $500.00 per month. And sometimes in between.

Q 40 That was in 1918?

A    Yes, sir.

Q 41 What did they pay, or on what basis were you paid?

A    We were paid 81 cents per ton, and I had two chalk-eyes working for me that I was paying eight dollars each per night.

Q 42 What is a chalk-eye?

A That is someone that I hired to work in my place in the mines, you see there are men who do not know enough to work by themselves, but if you put them with someone they work all right, and so I hired two chalk-eyes to help me in my room, and they used to work good.

Q 43 How much did they actually make for you?

A I generally drew $250 or $300 off them.

Q 44 And you say some months you would make as high as $500 per month?

A Yes, sir.

Q 45 But you had to pay your expenses out of that and you really did not make that much after all, did you?

A Well, yes, I had to pay expenses, but some months I would make that much.

Q 46 And you would actually put that much in your pocket?

A Yes, some other man's pocket; I never could hold it.

Q 47 How long did this happy period last?

A Well, I would work about six months and get enough money to go off on some spree.

Q 48 When did that period stop?

A I have not made anything to amount to anything since 1922.

Q 49 What is the cause of that?

A Well, I bought a car and went to taxiing then.

Q 50 How long did you taxi?

A About six or seven months.

Q 51 Did you then go back to mining?

A Yes, sir.

Q 52 What did you make?

A Four to five to six dollars per day. Some days I would make seven or eight dollars.

Q 53 That is $150 per month.

A I don't know. I never worked a whole month at a time. I was generally making about $90 or around $100 a month.

Q 54 How long were you making this $90 per month?

A    On up until this last cut, when it went on I never made that much any more.

Q 55 Beginning with 1923 and 1924, what happened that you did not make as much?

A    Well, we got some cuts.

Q 56 In wages, you mean?

A    Yes.

Q 57 How much?

A    First it was 81 cents per ton, and then it dropped to 71 cents per ton, and now it has dropped to 54 cents per ton. And then after you had your cuts taken out, there wasn't much left.

Q 58 When were these cuts in wages made?

A    I don't know.

Q 59 Was there any union here then?

A    There was one here, but they just quit paying their dues and it died.

Q 60 You say it has died out, that is the original one?

A    Yes, sir.

Q 61 What is the cause of this union dying?

A    I don't know.

Q 62 When did they cut to 54 cents per ton?

A    I don't know. I ain't never studied none about it.

Q 63 What is that?

A    I say I just ain't never studied about when it was.

Q 64 How long has it been since you have worked?

A    I am working now.

Q 65 Where are you working now?

A    Elcomb Coal Company.

Q 66 What do you get now?

A    Thirty-five cents per ton.

Q 67 How much would that be per day?

A    According to how much I worked that day as to how much I got.

Q 68 Roughly estimating, how much would you get?

A    I worked out last month $34.30.

Q 69 Is that the last month that you worked?

A    Yes, sir.

Q 70  Are you willing to work for that?

A    No, but it is work for that or starve.

Q 71  Can you get any other work to do?

A    No.

Q 72  Are you a member of the United Mine Workers?

A    Yes, sir.

Q 73  Any other union?

A    I belong to all of them.

Q 74  How did you join more than one?

A    I joined every one that came around.

Q 75  I don't see how you could do that. I thought if you belonged to one union that they would not accept you as a member of another union, that is, if they knew you were a member of another union. Isn't that the way it is?

A    Well, I belong to the Miners Union.

Q 76  And do you belong to any at present?

A    No. Not any at all.

Q 77  Are you a married man?

A    Yes, sir.

Q 78  How many children do you have?

A    None.

Q 79  Do you own your own home?

A    No.

Q 80  How much rent do you pay?

A    Six dollars a month.

Q 81  Do you live in a Company house?

A    No.

Q 82  In a Company town?

A    No. Well, maybe too.

Q 83  Where do you live?

A    On private property.

Q 84  When you get your money at the commissary, or office, do you get it in money or do you have to take scrip?

A    We get scrip.

Q 85  Does this store charge you more for the things you get?

A    There is some of the scrip that they give us.

Q 86 Do you get as much for scrip as you would if you traded with money at another store?

A No. You have to pay 11 cents per box for things we pay 20 cents in the commissary, and I can buy lard down here at the Piggly Wiggly store for nine cents, and have to pay two pounds for 35 cents with that there scrip in a Company store.

Q 87 What about butter?

A We don't have butter.

Q 88 What about bread?

A We don't buy bread.

Q 89 What do you do, you say you don't buy bread?

A We buy the flour, and pay for a 12-pound sack 40 cents, where we can get a 24-pound sack down here in town for 39 cents.

Q 90 Where do you get your clothes?

A That is a hard question to ask a man.

Q 91 Well, those are very good looking clothes you have on, where did you get them?

A Well . . .

Q 92 Have you had them a long, long time, or did you buy them or beg them or just how did you get them?

A I boot-legged and got these, but I have had them for about two years and I haven't done any boot-legging, or ain't sold any whiskey in about two years.

Q 93 How does your wife get her clothes?

A She don't have any.

Q 94 None?

A She couldn't come to town today 'cause she never had no shoes to wear.

Q 95 About what is the total of your earnings during the month?

A Some months I make more than others in spite of everything I can do.

Q 96 Will you average $30 per month?

A Just can't say, but last month I made $34.30.

Q 97 How do you manage to live?

A    We don't live, we just exist.

Q 98    Do you borrow any money?

A    No.

Q 99    Do you borrow any food, etc., from your neighbors?

A    No.

Q 100    Do you beg?

A    No. Nothing but the rent.

Q 101    Then what do you eat?

A    Beans, bull-dog gravy, and a little meat.

Q 102    What is bull-dog gravy?

A    That is gravy made out of flour and water.

Q 103    Have you had any trouble with your employers?

A    I don't know whether I was discharged or not. They had quit work when I got back one time up at Southern-Harlan Coal Company, at Lenarue, Kentucky, and about a month after that some one asked me to join the Union and I joined her.

Q 104    When was this?

A    About last June.

Q 105    Then what?

A    Well, I was away on a fishing trip, and had started back to work and when I got back they had done quit working there, and I went up the road to get a job, that was on Sunday, and they told me to come back Monday.

Q 106    Who is they, the foreman?

A    Yes, and superintendent.

Q 107    And then?

A    Well, I went back on Monday and they told me to come back a Tuesday, and as I started down the road to leave the foreman yelled at me, and asked me if I could not get a job, and I told him no, they didn't want me, or couldn't use me, or something like that. Then he and John Carroll went in a room and talked with the Superintendent, but he said he thought he better let me go on back and catch my fish.

Q 108    What did he mean?

A    I don't know.

Q 109 Haven't you any idea what he meant?

A    No. Only that he just wouldn't give me no job and didn't want me to work there.

Q 110 Have you been arrested?

A    Yes, sir. Twice.

Q 111 When was the first time?

A    I do not know the date.

Q 112 What month was it?

A    I do not know.

Q 113 Well, five or six months ago?

A    I don't know, but about three months ago.

Q 114 What were you arrested for?

A    Criminal syndicalism, so they said.

Q 115 Why?

A    I don't know, only I had ten or twelve *Daily Workers* in my hand.

Q 116 Were you on the street?

A    No, not exactly. I was on the railroad crossing over in Sunshine.

Q 117 What were you doing with twelve copies of that paper?

A    I was giving them away.

Q 118 Where did you get them?

A    Out of the Post Office.

Q 119 Were you distributing them?

A    Yes, sir.

Q 120 Were they addressed to you?

A    No.

Q 121 Well, what were you doing with these papers?

A    I was giving them away. I was over there and a carload of the law, four of them, drove up, and said for me to go back with them that I was going to jail. They took me up there with them in John Henry's office, and asked him what must they do with me and he said for them to put me in jail, and away back in there too. They did put me in for three or four days and then they brought me down before Hamp Howard and he dismissed me.

Q 122 Who is Hamp Howard?

A     H. H. Howard, is the County Judge, or something like that.

Q 123   What did he do with you, you say?

A     He turned me loose, on my bond, bonding me over to appear before the Grand Jury. He let me out on my own bond.

Q 124   Let you go, did he?

A     Yes, sir.

Q 125   Were you arrested again after that?

A     Yes, sir.

Q 126   How long after that were you arrested the second time?

A     It was while Court was going on over here, I just don't know exactly when it was. It was the second day of Court though that they come got me and arrested me again.

Q 127   What for this time?

A     Same thing.

Q 128   Did they search your house or anything that time?

A     No.

Q 129   Were you ever indicted?

A     No.

Q 130   Where were you when they arrested you the second time?

A     I was at the court house.

Q 131   What were you doing there?

A     Well, I was over hearing the trial, at the Court House, and they went over to my house to search, and my wife asked them if they had any search warrant, and they said they did, and she wanted to see it, but they only showed her just a little space where my name was, and on the way back home I met a man by the name of Alred and he asked me where I was going, and said that John Henry wanted to see me. And when I went back there and gave myself up, I was turned over to Bob Blair, and Bob started on up to jail with me and I asked him what they were putting me in for and he said there had been a lot of guns and ammunition found over at my house and a lot of stuff, and I asked him again and he said that time they were putting me in for literature that had been found in my house, and I told him that I sure would like to know where they found that—I never had seen none of it—and that I would like to have some of it to read, and I wanted to know about them guns and things, and told him I wished I knowed where they was at, 'cause I would have liked to have had them.

Q 132 What did they find in your house?

A They found some cards about holding your tongue, 13 application blanks for the Miners Union.

Q 133 Where did you get these cards about holding your tongue?

A I had them printed.

Q 134 What did it say?

A I can't tell you exactly. Just said something about a man's tongue getting his head cut off.

Q 135 Were you distributing these among the miners?

A Yes, sir.

Q 136 Did you give any of them away?

A Yes, sir.

Q 137 Anything else that they found in your house?

A Yes, the application blanks and a piece of a time book.

Q 138 They did not take any of your personal property?

A No.

Q 139 Did they break anything?

A I don't think they did.

Q 140 What did the Sheriff say to you?

A Said they had found a lot of guns and ammunition over there at my house and they were getting me for literature. I told him I sure would like to read some of it.

Q 141 What happened to you after that?

A They locked me up.

Q 142 How long did you stay in jail that time?

A Twenty days.

Q 143 Why did they let you out?

A They called me down to talk to "Baby" Jones and we talked a long time and then he said he would let me go if I would promise to leave the county and have nothing else to do with this National Union Organization, or the I. W. W., or Communists, because it was an unlawful organization and was trying to overthrow our government and set up a President, or something, over in Moscow, Russia. And he said for me to leave the county and he would see that there was nothing done with me.

Q 144 Did he say it was an unlawful organization?

A Yes, sir. He said it was against the Constitution of the United States, and I told him I had read the Constitution of the Miners Union and I hadn't seen nothing that was about the United States Constitution in it.

Q 145 What did you tell him you would do?

A I just went back to jail. He said if I would not take any more active part in it, he would let me go, but I just started right back up toward that jail.

Q 146 How long did you stay the last time?

A I don't know.

Q 147 Well, five days or a week, or just how long did you stay there?

A I said I didn't know.

Q 148 And did they bring you down before Judge Jones again?

A Yes, sir.

Q 149 And then?

A He tried to get me to promise to have nothing else to do with it or to take no active part in it.

Q 150 In what, in the National Miners Union?

A Yes, sir.

Q 151 Did you tell him you would not take any active part in it?

A Yes, sir.

Q 152 How long has that been?

A I don't know.

Q 153 What would you call "taking any active part in things"?

A I don't know.

Q 154 Well, for instance, would you think coming up here and testifying would be taking an active part in it?

A      Don't know.

Q 155  Well, suppose you were to get in jail again over this?

A      I reckon it will hold me.

*Questioned by Mr. Herndon Evans, of Pineville, Ky.:*

Q 1    During the time that you were making so much money
       and had those two chalk-eyes, how much did you make?
       How much did you pay these men to work for you?

A      I paid them eight dollars each per day to work for me.

Q 2    How much would you make off of them?

A      Oh, about $10 per day.

Q 3    Could they have gone to the company and gotten a job?

A      They could have but they couldn't do the work. You see,
       some men work pretty good if you put them in a room
       with some one else, when they don't know enough to
       work by themselves.

*Questioned by Mr. Bruce Crawford, of Appalachia, Virginia:*

Q 1    Were you doing what is known as contract work?

A      No, just loading coal.

*Mr. Herndon Evans:*

Q 1    Did you ever hire more than two men to help you?

A      No.

Q 2    Were you given a special place to work?

A      Yes, sir. I was given what they called a room then to
       work in. They are about 40 feet big.

*Questions by Mr. Maurer:*

Q 1    When you were in the Harlan County jail was there a
       Negro there or brought in while you were there by the
       name of Tom Epps?

A      Just after I got in.

*Mr. Ornitz:*

Q 1    Are you still under indictment?

A      Never was none made against me.

Q 2 How did they keep you in jail?

A Under a peace bond.

Q 3 Did you have a hearing?

A No. They kept me there 20 days for investigation by the Grand Jury.

Q 4 Have you ever had a hearing?

A No.

Q 5 And you were arrested for criminal syndicalism?

A Yes, sir.

Q 6 Were you indicted on that charge?

A No.

Q 7 You were simply put in jail and kept there for 20 days and then released, is that true?

A Yes, sir.

Q 8 Did you say that some one told you that if you joined the Union they would arrest you?

A No.

Q 9 Did any one promise you that they would let you go if you would promise to keep away from it and take no more active part in it?

A Yes.

Q 10 Well, if they turned you loose without trial, do you know what became of your case?

A There was no case against me. I was just held for investigation.

*Theodore Dreiser:*

Q 1 What do the words criminal syndicalism mean to you?

A I do not know.

Q 2 Well, what is your idea?

A Don't know.

*Mr. Ornitz:*

Q 1 You say you had copies of the *Daily Worker* in your possession when you were arrested?

A Yes, sir.

Q 2    What else did they find in your home?

A      Thirteen application blanks for the Miners Union.

*Theodore Dreiser:*

Q 1    Do you work for a mining company?

A      Yes, sir.

*Mr. Levy:*

Q 1    What did you do when you worked at the age of nine years?

A      I opened up doors for mules in the mine.

Q 2    Do they allow children of that age to work in the mines now?

A      No.

Q 3    What is the age limit, I mean, how young can they get a job in the mines?

A      Sixteen, I believe is the age, and they have to have their Mammy and Pappy sign a permit saying they want them to work.

*Mr. Herndon Evans:*

Q 1    Are you a member of the Miners Union, I mean the National Miners Union?

A      No.

Q 2    When you had these application blanks, were you working for them?

A      Yes, sir.

Q 3    Asking men to join and telling them they should?

A      Yes, sir.

Q 4    And you are not a member?

A      No.

Q 5    Had you distributed copies of the *Daily Worker* before?

A      I never gave away more than one or two.

Q 6    Where did you get them?

A      They were sent from Chattanooga to Mr. John Kimbell, and he gave us permission to get them out of the post office.

Q 7   Did you read any of the copies?
A     I read every one I could get ahold of.
Q 8   Do you subscribe to the view, suggestions and ideas advanced in the *Daily Worker* paper?
A     Some parts.
Q 9   Do you believe in the principles of the *Daily Worker?*
A     Some.


TESTIMONY *taken at the Lewallen Hotel, in the City of Harlan, Harlan County, Kentucky, on the 6th day of November, 1931, before members of the National Committee, for the defense of political prisoners. Theodore Dreiser, Chairman.*


## MR. HERNDON EVANS

*Theodore Dreiser:*

Q 1   What is your name?
A     Herndon Evans.
Q 2   Are you a resident of this city?
A     No, sir. I live in Pineville, Kentucky.
Q 3   What is your occupation, or position?
A     I am a newspaper man and printer. I also work for the Dailies, Cincinnati *Inquirer*, Associated Press, *Courier-Journal*, Louisville *Times*, and work as Reporter on anything where they are unable to send a special reporter.
Q 4   Is your work connected in any way with the coal operators of this district?
A     No.
Q 5   Have you any interest in any mine?
A     No.
Q 6   You are interested in what?
A     Arriving at the truth.
Q 7   Are you opposed to the National Miners Union, or the organization thereof?
A     I am opposed to Communists in every form.

Q 8    Are you affiliated with any organization?

A    No. But what do you mean?

Q 9    Do you subscribe to any religion?

A    Yes, sir. Of course.

Q 10    What?

A    Christian Church.

Q 11    Do you belong to any organizations?

A    Yes, sir. I am a member of the Kiwanis Club, Chairman of the Boy Scouts, and Chairman of the American Red Cross, Bell County Chapter, and take an interest in welfare work.

Q 12    Are you not interested in a coal company?

A    No, not now. Well, at one time I was in the coal business for about two months by buying some stock. They let me in on the ground floor when several men bought a $350,000.00 mine for $75,000.00, and later this coal mine was sold by the Sheriff for $10,000.00.

Q 13    What do you think of this situation in general? Do you think this strike now going on is equitable, or do the miners have reason to justify such a strike?

A    I do think there are irregularities on both sides and too much bitter feeling, but as for this particular strike . . .

Q 14    The Kentucky coal fields here?

A    I have expressed the opinion that under the present period of depression, I am not in sympathy with the strike during times we are now facing. I think it behooves each and every one of us to work all the harder, and we must share it alike. It is hard times for all of us and we ought to work all the harder.

Q 15    You have heard how much these people make, what do you say they should do? Work on that scale or try to better themselves?

A    My printing business have fallen off from 50 to 60 per cent during 1930 and 1931. We are faced with the same thing, that they are facing. Are we to make the best of it, or just give up? I think the main thing to consider is that both of us hold on until conditions are better.

Q 16 How much do you make a week?

A    I really don't know exactly.

Q 17 Do you get something like $200.00 to $300.00 per month? I would just like to know, if you are making as much as $100.00 per week, which would be around 200 to 300 per cent more than these people make.

A    If I were making $100.00 per week and which represents an investment of over $30,000.00, I could keep up and actually feel that I was very fortunate.

Q 18 Do you have outside interests?

A    Yes, sir.

Q 19 With all your outside interests, etc., do you make as much as $50.00 per week?

A    Can't say.

Q 20 Do you make $100.00 per week?

A    No.

Q 21 Well, $75.00 or $60.00 per week?

A    Average around $60.00 per week.

Q 22 That is $240.00 per month against $40.00 per, and you have money in your pocket to take advantage of the market. And do you expect them to take things just as they are and not try to better themselves any?

A    Every man should make every effort to better his living conditions and his wage condition, now especially.

Q 23 You think then a skilled worker is entitled to receive more?

A    Yes, sir.

Q 24 Do you oppose the union idea?

A    I am not opposed to it. I work six men in my business and have given them the privilege of joining the union if they so desired but they have never considered the Union.

Q 25 Would you employ a union man?

A    Just as quick as I would give any other man a job if he proved satisfactory and gave me service.

Q 26 Do you think it is wrong for them to join the union?

A    That is entirely up to the individual.

Q 27 Do you think a union is illegal?

A    Not especially, but I do think the right is reserved by the employer as to whether or not he will employ a man that is a member of a union. It is also his right to recognize or not recognize it just as he sees fit, but the right of the employer ends there, but he should reserve the right at all times to say whether or not he will recognize the union.

Q 28 Would you say that of the Standard Oil Company, or other large companys?

A    Well, the Standard Oil Company have their own union in their own company and they say to the National Labor Unions that they do not wish them to come in and disturb their organization, and they do not want the National Union.

Q 29 Do you think that is equitable?

A    I think my original proposition is fair.

Q 30 I am not speaking of propositions now, but equity, fair play, etc.? Do you think it is equitable?

A    Yes.

Q 31 Do you think it is equitable, or do you suggest that the U. S. not allow the A. F. of Labor to organize a company union? Do you think that equitable?

A    As long as the men are satisfied.

Q 32 What comeback have they?

A    They can most certainly quit, can't they?

Q 33 Yes, quit and starve. Would you have them do that? Men that can only hoard this much money and have the right to quit, they are in the same position that you are. Plans of this kind, do you think they are equitable?

A    There is this to be considered in it. How long can conditions exist of their own accord, how long can the employer afford to pay these men when he is losing money every day? As I said before, I have six men in my place of business, and business has fallen off something more than 50 per cent, something had to be done about it and the only man that I had that could be cut off had a wife and several children. It would mean that the children would have to be taken out of school if he did not have employment, so I called my men together and told them the circumstances and they each one agreed they would be willing to accept a cut in wages of enough to take care of this man's salary, in order that he might be kept on at his work.

Q 34 That is exactly what I wanted you to say. Now take the General Motors Corporation for instance, for I happen to know these to be facts, from the first hand information, that they had one hundred and fifty thousand men working for them, and during a period of good times they made in profits five billions of dollars and then came this depression and one hundred, fifty thousand men must be retrenched. Then came the time when they could not carry that many men and there came to them the question of either cutting off these men who had helped them make the five billions of dollars during good times or either cutting salaries in order to make up the retrenchment. In order to keep the company out of the red should they cut them off or merely cut their salary? Do you think that is equitable to cut them off in order to keep the company out of the red and still making money?

A I would say that they do the very best they can for the men until the last dime of the five billions of dollars went out.

Q 35 Would you say if these people organized against this that they were wrong to bond together?

A No.

Q 36 I would like to hear about the coal companies from 1919 to 1929, and from 1929 to now?

A Few of those that were in operation in 1919 are still there, and few of them that were in operation even in 1929 are still to be found. They have been sold, or sold at the Court House or passed into new hands in some method.

I doubt if there are any that are still in the same hands as they were ten years ago.

## Mr. Ornitz:

Q 1    What is a Company guard?

A    All I can say from what I understand, is this: Many of the men have been cut off or fired and while they are out they say that the Company shall not operate and in order to protect the men that are still working, the Company hires men that have been deputized, made Deputy Sheriffs, and given legal authority to guard the property.

Q 2    And the guards get the coöperation of the county authorities?

A    Yes, sir.

Q 3    They have been made Deputies of the Sheriff and have a right to protect the property of the Company?

A    Exactly.

Q 4    Don't you think it would be much more equitable to appoint some of the miners as the Company guards?

A    Yes, sir. That is done sometimes.

Q 5    Do you advocate that in your paper?

A    If I thought they would protect the property and not allow it to be destroyed, I most certainly would.

Q 6    It seems to me it would make it more balanced.

A    Yes, sir.

## Questions by Bruce Crawford:

Q 1    I believe you stated that in a period of depression you did not think a strike justified. Is that correct?

A    This is my theory.

Q 2    Then it should be done when they are making good wages?

A    If the Company is making untold profit. Yes, sir.

Q 3    Don't you think they should be protected and have the right to protection?

A    Yes, sir. At all times. Just as I am protected in my home by the fire department and police, etc.

*Mr. Dreiser:*

Q 1  Mr. Evans, I do hope you do not mind answering these questions.

A  Not at all. In fact I really enjoy it, but I would like to ask you a few questions, if you do not object?

A  Not at all.

*Questions by Mr. Evans. Directed to Mr. Dreiser:*

Q 1  You are a very famous novelist and have written several books. Would you kindly tell what your royalties amount to?

A  I do not mind. $200,000.00, approximately. Probably more.

Q 2  What do you get a year, if you do not mind telling?

A  Last year, I think I made $35,000.00.

Q 3  Do you contribute anything to charity?

A  No, I do not.

Q 4  That is all.

A  No, do not stop there, go right ahead and ask me something else. Would you like to know why I do not contribute to charity?

Q 5  Do you give any part of that to any organization?

A  Well, I give to the Civil Liberties Union, Old Age Insurance, and to Children's home.

Q 6  I see.

A  I will tell you something of my life. I happened to be from a large family. There were 13 children; three dead, and we worked like other people. When they became old, not being shrewd people, they saw in the papers that I had some money and, of course, they called on me for me to take care of them. I keep several of my near relatives.

Q 7  May I ask you what percentage of your income you give that way?

A  Five to six thousand a year.

Q 8  Do you give as much as one-tenth of your income?

A    Any one that has property must pay to keep it up. It costs to take care of it or throw it away. I am a writer, and I am mostly interested in the theory of equity. I would like to make this government one of equity. I employ four secretaries and I do not pay them any small matter for salary. They work continuously on facts and so do I. I am not dancing around at the Waldorf, but work most of the time. I am conducting this investigation at my own expense, as I do most of my investigations, and when it comes to the spending of money I think I will average among the rest of them.

Q 9    What I was trying to say was that me, with my $60.00 per week, give more to charity, and believe more in the standard of equity than you do with your $35,000.00 per year.

A.    No, I do not think so.

Q 10    Do you think you could maintain any standard of living if you only made $30.00 to $40.00 per month?

A    None.

Q 11    Do you agree with the principles of Communism?

A    They would not take me in, but I see in their form an equity, I call it equity, that is fine. I say let this country start with equity and work on from that.

Q 12    Do you believe in the Soviet government from Russia?

A    I have visited Russia and I believe their form of government is far better than any other I have seen in this country.
    As a matter of fact, for the first twenty years of my life I never made more than $14.00 per week. And out of that, had to pay room and board, but I weathered the storm. For five years after that I made $75.00 per month as a magazine writer, and they would not keep me because they did not like my articles, or my kind of articles. I then worked as an editor for two years and rose until I made $18,000.00 a year, for four years, but this company, who edited cheap magazines, quit and I was compelled to go back to writing, but my books never brought

me any money. I was fifty-five years old when I wrote my first success, "The American Tragedy," and up until that time, I never made more than $125.00 to $150.00 per month. Work it out for yourself.

Q 13 I have lived on less than that, and feel that I have contributed more to charity than you and that my life is more equitable than yours.

# TESTIMONY TAKEN IN HARLAN
## (*Continued*)

*Harlan, Kentucky, November 6, 1931*

TESTIMONY *taken at the Lewallen Hotel, in Harlan, Kentucky, before Theodore Dreiser, Chairman, and other members of the National Committee for the Defense of Political Prisoners.*

## HENRY THORNTON

*Questioned by Theodore Dreiser:*

Q 1    What is your name?
A      Henry Thornton.
Q 2    Where do you live?
A      On Clover Street in Harlan County.
Q 3    Were you born in this State?
A      No, sir.
Q 4    Where were you born?
A      Indianapolis, Indiana.
Q 5    How long have you been in this State?
A      17 years.
Q 6    How old are you?

A    Right around 48.

Q 7    What sort of work have you done?

A    Mining.

Q 8    Where?

A    In Kentucky.

Q 9    In Harlan or in Kentucky generally?

A    In Harlan County.

Q 10    You have been doing that for 17 years?

A    Here in this State.

Q 11    Are you mining now?

A    No, sir.

Q 12    What are you doing now?

A    Cleaning up the meat market in Kroger's.

Q 13    How long since you did any mining work?

A    Pretty close to last January a year.

Q 14    How does it come that you haven't done any mining since?

A    I don't know exactly how come.

Q 15    Were you discharged?

A    They called it laying me off.

Q 16    What mining company did you work for?

A    The Harlan Gas Coal Company.

Q 17    Did they give you any reason why they discharged or laid you off?

A    No, sir.

Q 18    How much were you getting a day?

A    I was loading coal by the ton.

Q 19    How much did you get a day?

A    Anything from $3.00 to $3.50 or $6.00.

Q 20    Did you make that every day?

A    No.

Q 21    How much did you make a week?

A    Anything from $15.00 to $17.00 a week.

Q 22    Did you make that regularly?

A    Not every week.

Q 23    If you didn't make $17.00 every week, how much did you make a month?

A    $30.00 or $35.00 a month.

Q 24 Did you make that regularly?

A    They didn't work regularly, you know.

Q 25 You don't know whether you made $35.00 a month?

A    No, sir, because they didn't work regularly.

Q 26 Could you say how much you made in the course of a year?

A    I didn't keep no tab. I don't know.

Q 27 Do you think that you averaged $20.00 to $25.00 a month?

A    I am afraid to say for I don't know.

Q 28 How many hours did you work a day?

A    12 to 14 hours.

Q 29 For six days a week?

A    Sometimes six; they didn't work regular.

Q 30 Sometimes six and sometimes not?

A    Yes, sometimes only four days.

Q 31 You would work as many as 14 hours a day or 12?

A    About 12 hours.

Q 32 Did you live in a company house?

A    No, sir.

Q 33 Did you buy anything from the Company store?

A    All the trading I done was at the Company store.

Q 34 You had to do it?

A    Under conditions.

Q 35 Were you paid in money or in some sort of book or scrip on the store?

A    I got a check from the office that would get you scrip from the office and trade it in the commissary.

Q 36 You did not get any actual cash?

A    Not unless you had a little over-plus on your pay-day. Between the 15th and 30th you got to the office to get the scrip and trade it in the commissary, and if you have any over-plus you can get it on the 15th or 30th, which is the pay-day.

Q 37 Was there anything left as a rule outside of your living expenses?

A    It was mighty light, sometimes a little bit.

Q 38  Did you get clothing with this?

A    No, sir.

Q 39  Just get food?

A    Yes, sir.

Q 40  What did you do for clothing? Didn't you buy any clothes?

A    Overalls at $1.50. If I had anything left over I would get some overalls.

Q 41  If you had anything left over, you could get clothing?

A    Yes, just overalls.

Q 42  Are you married?

A    Yes.

Q 43  Have you any children?

A    Two.

Q 44  Are your wife and children with you?

A    Yes, sir.

Q 45  Have they been with you all this time?

A    Yes, sir.

Q 46  Did you all live on this money that you made?

A    Not all together. Nine months at a time my boy was janitor at the colored school and got $25.00 a month.

Q 47  Did your wife do any work?

A    She had a small boy. She wasn't able to work. She had to take care of the house.

Q 48  How much rent did you pay for this house?

A    $15.00.

Q 49  At the time you were working, were you satisfied with your working conditions?

A    I can't say I would be satisfied. There wasn't no way for me to be satisfied.

Q 50  Did you feel that you were getting along very well?

A    I felt that conditions could have been better.

Q 51  Why did they lay you off from work? What reason did they give when they laid you off from working?

A    They didn't say.

Q 52  Had you done anything?

A   Not more than make two visits to the courthouse to the speaking.

Q 53  What speaking?

A   The union speaking.

Q 54  What Union people were speaking?

A   I couldn't call the names; just two speakings.

Q 55  Were they people from the American Federation of Labor that were speaking?

A   They told me they was United Mine Workers.

Q 56  And you went to the speaking?

A   Of course I didn't go to the speaking but I was off that day and they said I came and the Company stopped me on that account.

Q 57  Did you go to the meeting?

A   No.

Q 58  Do you belong to any organization of the United Mine Workers or the National Miners Union?

A   I joined the National Mine Workers.

Q 59  When?

A   I can't tell you exactly what day but pretty early after they discharged me.

Q 60  You don't know how long after?

A   No. I guess about four or five months after I was discharged.

Q 61  After you were accused of going to this meeting and were fired by this company, how did you make a living?

A   I didn't make no living. I just existed along among the people.

Q 62  Did anybody after that give you any trouble of any kind?

A   Later on after I had belonged to the Union they arrested me here.

Q 63  What for?

A   Drunk, they claimed.

Q 64  Were you drunk?

A   Not as I know of.

Q 65  When they arrested you, where were you?

A    In my house.

Q 66  They came to your house and got you?

A    Yes.

Q 67  Who came there?

A    A Deputy Sheriff.

Q 68  What did he say to you?

A    Not anything.

Q 69  Did he just ask you to come with him?

A    No, sir, he didn't ask me any questions.

Q 70  What did he do?

A    He took me up and took me on.

Q 71  Did he do you any bodily injury?

A    No, sir, no more than to knock me on the head.

Q 72  What with?

A    I couldn't tell you.

Q 73  Were you conscious when he hit you?

A    He knocked me on the ground.

Q 74  With his fist or a club or what?

A    I don't know what it was.

Q 75  Did you resist him in any way?

A    Not as I know of.

Q 76  Where did they take you? To the police station?

A    They said they were on their way to jail.

Q 77  In a wagon?

A    No, in a car.

Q 78  You don't remember them putting you in the car?

A    I remember that I couldn't tell anything about where I was. I could just discover I was getting up from a lick.

Q 79  How long did they keep you in this jail?

A    Five or six days before they tried me.

Q 80  Were you sick all this time?

A    I visited the doctor at his office and he dressed my head.

Q 81  Did they let you go out of jail to see the doctor or did they take you to him or did he come to you?

A    They taken me the first time. I was knocked in the head Saturday night and they taken me on Sunday night and after that they just opened the door of the jail and let me go to the doctor.

Q 82 How long did they keep you there?

A    They fined me ten dollars and costs, and they kept me there something like 12 or 13 or 14 days.

Q 83 Just sitting in jail?

A    Yes, sir.

Q 84 And then they turned you out?

A    Yes, they turned me loose.

Q 85 How long ago was it they let you out?

A    I never kept no tab.

Q 86 Since then you have been active in this Union that you joined?

A    No. I went to the meetings several times since then.

Q 87 Has anybody annoyed you since you went to these meetings?

A    No, that was the only trouble we had.

Q 88 Have you had more than one job since you left there?

A    I have had several jobs.

Q 89 What kind?

A    Well, this fellow would come along and want me to do a little work and that fellow would ask me to do some work, maybe for an hour or two, or an hour and a half, but I ain't had no regular job.

Q 90 How much do you make a week now?

A    I can't tell you.

Q 91 Do you make as much as $5.00?

A    I can't tell you. I cleans up for Kroger and they give me whatever they feel like giving me.

Q 92 In money?

A    No, sir, in provisions to live on.

Q 93 Do you and your wife live on that?

A    I told you my son is janitor at the school and that helps a little, but that is the only help.

Q 94 Without the assistance of your son, could you and your wife get along?

A     Not handy.

Q 95  Do you think anybody around here would give you a job of any kind?

A     I have an idea they wouldn't.

Q 96  Why?

A     Because I claimed to belong to an organization.

Q 97  And since you belong to that organization they wouldn't give you any work?

A     They refuse to employ me.

Q 98  Has anybody ever said to you that you needn't come to them for work?

A     No, not that.

Q 99  What did they say to you?

A     Some fellow said to me to let the organization take care of me.

Q 100 Was this some man that you had gone to for work?

A     I had talked to him about work.

Q 101 Do you object to saying who that man was?

A     I could say who he was.

Q 102 Do you think it would do you any harm if you did that?

A     It might.

Q 103 We won't ask you then to say who it was. Did he have a business of some kind? Was he an employer of labor?

A     Why, he had kind of a business all right, he was kind of a business man.

Q 104 He had a store or something?

A     No, sir, but he could assist me in working if he would have.

*Associated Press Reporter:*

Q 1   When you talk about getting scrip—was that a check that you could take to the bank and get cashed?

A     It was like this, you see. The scrip was a round piece of metal like this—

Q 2   That is a good half dollar.

A     Yes, but scrip is a piece of metal round like this.

Q 3   Did they give you cash for this?

A   No, we got it in food.

Q 4  If you had $15.00 in wages coming to you, would they let you have it, or would they let you have any cash at all?

A   No, sir, that is not the way.

Q 5  Just what is the way?

A   On pay-day if you have anything left over from the first two weeks, you can get that money. There is four weeks in the month, they count, and you work the whole month and the first two weeks they claim they pay you and you get the food and stuff from the commissary and if you get any cash it has to be left over from what you have already bought.

Q 6  In the meantime, they let you have the scrip?

A   Say, if I want to work this morning I haven't got any money. If I go to work on the 6th I haven't got any money and if I get any money it has to be left over at the end of the month after I have already got what I have out of the commissary and paid for it in scrip.

Q 7  Then if you have money coming to you you can get it?

A   Yes, I go to work this morning and then in the morning I go in and they give me the piece of metal that they call scrip and I take it to the store and trade it.

Q 8  If you have money of your own when you go to work to pay for things as you go along, then you can get cash for your wages?

A   Not until the month is out.

Q 9  You don't have to take that scrip if you don't want to?

A   If you have money you don't have to take it.

*Questioned again by Theodore Dreiser:*

Q 1  Do you mean they would give you either cash or scrip?

A   They would give you cash if you had anything coming to you at the end of the month.

Q 2  Do you know of any miner that ever had cash coming to him at the end of the month?

A   I don't know whether I did or not.

Q 3   Do you know of any miner that had money coming to him that was refused by the Company because he had joined the Labor movement?

A   Well, I don't know.

# 5

## FURTHER TESTIMONY IN HARLAN

In the afternoon, the coach of the Harlan High football team very politely invited the committee to go to the game, which was the big athletic event of the season for Harlan and Bell counties. Lester Cohen, Charles Walker and I went around to the Courthouse to try to get Judge Jones or Sheriff Blair to attend the hearing. Judge Jones was not to be found, Sheriff Blair was down in the basement counting ballots from the election, Mr. Ward of the Harlan County Coal Operators Association greeted us smoothly and said he would come over after the game; his boy was playing in the game and he felt he had to see it. As it turned out neither he nor Judge Jones were willing to talk to the committee. The statement of the point of view of the owners and the authorities came from Sheriff Blair, late that afternoon, and from the County prosecutor the next day.

Walking around the town we were spoken to on the street by a Dr. Nolan, who was chairman of the local American Legion post. He had been much impressed by Dreiser's remarks about a government of equity in his argument with the editor of the Pineville paper and felt that the hearing should be carried on in the town hall. He helped us dig up the town clerk, but it turned out that the mayor had already gone to the game and had carried off the key in his pocket.

Meanwhile over at the hotel miners kept on telling their stories.

*Harlan, Kentucky, Nov. 6, 1931.*

TESTIMONY *taken at the Lewallen Hotel, in Harlan, Kentucky, before Theodore Dreiser, Chairman, and other members of the National Committee for the Defense of Political Prisoners.*

## J. W. FREEMAN

*Questioned by Theodore Dreiser:*

Q 1   Are you a native Kentuckian?

A     Yes, sir.

Q 2   Where do you live?

A     Up here at Evarts.

Q 3   Are you a miner?

A     Yes, sir.

Q 4   Have you been for a long time?

A     Off and on the last thirty years.

Q 5   Are you working now?

A     No.

Q 6   How long have you not been working?

A     About eight months, I guess.

Q 7   Is there any particular reason why you are out of work?

A     I guess the reason now is they have me victimized.

Q 8   What do you mean by that?

A     I don't know. They call you that when you join the Union.

Q 9   How does that work?

A     It don't work. You don't work at all. They just let you rest.

Q 10  You mean you are on a black list?

A     I suppose I must be black listed. I haven't tried to get work but one time. I tried to get back where I was at and they wouldn't give me work.

Q 11  Did they say why?

A     No.

Q 12 How do you manage to live?

A    I have been getting a little off the Union and a little here and there.

Q 13 Are you married?

A    Yes, sir.

Q 14 Have you any children?

A    Six.

Q 15 Do you have to support them?

A    Yes, sir.

Q 16 Do you have to support them all?

A    No, sir, one of them is married and he supports himself.

Q 17 How do you manage to get clothing for them?

A    There has been some aid clothes got in and I have got a few clothes here and there.

Q 18 Is there any particular matter you want to tell this Committee?

A    None that I know of.

Q 19 Have you been assaulted at any time?

A    I have been arrested one time.

Q 20 How long ago?

A    The 6th night of last month.

Q 21 What for?

A    They accused me of selling liquor.

Q 22 Did you sell liquor?

A    No, sir.

Q 23 Why do you suppose they accused you?

A    I think they accused me of selling liquor on account of a little town race we had in our town and election. They thought probably I might be a Councilman on the Board against the law that was there, a Deputy Sheriff and a policeman in the town.

Q 24 You mean some law not favorable to the miners?

A    We call the Deputy Sheriff and the policeman the law.

Q 25 Did they object to being pushed out of their jobs?

A    All they said when they come on to Harlan with me was they said, "You are a candidate, aren't you?" and I said, "No, sir," and he said, "I thought you were a candidate for Councilman," and I said, "No, they have talked about running me but I ain't a candidate."

Q 26 Do you mean to say you can't be a candidate?

A You can't around Evarts. The law won't allow you.

Q 27 If all the people wanted you to have a political job, do you mean to say they couldn't nominate you and elect you?

A They might get me in jail.

Q 28 And you couldn't get into office without the consent of these people?

A No.

Q 29 Why wouldn't they want you to be in over there?

A They knowed I was against them. The Council hires the *Polices* and they knew if I got in I would be for another man.

Q 30 That hasn't anything to do with the mine trouble?

A No. I says to them when they arrested me, "I don't see what this means. Have you got it in for me because I belong to the Union?" and he says, "Damn the Union. I am a Union man myself," and I says, "You know I ain't sold no liquor."

Q 31 Were you locked up?

A Yes, sir.

Q 32 How long did you stay in jail?

A The half of the night they locked me up and all the next night.

Q 33 How did you get out?

A On bail. The next day they taken me to Pineville.

Q 34 Before a Judge? Who was this Judge?

A Judge Rollins.

Q 35 What did he say about it?

A I had a trial before him and he dismissed the case.

Q 36 Did they produce any witnesses?

A Yes, they produced affidavits.

Q 37 And he threw them out?

A Yes, sir.

Q 38 Were you ever arrested again after that?

A No, sir.

Q 39 Or annoyed by anybody?

A No, sir.

Q 40 Just by lack of work?

A Yes, sir, and I am going to tell the truth. I haven't tried to get any work but one time.

Q 41 Don't you think it might be worth while to try?

A I don't think I could get any work up in there. I don't believe I could.

Q 42 Why don't you leave this community?

A I own my own home and I can't afford to walk off and leave it without I am forced to and I have to do the best I can.

*Mr. Ornitz:*

Q 1 While you were in jail did they do anything to you in there?

A They didn't do anything to me only the night they put me in jail they locked my feet to a radiator like this one here, about that close up, and I laid in the floor the rest of the night.

Q 2 With your feet chained to the radiator?

A Yes, next to the room where the law slept. They said, "We ain't going to put you in that nasty jail down there. It is too nasty to put a human being in." There had been a man killed in there and they took me up to their room and there was a good bed in that room but they took me on back to an empty room and locked my feet to the radiator, about two feet from it, and I sat up in the window, to tell the truth, the most of the night, and they left me in there.

Q 3 Do you know anything about the dynamiting of the soup kitchen?

A No, I just know it was blowed up.

Q 4 You weren't there?

A No, I was home in the bed. I heard the shooting.

*Mr. Dos Passos:*

Q 1   Is there any connection between the law in Evarts and the Black Mountain Coal Company?

A   They work under the law. They claim there was eleven there the night they raided me. I only seen seven but my family seen eleven.

Q 2   Did they search your house?

A   Yes, sir.

Q 3   At the time they arrested you for being a candidate, they searched your house?

A   Yes, sir.

Q 4   What for?

A   They claimed for liquor. They shined their lights around a little.

Q 5   They didn't show you any warrant?

A   No, sir.

*Harlan, Kentucky, November 6, 1931*

TESTIMONY *taken at the Lewallen Hotel in Harlan, Kentucky, before Theodore Dreiser, Chairman, and other members of the National Committee for the Defense of Political Prisoners.*

## MRS. FLORA SHACKELFORD

*Questioned by Theodore Dreiser:*

Q 1   What is your name?

A   Mrs. Flora Shackelford.

Q 2   I suppose your husband was a miner and he is out of work?

A   Yes.

Q 3   Have you children?

A   Yes.

Q 4   How many?

A   Two of his and three grand-children to raise.

Q 5  Are they of school age?

A     Yes. One lacks just four months of finishing high school.

Q 6  Are they in school?

A     No.

Q 7  Why aren't they in school?

A     Because of working conditions; he was not making enough to support them.

Q 8  Is he working now?

A     No.

Q 9  Does he belong to the National Miners Union?

A     Yes.

Q 10  Has he had trouble?

A     He is black-listed.

Q 11  Has your house been raided?

A     Been threatened.

Q 12  Tell this Committee what you know about conditions as you see them.

A     Conditions are bad all over Harlan. People haven't sufficient food or clothing. Two years ago we bought a place, paid two hundred dollars on it and lost it. We have not been able to pay our store bill. The children can't go to school on account of not having sufficient clothing.

Q 13  Isn't there a law in this State to force you to send your children to school?

A     Yes.

Q 14  It hasn't been enforced?

A     No. They put up notices for them to be there.

Q 15  But the authorities are not forcing you to send your children to school?

A     No.

Q 16  What have you to live on?

A     What little aid the National Mine Workers give us.

Q 17  Have they given you aid?

A     Last month they gave us three sacks of flour, six pounds of lard and six pounds of sugar.

Q 18  What do you do about rent?

A    Son-in-law draws a compensation check and he pays the rent.

Q 19  He was hurt in the mines?

A    Yes.

Q 20  What do you do for clothes?

A    Just what people give me.

Q 21  Then you are a subject of charity?

A    Yes. When we would go to different places the law would follow us and when we got to church the law would be parked along the front and would blow their horns. The gun thugs are the law in this country now and not the judges and juries. At a mass meeting to be held here at the court house we were ordered away and hand grenades and tear gas were thrown.

Q 22  Why didn't they allow them to hold it?

A    Because they wanted to take away our American Rights, liberty and free speech and they ordered us away.

Q 23  For what reason?

A    Said they were not going to have it.

Q 24  What were you doing?

A    I was reading the New Testament to some ladies and they ordered me off and told me I didn't have any right there, had no business there. There was no mass meeting going to be there and they were going to throw tear gas. Asked me if I wanted to cry. I told them if God Almighty saw fit for me to cry I could cry.

Q 25  Who said this to you?

A    A Chicago gun thug. He was not a person any one knew from these parts; all the other men told me he was a Chicago gun thug.

Q 26  Was your house ever raided?

A    No; just threatened.

Q 27  Can you tell what you know about your own children or any other children?

A    Well, they are just suffering. A great many of them are suffering from want of sufficient food.

Q 28  What do they eat?

A    Just such things as pinto beans and corn bread made up with water; not even soda or salt in it. I went for over a week without anything to season pinto beans but lard.

Q 29  You know other families like that?

A    Yes. Families who have no shoes for their little children; no furniture in their house.

Q 30  Do you know any miners' children that are getting milk?

A    No.

Q 31  Do you suppose that if these men here would stop joining the National Mine Workers Union and could go back to work, would they go back to work?

A    If these men knuckle down to these conditions and put up with these yellow dog contracts, in less than a year from now they will be getting on their knees for a drink of water.

Q 32  Do you know the name of this Chicago gun thug?

A    No; they called him the Three Foot Gangster.

Q 33  Some of the members of the Committee got a rumor that there would be trouble at Wallins Creek Sunday afternoon; do you know any basis for any such rumor or how the miners feel about holding a meeting nowadays?

A    No.

*Dreiser:* I understand the gangster's name is Haywood.


*Harlan, Kentucky, November 6, 1931*

TESTIMONY *taken at the Lewallen Hotel in Harlan, Kentucky, before Theodore Dreiser, Chairman, and other members of the National Committee for the Defense of Political Prisoners:*

## J. D. MALICOAT

*Questioned by Theodore Dreiser:*

Q 1   Are you a resident of this County?

A    Yes.

Q 2   Are you a native Kentuckian?

A     No; I was born in Indiana; raised in this State.

Q 3   What is your trade or business?

A     Coal miner.

Q 4   Been a miner for how long?

A     Guess about thirty years.

Q 5   Are you a miner now?

A     Yes.

Q 6   Are you working now?

A     No; haven't been working since about the third or the fifth of May.

Q 7   Where did you work before that time?

A     At the Harlan Gas & Coal Co.

Q 8   Are you married?

A     No.

Q 9   Why did you lose your job?

A     Over joining the Union, I suppose. I joined the Mine Workers Union and then I lost my job.

Q 10  You didn't join it before?

A     I joined the Union and lost my job afterwards.

Q 11  Do you know whether or not you are on a black list?

A     I don't know; I haven't been able to get a job.

Q 12  Have you tried different places to get a job?

A     Yes, but they asked for a recommendation and the people I had worked for wouldn't give me one.

Q 13  Have you ever been arrested?

A     No.

Q 14  Have you ever been at the swimming pool?

A     Yes.

Q 15  Were you there when the men were killed?

A     No; I was there the following Friday; we were fixing to put the kitchen back.

Q 16  You were doing this for the National Mine Workers?

A     Yes.

Q 17  What trouble did you have?

A     Five or six gunmen came and held high powered rifles

and others walked around with guns on them and kept tantalizing us.

Q 18 What do you mean by tantalizing?

A Talking like they wanted to start something.

Q 19 Did they call you names?

A No.

Q 20 Were they all armed?

A Yes; had about two guns apiece.

Q 21 What actually happened after they walked around and threatened you?

A They looked all over the house to see what they could find and told us to get out they were going to close it up. One of them picked up the bottom of a barrel and hit it on the floor.

Q 22 Is that the only trouble you ever had?

A All I have ever had; that was the end of the soup kitchen.

Q 23 This was the soup kitchen for women and children?

A Yes.

Q 24 Are there any more soup kitchens around?

A No.

*Questioned by Mr. Walker:*

Q 25 Did you people have any knowledge beforehand that there was any threatening against the soup kitchen?

A We had heard rumors; nothing direct.

*Questioned by Mr. Dreiser:*

Q 26 After these men were killed why did you go to reopen the soup kitchen; didn't you expect trouble?

A We didn't know what might happen; we thought they would let us feed the women and children.

*Harlan, Kentucky, November 6, 1931*

TESTIMONY *taken at the Lewallen Hotel in Harlan, Kentucky, before Theodore Dreiser, Chairman, and other members of the National Committee for the Defense of Political Prisoners:*

## MRS. DEBS MORELAND

*Questioned by Theodore Dreiser:*

Q 1    What is your name?

A      Fannie Moreland.

Q 2    Are you a Kentuckian?

A      No, sir.

Q 3    What is your husband—is he a miner?

A      Yes; he has been a miner for the last five years.

Q 4    Is he working now?

A      Yes.

Q 5    Have you any children?

A      Yes.

Q 6    How many?

A      One.

Q 7    Is it an infant?

A      No; it is five years old.

Q 8    Do you live in a company town?

A      Yes.

Q 9    How much money per month does your husband make?

A      He is not making any now.

Q 10   How long has it been since he worked?

A      Last April.

Q 11   Has he tried to get work here?

A      I think so.

Q 12   Why can't he get work?

A      On account of the National Miners Union.

Q 13   Is he a member of the National Miners Union?

A      Yes.

Q 14 Is he black-listed?

A    Yes.

Q 15 Has he been arrested for anything?

A    Yes.

Q 16 How many times has he been arrested?

A    Once they arrested him and took him to jail.

Q 17 How long ago—since last June?

A    About a month ago.

Q 18 Do you know why they arrested him?

A    There was a car of the law came to the soup kitchen and found some literature.

Q 19 Where was this soup kitchen?

A    Down at Gulston.

Q 20 What did you have to do with the soup kitchen; did you work there or help run the soup kitchen?

A    I helped cook.

Q 21 What did your husband have to do with the soup kitchen?

A    He went out and collected food.

Q 22 And he did this to help out the miners?

A    Yes.

Q 23 Did anybody tell him not to?

A    No.

Q 24 Then why did they arrest him?

A    Because they found this literature in the kitchen.

Q 25 What was this literature?

A    *Daily Workers.*

Q 26 Did he distribute the *Daily Workers?*

A    No; just had them there in the kitchen.

Q 27 Did he take the *Daily Workers* by the year?

A    No.

Q 28 Then how did he come to have it?

A    I don't know how he came to have it there in the kitchen.

Q 29 Didn't they come and raid his house and search it?

A    Yes. They just found these *Daily Workers* and arrested him.

Q 30 What did they do to him?

A    Arrested him and took him to jail.

Q 31 How long was he in jail?

A    Thirty-four days.

Q 32 How did he get out?

A    They turned him out.

Q 33 Did you go to the Sheriff or the Judge or any one and speak for him?

A    Yes; I went to "Baby" Jones.

Q 34 What did this Jones say?

A    He said he would study about it and if he would agree to leave the county he might turn him loose.

Q 35 Did he agree to leave the county?

A    I don't think he did.

Q 36 Has he left the county?

A    They carried him away; they came to the house the fifteenth of last month and took him away.

Q 37 Have you seen him?

A    No.

Q 38 Is he alive?

A    Yes. But they beat him and left him for dead.

Q 39 Has he recovered from this?

A    Not hardly.

Q 40 For instance, did they knock out an eye or break an arm or is he going to be sick the rest of his life?

A    No, they bruised him up.

Q 41 Otherwise he is a good, strong man and will get well?

A    I think so.

Q 42 He can't come back here?

A    No.

Q 43 Do you intend to leave here and go to him?

A    I don't know yet.

Q 44 How do you live?

A    By people giving me things.

Q 45 How much rent do you have to pay?

A    Eight dollars a month, but I am not paying anything now.

Q 46 How do you get anything to eat?

A    Just what people give me.

Q 47 How do you get clothes?

A Don't get any; just wear what I had.

Q 48 How did you know that these men were the law, by the number of pistols they carried on their person?

A I knew one of the men.

Q 49 Did you see your husband beaten?

A No; they carried him to Cumberland Mountain.

Q 50 He was left there for dead?

A Yes.

Q 51 How long after they took him away did you hear anything about him?

A About a week.

Q 52 Did you hear from him or from some one else about him?

A Some one else about him.

Q 53 This man that you knew; was he an officer?

A He was the law.


*Harlan, Kentucky, November 6, 1931*

TESTIMONY *taken at the Lewallen Hotel in Harlan, Kentucky, before Theodore Dreiser, Chairman, and other members of the National Committee for the Defense of Political Prisoners:*

## BOB HOWARD

*Questioned by Theodore Dreiser:*

Q 1 What is your name?

A Bob Howard.

Q 2 Are you a married man?

A Yes.

Q 3 Is your wife alive?

A Yes.

Q 4 Have you any children?

A Yes; seven.

Q 5   Do you have to support them?

A   They are all married but one and he is in the Navy.

Q 6   Then you don't have to support them?

A   No.

Q 7   Do you own your own home?

A   Yes.

Q 8   If you did not work would you have any income of any kind?

A   Yes; I have a little property here in Harlan.

Q 9   How much does it bring you as an income?

A   About $25.00 or $30.00 a month.

Q 10   Are you a miner?

A   No.

Q 11   What are you?

A   A farmer, I guess; worked on a farm about all my life.

Q 12   Are you at all connected in any way with the clash here between the miners and the coal operators?

A   No; not interested in any way.

Q 13   Has it caused you any trouble?

A   No.

Q 14   You have not been arrested by anybody?

A   No.

Q 15   Been annoyed in any way?

A   No.

Q 16   Then I don't see how you are connected with this.

A   I was on the jury.

Q 17   Where was this jury sitting?

A   It was a coroner's jury up at the swimming pool.

Q 18   Was that here in town?

A   No; it was up at the swimming pool where they had a soup kitchen.

Q 19   How long ago was this that this coroner's jury was sitting?

A   I don't remember when it happened.

Q 20   Has it been since last August?

A   I think it has.

Q 21   What happened that this coroner's jury was there?

A     Two fellows were killed and another shot.

Q 22  Who were they; what were their names?

A     Joe Moore and Julius Baldwin.

Q 23  Were they miners?

A     I suppose they were miners.

Q 24  Does anybody know why they were killed?

A     No.

*Harlan, Kentucky, November 6, 1931*

TESTIMONY *taken at the Lewallen Hotel in Harlan, Kentucky, before Theodore Dreiser, Chairman, and other members of the National Committee for the Defense of Political Prisoners:*

## LLOYD MOORE

*Questioned by Theodore Dreiser:*

Q 1   What is your name?

A     Lloyd Moore.

Q 2   Do you live here in this town?

A     Yes.

Q 3   Have you always lived here?

A     Been here ten years.

Q 4   Are you a miner?

A     Yes.

Q 5   How long have you been a miner?

A     About ten years—ever since I have been here.

Q 6   Are you married?

A     Yes.

Q 7   Have you any children?

A     I have two children.

Q 8   Have you any work?

A     No.

Q 9   How long have you been out of work?

A     I believe I quit in March.

Q 10  You were not fired?

A   No, I quit to tend crop.

Q 11 There was more money in that than there was in working?

A   Yes.

Q 12 Do you own any property?

A   No.

Q 13 How much do you pay for rent?

A   I live with my father-in-law.

Q 14 You don't pay any rent?

A   No.

Q 15 I understand at the time Moore and Baldwin were killed in the soup kitchen that you were there?

A   Yes.

Q 16 What were you doing there?

A   I was just up there; I was just staying there at night.

Q 17 You were not helping them with their work in any way?

A   No.

Q 18 In regard to this shooting, will you tell us what you saw?

A   These fellows drove up in the evening after dark.

Q 19 Do you know how many drove up?

A   I could see two.

Q 20 What happened before this shooting?

A   Two men got out of the car smoking cigarettes.

Q 21 Were they armed—did you see any guns?

A   No. After they got out, they hollered, "Hands up," to the men standing there—about five or six.

Q 22 Can you tell who they were?

A   Johnnie Hall and Luther Lively.

Q 23 Were you one of the five? Were you one of them and this man that was killed?

A   Yes.

Q 24 Did you put up your hands?

A   No; I jumped in the door because they went to shooting before I had time to hold up my hands. I ran.

Q 25 Did you see any of these men shoot? Who had the gun?

A   Lee Fleenor.

Q 26 Do you know that the shot that he fired killed this man?

A   No.

Q 27 Could you identify the person as having fired the shot that killed the man?

A No; I couldn't tell that.

Q 28 What did you do after that?

A I ran.

Q 29 You didn't notify anybody—say for instance the chief of police or the sheriff?

A No.

Q 30 But why didn't you? With a man killed and another one wounded didn't you think the sheriff should be notified?

A Yes.

Q 31 Why didn't you notify him?

A I didn't think it would do any good.

Q 32 Did you think it would be dangerous for you to tell the sheriff?

A No.

Q 33 About when did this happen?

A About two months ago.

Q 34 Did any investigator come around to ask you any questions?

A No.

Q 35 Have you ever been arrested?

A No.

Q 36 Had any trouble of any kind?

A No.

Q 37 Have you ever been warned?

A Not personally but a rope was hung on my door about three weeks ago.

Q 38 Was it just a straight rope?

A It had a noose tied in it.

Q 39 Were you frightened?

A No; didn't pay any attention to it; my wife said something about it. I knew I hadn't done anything, it didn't frighten me a bit.

Q 40 There is a rumor in this community that your house was dynamited.

A   Yes. It didn't strike the house; it struck some forty or fifty feet of the house.

Q 41   Was it after the killing?

A   No; before the killing.

Q 42   Could you give any reason for this?

A   No.

Q 43   You must have some idea of why they would throw dynamite at your house. Do you feel that they were doing so because you had joined the National Mine Workers?

A   It could have been.

Q 44   Did anybody threaten or tell you you shouldn't join it?

A   No.

Q 45   Did you feel when you were joining that it might cause you trouble?

A   No.

Q 46   But it didn't turn out that way?

A   No.

Q 47   After the men were shot at the soup kitchen did they take them to a hospital?

A   I think this fellow's brother took him to the hospital.

Q 48   You cannot get work here?

A   I haven't asked.

Q 49   You do not intend to ask?

A   No.

Q 50   How do you expect to live unless you get a job back in the mine—you don't intend to leave this community?

A   No.

Q 51   Then you intend to ask?

A   Yes, I guess I will.

Q 52   You were a miner for ten years?

A   Yes.

Q 53   Was there a check weighman on the job at the last mine where you worked?

A   I didn't see any check weighman.

*Harlan, Kentucky, November 6, 1931*

TESTIMONY *taken at the Lewallen Hotel in Harlan, Kentucky, before Theodore Dreiser, Chairman, and other members of the National Committee for the Defense of Political Prisoners:*

## GEORGE RUTH

*Questioned by Theodore Dreiser:*

Q 1   What is your name?

A      George O. Ruth.

Q 2   Are you a Kentuckian?

A      No; I'm a Tennesseean.

Q 3   How long have you lived here?

A      I have worked in and around here since 1889.

Q 4   How long have you lived here?

A      Nine years.

Q 5   Are you a Union man?

A      Yes, have been since 1893.

Q 6   Are you working now?

A      No.

Q 7   Have you been out of work for some time?

A      Since the seventh of June.

Q 8   Where were you working then?

A      East Harlan Coal Co.

Q 9   Why did you stop working there?

A      You will have to ask the operators.

Q 10  Don't you know why you stopped work?

A      On a Sunday they came out to Black Mountain where a body of coal workers were marching with a flag.

Q 11  What flag?

A      The Stars and Stripes.

Q 12  Why were they marching?

A      To show their strength and Childress had them to come see what their strength was and on Sunday evening a deputy sheriff came around and notified us that there would be no work on Monday morning.

Q 13 Didn't some of them want to know why you were making a dummy of yourself by marching on Sunday?

A   Yes, and we told them that Sunday was a day set apart for rest and asked them if they didn't belong to a coal operators' union and told them we didn't see why we shouldn't have a right to go to our union.

Q 14 Were you ever arrested after that?

A   No.

Q 15 Did you do any work for the National Mine Workers?

A   Yes; I have worked for them lots.

Q 16 What did you do?

A   Took applications and wrote them up for them.

Q 17 Didn't you help them conduct the soup kitchen?

A   I fixed up the screen-doors and fixed up the table.

Q 18 Were you ever arrested at any time after that?

A   No.

Q 19 Was your house raided?

A   No.

Q 20 You haven't had any trouble with the law?

A   No.

Q 21 You haven't had any work?

A   No.

Q 22 How do you manage to live?

A   To tell the truth, I have been living off the neighbors.

Q 23 Are you living in the coal company's house?

A   Yes.

Q 24 Are you paying any rent?

A   No.

Q 25 Then why don't they turn you out?

A   I reckon it is because I fix the house up and keep it re-paired.

Q 26 Are you still a member of the National Mine Workers Union?

A   No.

Q 27 Why?

A Because I am not in shape to keep it up—pay my dues.

Q 28 Have armed men or deputies or company guards been patrolling the highways where you live?

A Yes.

Q 29 When did they stop?

A Two or three weeks ago.

Q 30 You haven't seen them since?

A No.

Q 31 There are mines working—some, several?

A Yes.

Q 32 What sort of men do they employ? Are they Union men?

A The sort of men who would take the place of their father or mother or brother or sister or relation of any other kind.

Q 33 Are all of these mines being operated by strike breakers so far as you know?

A No.

Q 34 Are they Union men?

A Some are, some are not; some belong to the National Miners Union and some belong to the United Mine Workers.

Q 35 Can you tell whether these mines here could go on with the kind of men they want? Do they make money?

A Not under conditions they have here. They get so much scrip and then their cuts and rents have to come out.

Q 36 I can understand a miner cannot make very much under these conditions, but I was asking whether these coal companies made any money.

A Sure. The commissary and rents of the miners will pay for the output of the mines.

Q 37 Is this something you have investigated? Are you a student of economics?

A I have been in a position to learn a lot of this.

Q 38 And you believe this can run the mines—the rents of houses and what money is made out of the commissary?

A Yes. You take a hundred and twelve houses at $8.00

and $6.00 a month and take one hundred and twenty per cent on the commissary and see what it makes.

Q 39  Wages have been reduced?

A      In December our wages were cut and one dollar was all we could draw. You had to make out your bill to the store manager; they made you fall in line and go to the book-keeper and if you had that much coming to you he would send you back to the scrip man and you fell in line again to get your goods.

*Harlan, Kentucky, November 6, 1931*

TESTIMONY *taken at the Lewallen Hotel in Harlan, Kentucky, before Theodore Dreiser, Chairman, and other members of the National Committee for the Defense of Political Prisoners:*

## ROBERT DEAN

*Questioned by Theodore Dreiser:*

Q 1    What is your name?

A      Robert Dean.

Q 2    Are you a native Kentuckian?

A      No, I am a native of Virginia.

Q 3    How long have you been in Kentucky?

A      About thirty-five years.

Q 4    How long have you been in this district?

A      About fifteen years.

Q 5    Are you a miner?

A      Yes.

Q 6    Have you always been a miner?

A      Yes.

Q 7    When did you work last?

A      We came out some time the last of March or the first of April.

Q 8    What do you mean by—"We came out"?

A       We were called out.

Q 9     Who called you out?

A       National Miners Union.

Q 10    Why did they call you out—through sympathy for those that got fired?

A       Yes.

Q 11    Were you dissatisfied with your work?

A       Yes.

Q 12    Why?

A       Because I wasn't making enough.

Q 13    How much were you making?

A       Probably two or three dollars a day.

Q 14    Are you married?

A       Yes.

Q 15    Have you any children?

A       One.

Q 16    Do you still have to school this child?

A       Yes.

Q 17    Is it in school now?

A       No, it isn't old enough; it is just four years old.

Q 18    You say you haven't been working since last March—how do you manage to live?

A       Had a little money.

Q 19    Do you own your house?

A       I own one on Poor Fork.

Q 20    About how much money did you have?

A       Had probably $190.00 and I sold my milk cow.

Q 21    How much does it cost you to live?

A       Not very much—about $4.00.

Q 22    How much of the $190.00 is left?

A       Not any—that is why I sold my milk cow two weeks ago.

Q 23    Have you ever had any trouble or have you ever been arrested?

A       Yes.

Q 24    What for?

A       Syndicalism.

Q 25    What does that consist of?

A   They got about a wheelbarrow full of papers out of my house.

Q 26  What kind of papers?

A   *Daily Workers.*

Q 27  What were you doing with them?

A   Taking them down town.

Q 28  I suppose the usual load of law came—did they break in?

A   They said they had a warrant. I wasn't there; my wife was there.

Q 29  Just your wife was there?

A   My wife and baby.

Q 30  Did they do any harm, break up anything?

A   Just broke a cake stand.

Q 31  Did they insult her?

A   No.

Q 32  How many times did they come?

A   Three times.

Q 33  On these occasions did they do any damage?

A   No. The last time they came they said they were hunting me.

Q 34  You didn't run away?

A   No.

Q 35  What did they say when they found you?

A   Nothing—just read the warrant to me and took me up here in this jail.

Q 36  Did they take you to the sheriff?

A   No.

Q 37  How long did you stay in jail?

A   Five days.

Q 38  How did you get out?

A   The doctor took me to the hospital; I took the flux and I was bleeding.

Q 39  Is it a comfortable jail as jails go?

A   There were too many in there.

Q 40  Did you sleep on the floor without a blanket?

A   One night I slept without any; four nights I had a mattress.

Q 41  Where did you go from the hospital?

A     The doctor told my wife to take me home.

Q 42  And there were no legal proceedings?

A     No.

Q 43  They haven't said anything to you since they arrested you?

A     Not until three or four days ago.

Q 44  What did they arrest you again for?

A     Because I am on one side and they are on the other.

Q 45  Did you get in an argument?

A     No.

Q 46  Where were you?

A     Standing on the street; a deputy sheriff read the warrant to me and took me to jail.

Q 47  This was on account of possessing unlawful literature?

A     Yes.

Q 48  How long did they keep you in jail?

A     Not long; I got a $5,000 bond and went back home.

Q 49  Where did you get money to put up the bond?

A     I didn't get it; they took me on my own bond.

Q 50  And you have had no help?

A     Had no way of living at all until I sold this cow. I applied for help to the United Mine Workers when I ran out of medicine and they said they were not putting out money for such propositions at all.

Q 51  When they arrested you on one of these charges didn't they accuse you of having ammunition?

A     No.

Q 52  Didn't the warrant say you were accused of having ammunition?

A     No.

Q 53  Were you around the soup kitchen when it was blown up?

A     No.

Q 54  Is that the place Lee Fleenor was supposed to have blown up?

A     No. This was at two-thirty in the morning. We heard the explosion and my wife said, "There goes your soup kitchen." I jerked on my clothes as quick as I could, the smoke hadn't cleared away but it was certainly riddled.

*Harlan, Kentucky, November 6, 1931*

TESTIMONY *taken at the Lewallen Hotel in Harlan, Kentucky, before Theodore Dreiser, Chairman, and other members of the National Committee for the Defense of Political Prisoners:*

## MRS. VIOLA GRACE

*Questioned by Theodore Dreiser:*

Q 1    What is your name?

A    Mrs. Viola Grace.

Q 2    Are you a representative of the National Miners Union?

A    I belong to it; I am working in the capacity of anything on earth I can do to relieve these poor, starving people.

Q 3    Did you hear Sheriff Blair say that the National Miners Union men have advocated robbing stores?

A    No.

Q 4    Sheriff Blair said the National Miners Union has advocated shooting to get food before starving and resisting evictions and that one or more of its members have been arrested for robbing stores. Do you know of any such instances?

A    No, I do not and I don't believe they can bring a National Miner up who has ever committed an offense other than to have a pistol or a shot gun or a *Daily Worker*.

Q 5    The possession of a pistol and a shot gun is legal in this State, isn't it?

A    Absolutely.

Q 6    What are the members of the National Miners Union asking?

A    They are asking for a little more bread and meat for the starving people, better homes to live in and Harlan

County a fit place to live in and coal miners regarded more than as jack rabbits to be shot at.

Q 7   Does the National Miners Union advocate the overthrow of the United States Government?

A     No. The obligation they give the miners I think I have by heart.

Q 8   Let's hear it.

A     Will you solemnly swear before your Almighty God that you will protect your brother and not scab against any one or take your brother's or sister's job and scab for less wages? Will you hold up for your rights, better conditions, better schools, warm meals in the schools, etc.?

Q 9   Is Tom Epps a member of the National Miners Union?

A     Not that I know of. If he is I do not know anything about his case. But that is all they have ever done—just asked for more wages.

Q 10  Have you any idea of how many people are out of work now in Harlan County?

A     No, I do not; so many have left.

Q 11  You mean left the county?

A     Yes. They took my husband out and busted his cheek bone and his whole head was black. The men that did it were turned over to the Harlan County authorities. They took his pocket knife; I can't even get his clothes; can't even get his grip.

Q 12  What became of his case?

A     Been no case; a miner can't get anything here.

Q 13  Do you know of any miner who ever served on a jury in Harlan County?

A     Yes; I know of several.

Q 14  Has any miner ever been called in a labor case?

A     No; those cases are sent to Manchester and other parts. But there have not been any of these sheriffs arrested for killing miners and you don't see any of those gunmen in jail.

Q 15  Was your husband arrested?

A     No; he was merely beaten. I said things that were not becoming a lady, but I was hot. When they started after him, one of them said, "Shoot him, G—— D—— him!" And I said, "And G—— D—— you, show your warrant." There was one old one-eyed—I don't know what you would call him, and I told the sheriff I didn't have a gun, but if I had a tea kettle of hot water I would scald that other eye out. Any of the other deputies are absolutely welcome to come and raid my house at any time, but he can't come.

q 16   You feel that is your privilege?

a      Yes. I won't have anything but hot water because they won't let me have anything else. They broke the locks on my doors.

# X. WHAT THE LAW HAD TO SAY

IN the late afternoon the committee trooped over to the Court House to talk to Sheriff Blair. He stood up against the wall for a long time answering questions and finally took the offensive himself by serving Bruce Crawford with a $50,000 slander suit. The next morning we drove up to Harlan again to talk to the county prosecutor. Harlan town didn't look so pleasant as the day before somehow. There were a good many tough-looking young men standing around with guns under their jackets. We got the impression that people's attitude had changed overnight. There was a war feeling in the air.

The attitude of the "better" people may be inferred from a talk I had with the County Supervisor and two other members of the Kiwanis Club in the hotel lobby. They solemnly assured me that there was no strike and that there was no real misery among women and children in the county, that all the trouble had been caused by a few malcontents who were too lazy to work anyway. I suppose they believed what they were saying. When we urged them to sit in on the hearings for a while, they became uneasy and sheered off.

The Mr. Jones who kept breaking into the conversation in Mr. Brock's office, was an attorney who shared the office with him. A brother of his, an employee of the Black Mountain Coal Company, was killed in the Evarts battle, and he himself had taken part in raids on the houses of miners suspected of being connected with the N. M. U. He had a group of friends in the hall during the conversation, and for a minute it looked as if there might be trouble. He kept us from forgetting that this was a war.

TESTIMONY *taken at the office of Sheriff J. H. Blair, in the Court House in Harlan, Kentucky, Nov. 6th, 1931, before members of the National Committee for the Defense of Political Prisoners:*

## J. H. BLAIR

*Questioned by Theodore Dreiser:*

Q 1  Mr. Blair, are you willing to answer some questions and to have the questions and answers taken down in shorthand?

A  Well, I don't know whether I am or not. I don't know what this is all about.

Q 2  We would like to ask you a few questions about the general situation around here in your county.

A  Well, ask the questions and I will see what they are.

Q 3  Mr. Blair, do you feel that there is any bias in the attitude of the Sheriff's office or the District Attorney's office or the courts here in their attitude toward these miners?

A  No, sir, I don't.

Q 4  Do you think that all of their complaints such as you know of are unjustified?

A  Well, there may be some personal conditions among them sometimes. I don't know.

Q 5  Do you know anything about the mine situation here?

A  Yes, sir.

Q 6  Do you know whether these mines have been paying any wages?

A  Well, they have paid reasonable wages, I think.

Q 7  What do you call a reasonable wage from a mining company?

A  It is based on what they get for their coal. They are not paying war prices for wages.

Q 8  Do you think that workmen anywhere have a right to organize as Union men?

A  Yes, sir.

Q 9    Have you any personal quarrel with any Union?

A    No, sir.

Q 10    No Union?

A    No Labor Union.

Q 11    You have no quarrel with the United Mine Workers of America?

A    No, sir.

Q 12    Or with the National Mine Workers?

A    I don't believe the way they do.

Q 13    What do you mean by that?

A    I don't believe in destroying property.

Q 14    Are you ready to state that the National Mine Workers in this district have destroyed property?

A    I don't know that they have. They have threatened to destroy property. Their leaders have.

Q 15    Would the fact that they were accused of destroying property elsewhere prejudice you against them unless they had destroyed property here?

A    What is your question?

Q 16    Would the fact that they were accused of destroying property elsewhere prejudice you against them unless they had destroyed property here?

A    No, sir.

Q 17    You wouldn't do anything unless they did something here?

A    No, sir.

Q 18    And have they destroyed any property here?

A    I don't know that they have, sir.

Q 19    It is said that you carry a lot of Deputy Sheriffs who have destroyed soup kitchens and searched houses and searched for such papers as the *Daily Worker* and National Mine Workers literature. Is that from your order?

A    What is done from the Sheriff's office is done by my orders. I am not responsible for Constables and County Patrolmen.

Q 20    What rights do you think the average individual has? What is free speech, as you see it?

A     Well, free speech is free speech.

Q 21  Do you think if a lot of men got up out in the court house square and advised these miners to quit work because of conditions and to join the National Mine Workers—do you think that they are entitled to do that?

A     Why, certainly if they would stop at that, but when they say, "If you get hungry, take your rifle and go to the store and get it," that is a different matter.

Q 22  Is it really against the law to say that?

A     Yes, sir.

Q 23  Do you really think that is against the law?

A     Yes, sir, you are making a threat against a man's property.

Q 24  Against whom? Against the State and the county?

A     Yes, sir.

Q 25  Does the reading of the law tell you that you can arrest these people?

A     Yes, sir.

Q 26  Under the laws of this State?

A     Yes, sir, to make a threat against any man or a man's property is against the law.

Q 27  What is free assembly?

A     You can assemble anywhere you want to so you don't hurt the other man's property; on the public highway or anywhere.

Q 28  Or in a public park?

A     Yes, sir.

Q 29  They can talk any way they please, but they can't threaten?

A     Yes, sir.

Q 30  They could talk about the unsatisfactory conditions under which they work?

A     Yes, sir.

Q 31  And they could say that they must do something to remedy it if they could?

A     Yes, sir.

Q 32  Or even strike?

A    Yes, sir.

Q 33 There is no objection to people striking?

A    No, sir.

Q 34 If they went to work then and struck and had no money, do you think they would be entitled to collect food and clothing and to sustain themselves in some way until they could compel the Company to take them back or find something else to do?

A    Yes, sir.

Q 35 Do you think they would be allowed to have a soup kitchen or should be allowed to have one?

A    Yes, if they wanted one.

Q 36 And do you think they have a right to go around and collect food and clothing without molestation?

A    Yes, sir.

Q 37 Do you think a paper like the *Daily Worker* is against the law of this State?

A    I think it creates trouble in the community.

Q 38 Do you think it is illegal for this paper to come into this district?

A    Yes, I do.

Q 39 It goes through the United States mail?

A    Yes.

Q 40 Is that illegal?

A    I don't know.

Q 41 Do you know that it does go through the United States mail?

A    No, sir, I don't know. They usually come in here in trucks and cars.

Q 42 They may have some special distribution here. And if the Government does admit it into the mails, do you think the Government considers it illegal?

A    There is a lot of stuff goes through the mails that is illegal.

Q 43 This paper has something like 40,000 circulation and goes into all States. I am not a Communist or connected with the *Daily Worker*. I am here to ask you what are the rights of certain individuals in this county and State.

There have been certain charges against you and I want to ask you those things without prejudice.

A    All right.

Q 44   We have had quite a little testimony about Deputy Sheriffs who have entered houses and searched for literature and have found *Daily Workers* and have brought these people to your office and they have been held under warrants for criminal syndicalism. Do you think the possession of the *Daily Worker* means criminal syndicalism?

A    The way we search, somebody makes an affidavit and the warrant is issued.

Q 45   Is it always on the allegation of some private citizen?

A    I don't know. I don't see the affidavit. The County Judge or the Magistrate or the Police Judge issues the warrant and places it in our hands and we don't question that because they are the court and that is part of their duty.

Q 46   How many Deputy Sheriffs are there in this county?

A    I couldn't tell you.

Q 47   Aren't they such by your appointment?

A    The Deputy Sheriffs are.

Q 48   Are there any Deputy Sheriffs in this county not appointed by you?

A    No, sir.

Q 49   How many are there?

A    It is a matter of record in the court.

Q 50   Don't you know how many Deputy Sheriffs you have?

A    No, sir.

Q 51   Your office pays, for them, doesn't it?

A    No, sir.

Q 52   Who pays for them?

A    Most of the Deputy Sheriffs are on a fee system.

Q 53   How do you know how many Deputy Sheriffs you have?

A    I always use enough to try to keep order.

Q 54   How many do you need?

A    I can't say. It depends on how much trouble I have.

Q 55   How many Deputy Sheriffs have you now?

A    I don't know.

Q 56 Do you keep order?

A The best I can.

Q 57 And you have a number of men doing that?

A Yes, sir.

Q 58 Is there any way this Committee could find out how many Deputy Sheriffs you employ?

A Yes, I reckon you could. It is in the County Clerk's office.

Q 59 Would they allow me to look at the record?

A I judge they would. You would find several of these Deputy Sheriffs have been killed. If you didn't know they were dead you would think they were still living and doing duty.

Q 60 Are any of these Deputy Sheriffs paid by the coal companies?

A I judge some of them draw salaries from Coal Companies.

Q 61 Under whose jurisdiction are they when they draw a salary from the coal company?

A The official end of it is under my jurisdiction.

Q 62 The official end is under you?

A Yes, it is like a man who is working and he can make a little on the side and maybe they can look after order in the camp, and he is paid on the fee system for his work as deputy. If he does anything he gets paid for it and if he does nothing he does not get paid.

Q 63 The coal company doesn't pay them so much a week?

A Not as Deputy Sheriffs.

Q 64 I would like to know what the fees are?

A The Statute fixes the fees. There is $2.00 for an arrest and 25 cents for summoning a witness, and in some cases 20 cents and some 60 cents, and on a notice we get 25 cents.

Q 65 For instance, if they wounded a man, is that a special fee?

A Wounded a man? No, sir.

Q 66 Does that come under the head of making an arrest?

A No, sir, not unless they arrest him.

Q 67 If the man resisted and he wounded him, he would get a fee for the arrest?

A  No, sir, he wouldn't get anything in the fee line unless the man was brought into court and found guilty.

Q 68 If he is wounded that hasn't anything to do with it?

A  No, sir.

Q 69 Do you know how many of these men are working for the companies?

A  No, sir, a lot of them work for the companies. If you do any work at all here you do it for some company.

Q 70 I mean these Deputy Sheriffs working for the companies under your jurisdiction—how many of them are there?

A  I don't know.

Q 71 Some of them you say are paid by the county and I can find them in the Clerk's office?

A  They are paid by the fee system, as I told you. I pay my salaried men who work here in the office.

Q 72 And the others are not paid by the companies, are they, but by you?

A  You don't understand. If I am working for the coal company or a lumber company and I have a chance to be appointed a Deputy Sheriff and work for some fees on the outside of my other work, or if the coal company is interested in having some one preserve order in the camp and take care of things and I can get the job, I will be glad to have it and get the fees for making arrests, etc., but I get my salary from the coal company and not a salary as Deputy Sheriff. What I would do as Deputy Sheriff in that case would be on the outside and paid on the fee system.

Q 73 Are you yourself paid fees?

A  That's all I get. I am on a fee basis. About the Deputy Sheriffs, say that I am working at Black Mountain and a man comes into the camp selling liquor and I arrest him and bring him to town here and he is tried and found guilty. Then I get $5.00 for that fee.

Q 74 Can you tell me whether any of the deputy sheriffs that these coal companies pay or that you pay fees are from any detective agency or any strike-breakers' agency from outside cities or outside of the State of Kentucky?

A     I beg your pardon—I don't get the question.

Q 75 These Deputy Sheriffs working for the coal companies and collecting fees from you, or that you say work for you on the fee system, did you get them from strike-breakers' agencies?

A     No, sir, they are citizens of Harlan County.

Q 76 Are they all citizens of Harlan County?

A     Yes, sir.

Q 77 It has been charged over and over that they are not.

A     So I understand.

Q 78 And you say that that is not true?

A     No, sir, it is not. They are living here and they are citizens and were before this all ever came up.

Q 79 Do you know the histories and characters of the men you deputize?

A     Yes. I know they are men of good reputation here or I wouldn't put them in and I do put them in and if a man does something that I think is not the right thing to do as a Deputy Sheriff I put him out.

Q 80 Is there any man working for you as Deputy Sheriff who has a prison record?

A     Not that I know of.

Q 81 Does Bill Randolph work for you, or did he?

A     Not this present term of office. He worked for me when I took office in 1922, but in this term of office he has not.

Q 82 He did work for you at a previous term?

A     Yes, sir.

Q 83 Did you succeed yourself as Sheriff?

A     No, sir. You can't succeed yourself here as Sheriff. You have to lay out four years.

Q 84 But you were Sheriff once before?

A     Yes.

Q 85 And he did work for you?

A     Yes. I put him in a while and then I discharged him. He arrested a man and hit him over the head with a pistol and I didn't think that was necessary at all and I discharged him.

Q 86 Was he accused of killing a man named Chasteen?

A    Yes, he was tried by a jury and turned loose.

Q 87 And the verdict was not guilty?

A    Yes, sir.

Q 88 It is charged that you engaged Bill Randolph as Deputy Sheriff at a time when he was bonded out on a prison charge in another county. Is that true?

A    How was the question?

Q 89 It is charged that Bill Randolph was a Deputy Sheriff for you and that at the time you took him he was bonded out on a criminal charge in another county?

A    I answered that in a previous question when I said that I discharged Bill Randolph in the term of office which I began to serve in 1922. He was a young man then and had not had any trouble. Since I discharged him I think he has killed three or four men, but he has never been a Deputy Sheriff under me again.

Q 90 Does the law of this State require that a Deputy Sheriff has to be a citizen of the State for at least one year?

A    He has to be a citizen of Harlan County.

Q 91 How long do you have to be here to be a citizen?

A    You have to be in the State one year and in the county six months and in a precinct 60 days, before you can vote.

Q 92 Do you always determine the citizenship and residence of your Deputy Sheriffs before appointing them?

A    I usually know about a fellow or have some recommendation from some one I trust.

Q 93 Have you a Deputy Sheriff named Haywood?

A    Yes, sir.

Q 94 Can you tell me anything about him?

A    Yes, sir.

Q 95 Has he ever committed a crime of any kind?

A    Not since he has been in this State.

Q 96 Do you know his history before he came into this State?

A    No, sir.

Q 97 You don't know anything about him?

A    Yes, since he came here.

Q 98 It has been charged that he has been operating as a deputy and is connected with an agency that has sold his services from time to time in different strike troubles. Do you know that?

A    No, sir.

Q 99 You never heard anything like that?

A    No, sir.

Q 100 No agency, so far as you know, sent him to you?

A    No, sir, he came in here and brought his family, his wife and two kids, and has been here a good long while.

Q 101 More than a year?

A    He had been here about a year or more when I put him in.

Q 102 You know about that soup kitchen being blown up with dynamite at Evarts?

A    Yes, sir.

Q 103 Do you know who did that?

A    No, sir, I tried to find out.

Q 104 Take this case of this soup kitchen where Lee Fleenor did the shooting and killed a man and wounded another one.

A    There were two men killed.

Q 105 Why did Lee Fleenor kill that man?

A    He claimed he shot in self-defense.

Q 106 And the fellow that was wounded in the shoulder he shot in self-defense also?

A    Yes, he said they came out with their guns on them and they shot and he shot back.

Q 107 There were as many as three soup kitchens in your county?

A    I think there were more than that. There was one at Evarts and one at Wallins and one at Panzy, one at Elcomb and one at what they call Clovertown, where the killing was.

Q 108 Are any of those soup kitchens still in existence?

A    I don't know.

Q 109  I understand that none of them are in existence, that they have all been annoyed by Deputy Sheriffs and have all given up. Is that true?

A    My understanding was that they couldn't finance them.

Q 110  They were never annoyed, so far as you know, by Deputy Sheriffs?

A    No, sir.

Q 111  You didn't send any Deputy Sheriffs there to search the place for literature?

A    I don't remember whether we ever searched there or not. The search warrants and affidavits in the court will show.

Q 112  I understand that after Lee Fleenor killed this man he came here and gave himself up and was discharged?

A    He gave up to me and I kept him until next morning and took him to the court and the court fixed his bond to answer indictment. We were in the last day or two of our Grand Jury and I taken the Coroner's list of witnesses and I got a subpoena to bring the people in before the Grand Jury and they were away on a burial. They had taken them to Tennessee to bury these fellows and the Grand Jury adjourned before they came back and the fellow is still under bond to answer indictment and we haven't had a Grand Jury since.

Q 113  When do you have a Grand Jury next?

A    In November.

Q 114  Is it your intention to prosecute this case?

A    It is not my duty to prosecute the case. We are going to present to the Grand Jury all the evidence we can find.

*Mr. Ornitz:*

Q 1  He is still a Deputy Sheriff under you?

A    Yes, sir.

Q 2  You have not discharged him?

A    No, sir.

Q 3    He is still a Deputy Sheriff while you are investigating him as a murderer?

A    Yes. A man is not guilty here until he has been proven guilty.

Q 4    And he is still employed although the Coroner's jury found him guilty?

A    I think they found that he shot in self-defense.

Q 5    A member of that jury testified before us today.

A    You can go to the court and get the report of it. I have never seen it.

*Theodore Dreiser:*

Q 115    Do you hold that workers have the right to have picket lines?

A    Yes, sir.

Q 116    Do you protect them in that?

A    They don't picket in this country at all.

Q 117    Have company guards the right to practice their profession outside company territory?

A    If he is not an officer he hasn't, but if he is a Deputy Sheriff he has jurisdiction in the county.

Q 118    He can go anywhere in the county?

A    Yes, for he is a full-fledged Deputy Sheriff.

Q 119    There have been instances of newspaper reporters who have come in here and have been shot. Why were they shot?

A    I don't know, sir.

Q 120    It is charged that they were shot by these Deputy Sheriffs?

A    Yes, I know, it was charged in the papers.

Q 121    Why should they fire at outside newspaper men for coming here?

A    I can't say, sir. I deny the charge of any Deputy Sheriff shooting any newspaper man.

Q 122    This girl that was taken here, Jessie Wakefield. She came in here for some newspaper or magazine. Why was she arrested?

*Mr. Ornitz:*

Q 1 She was charged with threatening to blow you and Judge Jones off the face of the earth and leave no trace of either one of you, and she was released merely on her promise to leave the State. Is that true?

A I don't know. That is not in my jurisdiction. She was arrested and indicted by the Grand Jury, I think, and charged with criminal syndicalism.

Q 2 If she was charged with criminal syndicalism, is it possible that she could just be dismissed and walk out? That is rather a serious charge, is it not?

A Yes, sir.

Q 3 Why should they say to her that if she would get out of here that would be the end of it? What became of it?

A I didn't have anything to do with her release, but I can give you my understanding. I understood that she made the proposition to the court herself that she would leave and never come back if they would release her.

Q 4 Did she make that proposition to you?

A No, sir, that is just information.

*Theodore Dreiser:*

Q 123 There is instance after instance. I have listened to nothing but testimony of how these Deputy Sheriffs have acted, and for instance, that a man would be a miner and would be active in promoting the welfare of the National Mine Workers—you have no objection to that, have you?

A No, sir.

Q 124 You have no objection?

A No, sir, not if they were orderly about it, but the members of the organization would threaten and we had wholesale store robberies up here. They would go and take a whole commissary and they advocated it in the meetings. There is no objection to any labor organization here that is orderly, but when they carry out at

night what they advocated in daylight by threats and
go and rob stores and things like that, I do object.

*Mr. Ornitz:*

Q 1   Have you any proof that the Mine Workers Federation
      did that?
A     Several of them have been indicted and others were
      bonded in the court.

*Theodore Dreiser:*

Q 125 Have you convicted any of them?
A     There hasn't been any of them tried.
Q 126 Have you any of their literature in your possession?
A     Yes, sir.
Q 127 Will you let me see it?
A     No, sir.
Q 128 Why not? Is there any objection to my seeing or the
      press of the country knowing what this was?
A     What I have got is for my private files. I will show
      it to you though if you want to see it.
Q 129 I would like to see it. If it is as bad as you say and you
      could arrest these people for it, then I would like to see it
      and know what the nature of it is.
A     I told you that the arrests made were on warrants from
      the court. You might be as innocent as anybody but if
      the court came in here with a warrant for your arrest I
      would not be the one to pass on it. I would make the
      arrest.
Q 130 When these men went out and stopped a man going
      around collecting food for those soup kitchens, it was
      charged that he was held a few days and let go, and it
      was charged that a man would have a *Daily Worker* or
      something like that in his house and a car-load of Deputy
      Sheriffs would come up and search the house and find
      these things and arrest him and in a few days or a month
      he would be let go and that would be the end of it, but

he was annoyed in this way and made miserable. How would these things occur?

A    I told you that the courts would usually issue a warrant. We have a warrant or a man commits a violation in our presence before we make an arrest.

Q 131 You don't let him go?

A    No, sir, I take him to the court.

Q 132 It has been sworn to that they would be arrested in that way and they would not be taken to any judge and would be let go and occasionally would be taken before a judge.

A    In a few instances a Deputy Sheriff will arrest some fellow and bring him in and unless I think he has a case that will stand in court I don't let him go into court with it and take the time of the court. I make sometimes a complete investigation and turn him loose.

Q 133 If these miners were really under-fed and could not exist on these wages, would you like to see them win this strike?

A    We haven't got any strike that I know anything about.

Q 134 Would you like to see them organized nicely and comfortably under the National Mine Workers?

A    I wouldn't want to see the National Mine Workers organizing in this county for the reason that they are disorderly and have advocated stealing property.

Q 135 Have you evidence that they have advocated stealing and destroying property?

A    I have heard it myself.

Q 136 Have you handbills and circulars or anything of that kind?

A    I can get you plenty.

Q 137 How can I get it?

A    I can get you some affidavits. I heard one man myself out here in front of the court house and he said, "Don't starve. Take your guns and get the stuff if you get hungry." Another man had an eviction case in court and he made a speech on the steps of the court house and made the remark that if they got a judgment against him the man that came to put him out would die. They got a judgment against him and that evening he was put out and he and I are both still living.

Q 138 Since this trouble, have any of these coal companies served notice on you that you would have to protect them?

A    They don't serve notice on me that I have to protect them.

Q 139 They do that in Pittsburgh.

A    I don't take orders from anybody except the Statute of Kentucky and I try to follow it.

Q 140 You don't have notice from any coal operator that you would have to look after him or he would hold you personally responsible?

A    I think I have a telegram here from you and that is the strongest order I have ever had except from the Statutes.

Q 141 Do you know why Bruce Crawford was shot?

A    No, sir, I didn't know he was in town. The papers circulated that I saw you, Mr. Crawford, and that you saw me, but I did not know you were in town.

Q 142 Did you go to his office?

A    Yes, sir, to see about an article in his paper.

Q 143 Did you object to that?

A    Yes, sir.

Q 144 Was it false?

A    It was false.

Q 145 What did he say about it?

A    He said it was written by a fellow living here in town.

Q 146 Did you tell him that it would be dangerous for him if he came over here?

A    No, sir.

Q 147 Or to be seen in this county? You didn't tell him that?

A    No, sir, I went to see him about the article and we were talking about it and he said a young fellow here in town wrote the article and his name is Tess Huff and he just signed the article "Tess," and it being false, I didn't like it.

Q 148 Is it absolutely true that Bruce Crawford can come back and forth at any time?

A    Any time that he is coming and will let me know I will meet him at the State Line.

Q 149 He runs no risk whatsoever in coming in here?

A    No, sir, I think not. I came in here about 6.30 that morning and had a lot of work pressing me and it was around 10.30 when I heard about him being shot. A fellow that worked here at the desk went to the post office to get the mail and Mr. Mullins asked Mr. Ward, the man that went to the post office for me, how bad that fellow was shot and he came back and told me, and I tried to find Mr. Crawford and I could not get in connection with him.

Q 150 Is this the first time you have met Mr. Crawford since you saw him in his office?

A    Yes, it is the first time I have seen him, isn't it, Mr. Crawford?

*Mr. Crawford:* It is the first time we have met.

*Mr. Ornitz:*

Q 1  Four or five people have testified before us that on at least six occasions which we can submit to you, that your Deputy Sheriffs entered their homes and ransacked their personal property and that these Deputy Sheriffs were drunk and were cursing in the presence of women and children, and that they made arrests based on these illegal seizures, and that they were then discharged by the courts. Have you any information about this?

A    No, sir.

*Theodore Dreiser:*

Q 151 You have never heard of this before?

A    You can hear anything.

Q 152 Is it not a fact that men arrested by your men were later discharged?

A     A lot of people beat their cases in court.

Q 153 Do you know of any cases where men were discharged because your Deputy Sheriffs made illegal arrests and on evidence obtained without search warrants?

A     I know of some cases where somebody made an affidavit for search warrants and they wrote the search warrants on a liquor warrant to search for liquor; and for stolen property or anything else is on a different form and not on a liquor search warrant, and they dismissed them out of court because they were on the wrong form.

Q 154 Do you know of any other cases except in this liquor instance of discharges by the court where your men made illegal arrests?

A     No, sir.

Q 155 If we presented this evidence to you and you found it to be true of the annoyances we have told you about and the practices of your deputies would you discipline these men?

A     Yes, sir.

Q 156 If we will bring to you three women who will tell that Lee Fleenor has made a practice of waiting for women on the highways, one man blowing the horn and Lee Fleenor and another man meeting the woman and hemming her in, and crowding other people off the road, would you investigate Lee Fleenor?

A     Yes, sir.

*Mr. Ornitz:*

Q 1   Would you believe me if I told you that these facts had been published in Nashville newspapers and other magazines or papers?

A     I do not know that they are facts. How do you know them to be facts?

Q 2   I didn't say they were facts. I said would you investigate these charges?

A     I would like to have that question read and see if you did not say facts. Am I right or is he? (To the stenographer.)

*Stenographer:* You are right, Mr. Blair.

Q 3    Would you make an investigation of these things?

A    I told you that I would make an investigation on Lee Fleenor or anybody else. Any time there is a charge coming in I will investigate it.

*Theodore Dreiser:*

Q 157    You say that always when a Deputy Sheriff goes into a house to search for literature it is because somebody has filed a complaint?

A    Yes, on some information.

Q 158    Have you records of all the people that have filed complaints in all these cases?

A    I told you in the beginning that I didn't have any of those records. Somebody comes before the court that issues the warrants.

Q 159    If it was assumed that somebody was stealing or was distributing inflammatory literature and I wanted to do something about that, what is really the proper legal course for me in this State? Do I have to go to a court or what do I do if I believe that somebody is bringing in or distributing inflammatory literature?

A    You would go before some court that issues warrants and make an affidavit and describe the property.

Q 160    I can't do it on belief? I would have to do it on personal information?

A    Yes, you would have to have information.

Q 161    I would have to know the stuff was in there?

A    No, sir, the laws of this State don't require that. They require information to the best of your knowledge. I might tell you that a fellow over here had it and you could go and swear out a warrant.

Q 162    And the court would give me a warrant to have that house searched?

A     Yes, if he thought it was all right.

Q 163  There is no other method except that for having a house searched?

A     No, sir.

*Mr. Ornitz:*

Q 1   Is Tom Epps in the Harlan jail?

A     No, sir, he was discharged a long while ago.

Q 2   The allegation is made that he was held for two months without a hearing or indictment—do you know about that?

A     Yes, sir.

Q 3   Is there any truth in that allegation?

A     I think that was in the store robbery of the East Harlan Coal Co. About 250 men went into the store and robbed it. This fellow was indicted and there were five or six men indicted with him.

Q 4   How long ago was that?

A     Back in May of this year, I expect. It was at the August term, I believe; and in drawing that indictment where there is more than one they style the case on the back of the indictment and show "Tom Jones, &c." for instance and then they put all the names in the indictment. In this case they put Jim Reynolds, &c., on the back of the indictment and Tom Epps was included in the indictment and they issued a bench warrant from this indictment and we had it and I think we made two arrests and Tom Epps was one of these and he couldn't make bond and we put him in jail.

Q 5   Did somebody come in and accuse him as one of the men that robbed the store?

A     That was before the Grand Jury and Mr. Middleton from Evarts, came down here and wanted to make a bond for this fellow and get him out and the Clerk ran through his indictments and couldn't find any against Tom Epps, and he went to the Commonwealth's Attorney and Brock came up to see why he was in jail and

I said we had a warrant with the other names and I got the warrant and showed him where Tom Epps was arrested and put in jail and couldn't make bond, and he went on to the Clerk's office and made bond and Tom Epps got out.

Q 6 Then you would say that he was forgotten in jail because of a technical error?

A No, he never offered to make any bond. They have a chance to make bond within an hour after they are indicted and he never offered to make any bond.

*Theodore Dreiser:*

Q 164 Why did the District Attorney ask you why the man was in jail?

A The Prosecuting Attorney don't have the records.

Q 165 It seems to me that he was lost in a series of names on one indictment.

A No, I didn't say that.

*Mr. Ornitz:*

Q 1 Was a separate entry made of his incarceration?

A He was indicted jointly with five or six others and Tom Epps and others were on it and we found Tom Epps and most of the others left the State, and this indictment was styled on the back Jim Reynolds, &c, and in the body of the paper appeared the name of Tom Epps. But his name does not appear on the back of the folded paper.

*Theodore Dreiser:*

Q 166 It looks as if he must have been forgotten.

A No, he was not forgotten. He got out when the fellow came to make his bond. Here is the warrant. The indictment of the Grand Jury here is against Haskall Stewart, &c., and I don't know without opening it who is on the inside. Then I open it and see the names of Paschal Sweeney, Jaff Tackett, and Chester Colson on the inside of that paper. This fellow was absolutely not forgotten. He got out of jail within one hour from the time the man came and made the inquiry about him to make his bond but the papers had full account next day that he had been forgotten.

Q 167 Why didn't he have a preliminary hearing?

A    We don't have a preliminary hearing on indictments.

Q 168 Why wasn't he brought into court? Don't they do that in this State?

A    Yes, sir.

Q 169 Don't people plead to the court?

A    I can't say whether he plead or not. If his bond is endorsed on the warrant we take his bond and if it is not, we deliver him to the jailer. Court was not in session.

*Mr. Ornitz:*

Q 1   Do your Deputy Sheriffs make a report to you of the amounts they collect in fees?

A    No, sir.

Q 2   That is their own business?

A    Yes. If I have got a fellow out here in a rough place in the country he gets all the fees and I keep check on him to know that he is not grafting and turning them loose.

*Theodore Dreiser:*

Q 170 There are going to be two meetings of the National Mine Workers, one at Evarts and one at Straight to-morrow afternoon and on Sunday I had a communication from some one that if the one at Wallins Creek was held there would be trouble. Suppose that it is held and I am there with this Committee and others and there is trouble, what would you have to say about that? Can you prevent that?

A    I think I can guarantee that there won't be any trouble at either place. In fact, I don't think we will have any more trouble.

Q 171  Why not?

A      Because the people are working and things are going along pretty well, with the exception of a very few.

*Mr. Ornitz:*

Q      Do you know of any instance of machine guns being mounted on Company cars with your Deputy Sheriffs behind them?

A      We have got some automatic guns we take out sometimes.

Q 2    I mean on Company cars.

A      If the companies have any cars except individuals, I don't know anything about it.

Q 3    Would you deputize a Union man on picket duty and make them Deputy Sheriffs so that they could protect Union interests?

A      If there is anybody in this county that is trying to picket, I don't know it.

Q 4    Suppose the Union men would say, "We can't go out and meet machine guns and Colts and other weapons with our bare hands but we want to be Deputy Sheriffs with guns." Would you deputize Union men?

A      I wouldn't deputize anybody just so they could be Deputy Sheriffs with guns. What kind of Union men do you mean?

Q 5    That is not my question. Suppose they were United Mine Workers. Would you deputize Union men?

A      I would deputize Union men but from all the evidence I have got of the National Miners Union I wouldn't deputize them.

Q 6    You told me not to convict Lee Fleenor before he was found guilty. Aren't you convicting the National Miners Union before they come to trial?

A      I didn't say that to you.

Q 7    Well, something like that. When I asked you why you continued to employ Lee Fleenor you told me that in your State or in this county a man is innocent until he is proved guilty. Doesn't that rule apply to the National Miners Union?

A    No, sir.

Q 8    Why not? I will bring three men here who will say that Lee Fleenor shot first and that they saw the blaze of his gun in the dark; that they didn't see the gun but they saw the fire.

A    I told you he has not been tried yet.

Q 9    Why wouldn't you deputize men of the National Miners Union?

A    From their conduct and what they say in their open speeches and the store robberies that have taken place I wouldn't do it.

Q 10    Could you be restrained by court order from interfering with these people?

A    I don't interfere unless we find them guilty of violations of the law.

Q 11    You would refuse to protect them on the ground that they were violators. If that is proven, wouldn't your position be a little queer?

A    You misunderstand. I would like to ask you a question.

Q 12    All right.

A    Say I own my home out here. Suppose I don't want you out there. The law of this State protects my home and property and if you were to enter on it, do you think any officer would come out there and make you a Deputy Sheriff to look after my property?

*Theodore Dreiser:*

Q 172    Suppose it is a public highway. In Pittsburgh they were picketing this highway and these Deputy Sheriffs of companies actually provoked quarrels with them and shot them and called them names in the bargain and they were there not to hurt scabs but to ask them not to take their places. Do you think these pickets would be entitled to protection from Sheriffs as much as the companies would be entitled to protection for their property?

A    I think they would if they were entitled to be protected on the road.

Q 173 How would you protect them? By armed Deputy Sheriffs?

A    Yes, I would give one man entitled to protection the same protection I would give any other man who was entitled to it. Just like I would give you.

*Mr. Ornitz:*

Q 1    We have many people who have come here and made sworn statements of this fact: That Deputy Sheriffs and company guards kill and are discharged on the ground of self-defense, but in all the cases of miners who are arrested on charges of murder there has not been a single instance of self-defense in their cases. Is that clear?

A    No.

Q 2    That Company guards have been charged with killing people and their defense is always self-defense. Take the case of Lee Fleenor—he hasn't been indicted, has he?

A    No, the witnesses haven't been before the Grand Jury.

*Theodore Dreiser:*

Q 174 How many Deputy Sheriffs have been killed in this labor war?

A    You mean over the labor troubles?

Q 175 Yes.

A    I think I have lost five or six.

Q 176 How many miners have been arrested or indicted for the murder of these men?

A    Quite a number. It is a court record.

Q 177 Would you say more than forty?

A    I don't think so.

Q 178 How many miners have been killed in this war?

A    I think three.

Q 179 How many people have been arrested for their deaths?

A    Two.

Q 180 Have there been any indictments?

A    Yes, two indictments.

Q 181 Have they been disposed of?

A    No. One miner I think was killed in the Evarts fight up there.

Q 182 Who is charged with this murder?

A    Nobody. I think it is possible that their own side could have killed him the way they were shooting and it is possible that our fellows did it. I don't know. There is nobody indicted in this case.

Q 183 Do you consider that the miners have the right of self-defense?

A    Yes, sir.

Q 184 Do you consider the International Labor Defense an illegal organization as you do the National Miners Union?

A    I don't know anything about it.

Q 185 Do you believe that you have the right to rule the National Miners Union an illegal organization before there has been an adjudication by the court?

A    What do you mean by that?

Q 186 You said you wouldn't permit them to organize because they made threats and other things that you considered illegal.

A    I don't think I said that.

Q 187 It amounted to that to me. That's what it means to me, what you said.

A    I said I wouldn't appoint them Deputy Sheriffs.

Q 188 And in your previous answers you said something to the effect that you wouldn't consider them being in the county because you considered them dangerous. That's what you said in effect. That's how it seemed to me.

A    I didn't say I wouldn't permit them to stay in the county.

Q 189 You would allow the National Miners Union to come here?

A    Certainly. They are here.

Q 190 You say they are here?

A    Yes, and they have not been intimidated in any way.

Q 191 You have summoned Mr. Bruce Crawford to be here in ten days. Will you explain what this is?

A    This is a summons issued from the Circuit Court Clerk's office up here on a suit I filed there this afternoon on a slander charge against Mr. Crawford and *Crawford's Weekly* on a slander charge which he printed against me in his paper, and a copy of the article is filed with the suit.

Q 192 If he comes here and answers this thing, will he be fully protected?

A    Yes, I will meet him at the State Line at any time and bring him in and take him out. I want to get my damage off of him.

*Mr. Ornitz:*

Q 1  How much damage are you asking?

A    $50,000.00 He can answer at any time between now and the November term of court, beginning the 4th Monday in November.

*Harlan, Kentucky, November 7, 1931*

TESTIMONY *taken at the office of William E. Brock, Prosecuting Attorney, in Harlan County, Kentucky, before the National Committee for the Defense of Political Prisoners, Theodore Dreiser, Chairman, and others.*

## PROSECUTING ATTORNEY BROCK

*Dreiser questioning :*

Q 1  In regard to this particular situation here, I would like to know what people have a legal right to organize as a union?

A    To what do you have reference?

Q 2  In defensive labor unions.

A   Before I can answer that, I would have to know the particular union referred to.

Q 3   The United Mine Workers of America.

A   They have a legal right.

Q 4   The National Miners Union?

A   I am a little in doubt about it. I think they are an illegal
organization.

Q 5   Is this a private opinion?

A   That is an opinion I have arrived at by reading their present reports.

Q 6   If they are not interfered with elsewhere, do you think
you should do so?

A   I do not interfere with them if they don't break any law
but I think some of them have been guilty of Criminal
Syndicalism.

Q 7   Have they a right to organize in this locality and function as an organization so long as they don't break any
law?

A   Yes, I think under such circumstances they have a right
to be here.

*Ornitz questioning:*

Q 8   You said that they had been guilty of violating a law.
Is that an adjudication or an opinion?

A   I said I considered that amounting to a violation of the
law of Kentucky. That is my opinion.

Q 9   Have you had any convictions of this organization?

A   We have not convicted any of Criminal Syndicalism yet.
Gibbs, Johnson and a few others were very guilty but
we . . .

Q 10  Is Arnold Johnson a member of the United Miners
Union?

A   I don't know.

Q 11  Is he a member of the Civil Liberties Union?

A   I don't know.

Q 12  Does anybody here know whether Arnold Johnson is a
member of these organizations?

Gannes answered: He is not a member of National Miners
Union but he is a member of the Civil Liberties Union.
He is not a member of the Communist Party. Civil Lib-
erties Union in no way is affiliated to the Communist
Party or the National Miners Union.

Mr. Brock: The organization he belongs to is communistic.

Jones: Under the laws of the State of Kentucky, the literature
circulated by Johnson and the actions carried on by him
can be construed as communistic under the Criminal Syndicalist act.

Q 13 Gannes: Is circulating communist literature a crime?

Brock: Yes, it is.

Q 14 Is it your conviction that Arnold Johnson, whom you
have already characterized as a communist, is guilty? Has
there been any legal judgment to that effect?

A    We had him arrested on a warrant and he stated in jail,
he admitted to me that he was communistic. Some good
people from up at Berea College came up to see me to
intercede in his behalf and him being a young man, Judge
Jones and I agreed that if he quit his activities, we would
let him go. Then these people went over and spoke to
Johnson and they came back and told me that he was
stubborn and they could not do anything with him and
so they went back.

Q 15 What is the punishment for Criminal Syndicalism?

A    Not less than two nor more than 20 years.

Q 16 How do you construe free speech under the constitution
of this State?

A    So long as a man speaks within the laws of the land, then
it is free speech, but when it becomes a violation of the
laws of the land, it is a speech to be prohibited. If a man
goes out here and makes a speech and advises the overthrow of this government, then his speech is not a free
speech. It is a speech prohibited by law.

Q 17 You admit the right of individuals to speak except where
they advocate an overthrow of this government.

A    They have got that free right.

Q 18  Is advocating an overthrow of the government the same as to advocate a change in the government?

A     The change of the government peaceably is not criminal if there is not force. When there is force it then becomes a crime.

Q 19  What do you mean by force?

A     Force means a man picks up his gun and says to the fellow on the other side, "You come on our side or you die." Some of the miners did that. This fellow Gibbs. We found him with this communist literature in his possession, his membership card in that party, five high powered rifles and pretty near half a bushel of cartridges. He got on the witness stand and said he thought more of the Russian government because it was a better government and if he could go there he would go there.

Q 20  Do you think it advisable to change this government in any way?

A     I think this government is exactly right.

Q 21  There is nothing to change in this government, to bring it in line with human equity?

A     No, sir. If the people want any change there is a proper legal way of doing it.

Q 22  Then anybody could advocate a change in government and go out and speak for it?

A     (Jones) No, not in the way that some of them did here.

Q 23  You admit the right of individuals to speak until they advocate a change in government?

A     Yes, sir, by force and violence.

Q 24  You consider advocating a change in government so as to make it more equitable as advocating an overthrow in the government?

A     To teach any change in the government peaceably by free speech is permissible; when they advocate force and violence as they did here, then it becomes a violation. Some of them say to use guns and come out and demand they fight.

Q 25  Have the miners done this?

A    Yes, I told you about Gibbs.

Q 26 Would you say that the miners have the right to strike?

A    The miners have a right to strike as long as it is peace-able and without force. Absolutely, we are strict in main-taining their right to strike.

Q 27 If they go out on strike, would you say they had a right to organize unions or join one to protect themselves? To collect money to feed themselves, is that legal?

A    So long as the miners' acts are peaceable and within the law, they are within their rights to organize.

Q 28 If they were hungry, would you admit that it was proper for them to collect clothing and food from whomever they could, so they could live?

A    It is absolutely right and Christianlike to get food for the strikers.

Q 29 If they organize a soup kitchen, is that within their rights?

A    Yes, sir.

Q 30 Is it legal to conduct soup kitchens?

A    Yes, sir.

Q 31 There were five soup kitchens here that were blown up. In one of them, a man was murdered and another shot in the shoulder. The sheriff said that some of them, the Deputy Sheriffs, who were involved in the shooting were paid by the coal companies. He said he does not know but he feels sure that those Deputies were not involved with the blowing up of the soup kitchen.

A    I am sure that none of those Deputies interfered with the soup kitchens. I have investigated this and I have not found any of them to interfere with their legal rights.

Q 32 Was Mr. Lee Fleenor a Deputy Sheriff?

A    Yes, sir.

Q 33 He went down to Sheriff Blair and admitted he killed this man Baldwin in the swimming pool soup kitchen.

A    Yes, sir, he did. He said in self-defense.

Q 34 Has he been prosecuted?

A    He surrendered to the Sheriff and the Grand Jury in-vestigated the case. With the exception of one witness we could not get, the Grand Jury heard the testimony of all the witnesses and dismissed the case. I entered on my own motion in order to refer the case to the next Grand Jury for further investigation simply because some of the people were interested in the prosecution and said that this man who left would be a stronger witness for the Commonwealth than the fellows who testified.

Q 35 I understood that the fellow who left knew more about the facts than the fellows who testified. Why didn't you withhold it until this man could get back?

A That is why I recommended it be withheld for the next Grand Jury.

Q 36 Was any effort made to find the other man in the car with Fleenor?

A I don't know of any other man.

Q 37 Did you prepare any of the briefs for the Grand Jury?

A I have got a copy of this testimony. When Lee Fleenor gave himself up, he made a statement how it happened. I discussed it privately with every man that was there and saw it. I heard each one of them go on the stand. I have got their written statement. I did not call the brother of the man who was killed.

Q 38 Did you get a hold of any of the other three in the car?

A There was no testimony about the other three being in the car.

Q 39 How could we get a copy of the testimony before the Grand Jury?

A I have a copy of this testimony.

Q 40 Would you mind giving us a copy of this testimony?

A I wouldn't care a bit giving you a copy of the Grand Jury testimony. I can give you a copy.

*Dreiser questioning:*

Q 41 How do you construe free assembly?

A I construe the right of free assembly to mean that any number of persons may assemble together so long as the object of that assembly is peaceable and lawful.

Q 42  Would it be lawful to discuss a political or social ill?

A    If it was merely some fellow expressing his opinion, it would not be illegal. But if he went to teaching and undertaking to show we would do so and so by force, that would turn out to be against the law, that would turn out to be unlawful assemblage.

Q 43  Supposing some one said the rich were too rich and the poor were too poor; and that there should be some change in this government to make it more equitable; that it should be made impossible for individuals or corporations to collect enormous wealth, would you think that was an illegal speech?

A    I don't think that is illegal.

Q 44  It would be all right to do that?

A    I want to go a little further and quote an instance that occurred in this town. At the court house door the miners had a mass meeting. One of their speakers got up and said, "Boys, you see this row of banks,"—he pointed over to the First City Bank, to the Harlan Bank and to the Citizens National Bank—He says, "They have got thousands and thousands of dollars in that bank. They have got that in the wrong name. It is your money. You dug it out." I consider that a statement unauthorized. That was not true. It was not their money.

Q 45  Did you interfere with that man?

A    I did not interfere with that man. Nobody did.

*Mr. Ornitz questioning:*

Q 46  Why did you not prosecute this man? There were reports of individuals having literature in their possession who were illegally raided. Here you have a case of a man who you claim was making an illegal speech, why wasn't he arrested?

A    The reason that man was let go is there were three or four thousand men armed in the crowd there and anybody trying to make an arrest would be committing suicide.

Q 47 Is he still living in the community? Is he a resident here?

A He lives about here.

Q 48 That man would have been arrested if he were not surrounded by these other men?

A He was arrested later for distributing communist literature.

Q 49 What happened to him?

A He was arrested with many others. We discharged every one of them.

Q 50 Why?

A They agreed to live a quiet life and agreed to go home and not to take part in the organization of the Communist Party.

Q 51 Is that the duty of your official office, to change the opinions of these miners?

A An officer has discretion, and he can use that discretion on account of a man's family suffering for him. If he wants to discharge him to be a man, to test him and give him a chance to prove himself, he can do that.

Q 52 Do you do that in the case of larceny?

A We do not do much of that in larceny cases. It has all been done in behalf of the miners.

Q 53 It is not being done to keep these miners from forming the National Miners Union?

A No.

Q 54 On the condition that they will quit the union activities, and leave the county, and in that way to get rid of them?

A No, sir. We don't ask men to do that. We only did it in one case where the man was organizing this Communist Party here. That is the only thing we have asked them to cease activities in.

Q 55 Yesterday there was testimony given, by the miners and their wives to this effect: they said they were arrested for having the *Daily Worker* in their possession, or for having an N. M. U. card in their possession. They were kept in jail varying from 5 to 30 days, and then told, "If you

agree to quit the union, we will give you your liberty."
Do you know of any such instances yourself?

A    No, sir.

Q 56 These men, then, were not telling the truth?

A    I don't know.

Q 57 Didn't you bring an indictment against Jessie Wakefield?

A    Yes, sir.

Q 58 Did you charge her with desiring to blow you and Judge
Jones off the face of the earth?

A    The Grand Jury heard the testimony. I did not hear the
testimony before the Grand Jury. The case was investigated at a time I was not present.

Q 59 Do you have any recollection of the minutes of that indictment?

A    I don't know. I could get it. The county attorney takes
the minutes before the Grand Jury. The Grand Jury
handed me the minutes indicting her for criminal syndicalism.

Q 60 Do you know if any offer was made to Mrs. Wakefield to
free herself from these serious charges on condition that
she would leave the county and Kentucky?

A    She sent word downstairs—she was up in the jail, she
wanted to talk to Judge Jones. And Judge Jones had her
brought down into court and talked to her. She said she
had been informed if she would cease activity and leave
here, she could go home, and she would be turned out.
The Judge told her that was true. She said she would.
She said, "I will go home and stay away from here." He
told her, "All right," he would let her go. She says, "I
don't want to go right now today. I would like to go
down to Pineville to rest for a day. I would like to have
a day." The Judge said, "You can have a day or two
days, or a week." She was discharged on that statement.

Q 61 Do you know who informed her that she could obtain
her liberty at those bargain rates?

A    We had been turning out some previous to that on such
statements, that they could go home, if they quit their

activity. She, somehow, had found out about that. So she sent word down that she wanted the same proposition. She came down, and that was her statement.

Q 62 We are going to make a report, and we feel we have a picture of an extraordinary legal procedure, that in this case, involving lives, the threat against the lives of county officials, where a charge of Criminal Syndicalism has been made for advocating the overthrow of the government, that you do a god-like thing such as giving them their liberty on the mere promise that they leave the county and quit their activities; telling those people to go home and sin no more. We want to know whether that has not been done here. Why isn't that done with the poor devils who merely steal and do not want to overthrow the government?

A These fellows who are indicted for being with the Communist Party were maybe from some other place, from New York, Chicago, Chattanooga, Tennessee, and being strangers here, and having gotten into this trouble, it looked, when they saw their wrong, and pleaded for mercy, a man could grant them that mercy.

Q 63 You don't do this in any other case, do you?

A We have let many boys off by this promise to be good.

Q 64 You now have reference to the probation system? But these people have not pleaded guilty in any instance, have they?

A They have not pleaded guilty, but after they pleaded and said, "I will cease activities and have nothing to do with the organization of the Communist Party, we let them go under those conditions.

Q 05 Probation, understand, is quite a different thing, you know that?

A Yes.

Q 66 This cannot be considered probation. A boy is arrested for stealing, and he is taken to court and confesses; he pleads guilty. He is then given probation, to give him another chance. But that was not followed in these Criminal Syndicalist cases, and the case of threat to assassinate, was it?

A It has been proven that they were threatening the lives of Brock, Jones, and they were willing to let them go, if they left Kentucky. No human heart could not get sorry for some of these prisoners who did not understand what they were involved in, being drawn into this Communist Party.

Q 67 In the case of the people who were allowed to go home there was no adjudication of guilt?

A We did not try these cases, but we had proof they were guilty; I believe they were guilty.

Q 68 You charged Mrs. Wakefield and Arnold Johnson with being Communist Party organizers; they denied that charge?

A No, sir. Johnson admitted that he had been active in the Communist Party.

Q 69 Johnson is a theological student; he came from a theological seminary where he was studying for the ministry, and came down here for the Civil Liberties Union?

A I don't know nothing about that.

Q 70 You didn't. . . .

A I do know that a professor came down here and they claimed to know him. They came here to beg for him. I agreed to discharge him if he stopped activities in the Communist Party. They said we will go to the jail and talk to him. They went to talk to him and said he was stubborn as could be and they could do nothing with him. But finally he pleaded for mercy.

Q 71 Did he confess he was a communist organizer?

A He said he was working for the organization.

Mr. Jones: Let me tell you something about what I think about you fellows—

Q 72 We are not questioning you, Mr. Jones. We will talk to you later.

Mr. Brock: I said to Mr. Johnson, "Are you helping to organize the Communist Party here?" He said, "Well, I have been with them for three weeks," and he could not evade; though he did not give me a direct answer. You could see between the lines he was working in it.

Q 73 Would you admit such an opinion in evidence, "reading between the lines"?

A    No, sir. We are not giving evidence here.

*Questions by Mr. Dreiser:*

Q 74 What do you consider Criminal Syndicalist literature?

A    I consider Criminal Syndicalist literature the literature circulated by this man Gibbs with Lenin's picture on it, and under that picture telling, step by step, how to make a *coup* in the government and take it over. I call that Criminal Syndicalism.

Q 75 You mean that illustration of Lenin?

A    Another example is—one that I would convict on—I would convict a fellow that would go out and organize a party, make an organization, which organization would teach their membership to overthrow the constitution of the state, or to overthrow the constituted authorities of the state, and place themselves in authority.

Q 76 Have you come across such literature?

A    Not in words, but in substance.

Q 77 What was it?

A    It was a circular gotten out. I don't know where they were gotten out.

Q 78 Did you make any convictions?

A    We didn't try any man on it. We let them go.

Q 79 There has been testimony here that men would have copies of the *Daily Worker* in their home. Their homes would be raided and copies of the *Daily Worker* would be found, and they would be arrested and held in jail. Do you consider possession of the *Daily Worker* illegal or a subject for Criminal Syndicalist charges?

A    Does the *Daily Worker* teach Communism?

Q 80 A great deal of it teaches social equity and a new equitable arrangement of American institutions. Would you say that if that paper was found they should be arrested?

A   Suppose a man is found with 50 or 300 copies, and he is distributing that paper, and that paper teaches Communism, then would he not be teaching and advocating the overthrow of the government?

Q 81  It is admitted to the United States mail for distribution. It has mailing privileges which have not been interfered with, would you consider that as illegal for distribution? It has a circulation of 40,000 copies and has not been interfered with in New York or elsewhere. Do you think that you are justified in restricting it?

A   There are things going through the mail that are not legal. That is one of them.

*Ornitz questioning:*

Q 82  Does the *Daily Worker* violate the Kentucky Criminal Syndical Law? Don't you think that it is arbitrary for you to arrest people for distribution of the *Daily Worker* and not get an adjudication on it? If you release all prisoners who possess the *Daily Worker* on the promise not to read the *Daily Worker*, you are enforcing a law that has never been ruled upon. You are making a decision without legal ruling.

A   There have been decisions. This is what I am going to do. Whenever these men return, I propose to try them right on the evidence we are now discussing.

Q 83  We heard witnesses who charged criminal acts against company guards who are Deputy Sheriffs receiving pay from the companies as well as against regular Deputies in Brock's retinue. If you hear charges of crime against these Deputies will you prosecute?

A   Yes. In fact, I have heard charges on both sides. The first overt act came when some one waylaid Scott and wounded him. After that trouble began to grow.

Q 84  The wife of a miner testified that six drunken men claiming to be Deputies came into her home, ransacked her trunks, drawers and closets. They did not have a search warrant. Is this a crime?

A   Absolutely.

Q 85 If we submit this evidence, will you investigate?

A   In case you can prove that a law has been violated, then we will investigate this.

Q 86 Why did you not prosecute a Deputy Sheriff who Judge Whitehead ruled entered a house and took something away without a legal search warrant?

A   I don't think that is so, but . . .

Q 87 Why did you not prosecute in that case?

A   If the party goes before the Grand Jury, then we will go on.

Q 88 These witnesses told us they were afraid to speak. If you recall we sent you a telegram asking that you give us assurance that they would be protected. They said they had lost respect for legal machinery here because they said it was in the hands of the coal operators. They said that not one Deputy had been arrested and indicted for crime while about 50 miners have been arrested for the alleged killing of Deputies.

A   Why don't you listen to my story? You are only getting one side of it. The first act was when a Deputy Sheriff, three of them, were attacked on the road. A man was taken out on the public road and whipped because he went to work. They demanded that he stay away from there. Do you justify that?

Q 89 Has there been any conviction in that case?

A   That has been sent to another court.

Q 90 Why was that case sent away? It was sent 200 miles away. Why was it sent so far?

A   In the County of Harlan, in the County of Bell and in Perry, they have coal and we had an election here in which the issue made was whether these men were justified, these Deputy Sheriffs, and Charles Finley, Congressman, made that his issue and the people here were trying this here case in the election and I wanted to take this case into a district where these men could have a fair trial, where there was no coal. The people voted against these miners so I took them away where they can have a fair trial.

Q 91 The prosecution will receive money from the County treasury with which to defer expenses for witnesses' transportation, etc.?

A    The prosecuting attorney takes charge of it where the cases are.

Q 92 The prosecution witnesses will be allowed transportation and will receive compensation?

A    They will get a stipulated amount and mileage.

Q 93 Who will pay for the transportation and upkeep of the witnesses for the defense?

A    The defense will pay for this.

Q 94 These defendants are very far away and it will be expensive to get the witnesses there. Do you think they will get a fair trial if they are penniless and therefore cannot get their witnesses?

A    If they file a statement saying that they have no means to get the witnesses, the judge will order the Sheriff to bring the witnesses.

Q 95 Where would these poor persons get money to prepare the affidavits that would be required and get the attorneys to take care of this?

A    These people had a lot of lawyers here.

Q 96 Was there no place nearer you could send them to?

A    No county that would be free of sentiment.

Q 97 What union do these men belong to?

A    I don't know. I think the National Miners Union.

Q 98 When did this all happen?

A    In May.

Q 99 The National Miners Union was organizing in May?

A    The National Miners Union I think was organizing at that time.

Q 100 What investigation did you make of the dynamiting of Mrs. Wakefield's automobile?

A    We sent the Sheriff over there and he talked to every one around. The Sheriff could not point to a witness that knows who did it.

Q 101    What about the soup kitchen which was dynamited?

A    In neither of these cases could we find anybody guilty.

Q 102    Did you find any indictment against any Deputy who illegally raided the miners' homes?

A    We never had any indictment. There never was any complaint made about the miners' homes being raided.

Q 103    Have you found any indictment of any Deputy Sheriff who raided the homes of miners without warrants?

A    There was no complaints.

Q 104    Have you ever found indictment against persons for shooting Boris Israel, a newspaperman?

A    We investigated the case but could not find the person.

Q 105    Was there any indictment against persons for shooting Bruce Crawford?

A    No, sir. We don't know who did it.

Q 106    How many men were indicted for shooting Deputy Sheriffs?

A    I don't know the number.

Q 107    More than 20 or 30?

A    Might have been.

Q 108    There have been no indictments for acts of violence committed against laborers or sympathizers of laborers?

A    I don't know whether or not this is so.

Q 109    Have no charges or indictments been made against Deputy Sheriffs?

A    It has been charged but we never found out who did it.

Q 110    What about . . . ?

A    Now wait a minute, let me talk. You are only inquiring about one side of this. Why don't you ask about the men who were killed as officers of this county?

Q 111    While investigating we have found that the situation has been one-sided in this county against the laborers; indictments are numerous against them, the laborers, and not against the other side. Why was not Lee Fleenor indicted?

A    Fleenor is under investigation.

Q 112    Is he still a Deputy Sheriff?

A    I don't know.

Q 113    Sheriff Blair tells us he is. Don't you think he should not be retained as a Deputy Sheriff?

A    A man is not a criminal when he is charged with crime. He is innocent until he is proven guilty. However, if I were a Sheriff and had a man whose guilt was questioned, I would lay him off until it was over.

Q 114    Do you know anything about Tom Epps?

A    Yes, sir.

Q 115    Do you know that he was in the County Jail for a considerable time on no charge at all? Is he still in jail?

A    I don't know whether he is in jail now.

Q 116    There seems to have been some mix-up. He was arrested for something and apparently forgotten. Somebody came and filed a bond for him and then he was released. How do you explain this?

A    I know we did something about the case but I don't remember what we did. There were so many of these cases—the court was overwhelmed with cases.

Q 117    A man could be held in jail indefinitely without a proper hearing?

A    Our court lasts thirty days and he might lay in there for thirty days.

Q 118    Even though he was not guilty, he would have to wait that long waiting for a hearing?

A    (No answer.)

Q 119    We have copies of two affidavits, one from Jim Grace and another from Debs Moreland, both claiming they have been beaten and driven out of this county. We are giving copies of these to the press. We think they call for an investigation. If these men return to make charges, will you assure us that these people will not be hurt? How could we assure these men that this won't happen to them again? Mrs. Grace has also told us about the facts in connection with her husband. In what way could we get them into Harlan so they won't be afraid?

A    Nobody will harm them and if there is any threat of their being harmed, I don't know it. You have only been inquiring about one side of the whole thing and you only been over a very small part of one side of the trouble and you have been over the miner side of it. You have not asked about the outrages committed by these Communist people.

Q 120  We are here now to get evidence for the other side.

A    You are not treating the situation fairly. You are not bringing out anything except what is on one side of it.

Q 121  Well, let us hear what you have to say.

A    You are only bringing out one side of it, the miners' side. You are not being fair. I want to tell you more about it. When this trouble was started by Estes Cox getting killed and shot from ambush—he is a Deputy Sheriff—when he was driven out of a mine at Black Mountain. A day or two after that a lot of men had been notified not to go back to those mines to work. If they did they would be killed. A man went back and worked and a bunch of fellows came in broad, open daylight, and whipped and beat him brutishly. And the Deputy Sheriff up at Black Mountain came down to town and got warrants for them and when they went up to arrest them, one of these miners shot him down like a dog, without a bit of justification. When that man was shot down sentiment began to reach a pitch on both sides and the proof showed before the grand jury. I think the sworn testimony that W. B. Jones, who was some kind of officer in one of these labor organizations, I think he belonged to the Communist Party, he called his men together, and had what he called a private meeting, he and Bill Hightower, president of the local. In W. B. Jones's house was found a lot of this literature that teaches Communism. He called the men together that night and told them to get ready for the next morning, as the law came down from Black Mountain every one had to die. He sent out his men, about 50, and they took a position along the public highway, behind rocks and houses and fences. As the officers came along, driving in a car, and coming down from Harlan, they fired and they killed three; and one of their men got killed. The officers fired back. Four men were killed in open daylight. After that killing we got warrants for the men we could find that was connected with it. When our grand jury sat we indicted every man that was in that meeting, or went down there with a gun that day. There was 20 of them. There was men in that we could never get their names. A lot of them immediately left this county. That killing was made an issue in the campaign, and it was claimed they were innocent and that they fired in self-defense and that the officers fired and commenced the trouble. The people overwhelmingly voted they were guilty by electing the man who argued the case of prosecuting these men. That is why I sent these cases out of this county. I wanted them to go down there and have a trial where there was nobody concerned either way. I think the laws of Kentucky justifies that. After that I heard more of the Communist Party. It kept getting more active about here. These Lenin pictures, these circulars with Lenin's pictures were being distributed and circulated.

Q 122 Has any judgment in court been made and these facts established?

A     Let me continue. We commenced investigating them before the Grand Jury and if we found a man with that we arrested him. They have been turned out because they have begged for mercy. Sentiment died down; soldiers came down; and the governor brought them down here without giving notice to any officer, and he took them out before I had any idea he was going to take them out; and they were taken out for no other reason except to permit the Communist Party to organize under terms they would vote for the man the governor was for. Every indication showed it. So the people overwhelmingly voted it down. I thought they ought not to pass on these men's cases after they decided in the election against them. I think I did right. I am going to stand by it.

*Mr. Ornitz questioning:*

Q 123 I would like to ask one question in connection with the statement of facts. Has any judgment in court been made to establish the facts? I don't mean indictments; I mean facts.

A After the thing occurred, just before the soldiers were sent in here, when these reds were in here, you would find a bunch of men on the highway with high-powered rifles and guns. If a man came along, he was halted, asked where he was going. If he was a fellow who was going to a mine to get a job to work, they told him, "The other way!" And if he didn't go, they made him go. We indicted people like that for banding. We indicted lots of them on that charge. So we haven't tried any of those cases. We sent some of them away from here to be tried. The rest are pending here. I thought I would let them try those cases in the county, and see whether or not if they are convicted—and if they decide those men are innocent I am going to dismiss these cases.

Q 124 Do you know Jones and those associated with him were members and officers of the U. M. W. of A.?

A They claim to be officers of the U. M. W. of A. As long as they claim this I am for them because I am a U. M. W. of A. man myself. I am with the U. M. W. of A. in principle. I helped to organize them in the county. Once we organized and had a 90 per cent organization. We forced them to settle in 1917. We struck and got a settlement. That was the 1917 scale. It is a patriotic organization. I don't think you could get one of them to advise a killing here or an illegal act.

Q 125  Jones and Hightower claim they were members of the
U. M. W. of A.

A      Yes, sir, they did. I think they belonged to it when it
went far enough until they struck, and they could not
get along and they could not get any relief from the
U. M. W. of A. to buy provisions. They stopped right
there. This other organization, the National Miners
Union said, "We will feed you, give you support, if you
join us." They joined them. I saw a published statement in the *Daily Worker* where they had joined the
I. W. W. and they were complimenting them in the
*Daily Worker;* and they said they were sending them
money. I think Hightower and Jones, my judgment is,
belonged to the U. M. W. of A. I believe they quit and
I believe they joined the other organization. I think
they joined the Communist Party. I think they joined
the I. W. W. I think Jones and Hightower is the brains
and instigators and the conspirators of the murder.

*Mr. Dreiser questioning:*

Q 126  That is all, Mr. Brock, thank you.

Mr. Jones: Just one minute. Let me ask you something? (To
Mr. Ornitz.) Are you a citizen of the United States;
when were you naturalized?

Mr. Ornitz: If it will interest you to know it, I am a native
citizen in the United States.

Mr. Jones: Where were your parents born? Have you any kin
in Russia?

Mr. Ornitz: Yes.

Mr. Jones: I thought so.

Mr. Ornitz: And I have kin in Kentucky, in Germany, in
France and in many other countries. But what has that
to do with the conditions in Harlan?

Mr. Jones: I thought you were connected with Russia.

Mr. Ornitz: Is there anything else you would like to know?

Mr. Jones: No, we know enough.

# XI. THE FREE SPEECH SPEAKIN'S

## by John Dos Passos

ALL the women in this coalcamp
Are sittin' with bowed down heads,
All the women in this coalcamp
Are sittin' with bowed down heads,
Ragged an' barefooted
An' their children a-cryin' for bread.
No food, no clothes, for our children,
I'm sure this ain't no lie.
No food, no clothes, for our children,
I'm sure this ain't no lie.
If we can't get no more for our labor
We will starve to death and die.

Straight Creek is the section of Bell County that has been
organized fairly solid under the National Miners Union.
Owing, the miners say, to the fair-minded attitude of the
Sheriff, who has not allowed the mine guards to molest them,
there has been no bloodshed, and a three weeks' strike ended the
week before we got there with several small independent operators signing agreements with the union at thirty-eight cents
a ton and allowing a union check weighman.[1] (The boy who
was check weighman told me that in the mine where he worked
one cwt. weighed eighty pounds when he took over the scales.)
They say that thirty-eight cents is not a living wage but that
it's something to begin on. The committee had been invited to
attend a meeting of the N. M. U. local at the Glendon Baptist
Church and walked around the miners' houses first.

---

[1] Since then the miners of this section have struck again. They claim that
the coal operators (influenced by Judge Jones and the Harlan County Coal
Operators' Ass'n) have refused to carry out the agreement.

Straight Creek is a narrow zigzag valley that runs up into the mountains from Pineville. The mines are small and often change hands. The houses are low shacks set up on stilts, scattered in disorderly rows up and down the valley floor. They are built of thin sheathing and mostly roofed with tarpaper. A good many have been papered with newspaper on the inside by their occupants in an effort to keep the wind out. The floors are full of cracks. I have seen similar houses in Florida shantytowns, but here in the mountains the winter is long and cold. It's hard to imagine how the miners and their wives and children can get any semblance of warmth out of the small coal-burning grates. They have to pay for their coal too, though some of the operators allow the women and children to pick up what they can around the tipple. It wrings your heart the way the scantily furnished rooms have been tidied up for the visitors.

The visitors form a motley straggle through the little dooryards (there have been cows and pigs kept in some and you have to be careful where you step); a certain Mr. Grady, who I believe is the same gentleman who made such a fuss last year about losing his job as technician in Soviet Russia, has turned up and is putting everything down in a little notebook. When somebody asked him who he represented, he replied: "I have nothing to do with you people, I represent American citizenship." It would be interesting to know who is paying Mr. Grady's carfare now that he has been fired by the Soviet Government.

The A. P. man and the gentleman from the *Courier-Journal* have a harrowed look on their faces; they keep looking around behind things as if they felt the houses had been put up to hoax them. They refuse to believe that people can be so badly off as that. They crowd into the door of one shack to hear what Aunt Molly Jackson, the local midwife, has to say, but you can see them getting ready not to believe what she says, what their own eyes see.

*Straight Creek, Kentucky, November 7, 1931*

## Testimony of AUNT MOLLY JACKSON

Q 1  What is your name?

A    Aunt Molly Jackson.

Q 2  What do you do?

A    I am a nurse.

Q 3  A graduate nurse?

A    Yes.

Q 4  Can you tell us something about the condition of the people in this hollow?

A    The people in this country are destitute of anything that is really nourishing to the body. That is the truth. Even the babies have lost their lives, and we have buried from four to seven a week all along during warm weather.

Q 5  Due to lack of food?

A    Yes, on account of cholera, famine, flux, stomach trouble brought on by undernourishment. Their food is very bad, such as beans and harsh foods fried in this lard that is so hard to digest. It is impossible for a little baby's stomach to digest them. The digestive organs are not strong enough to digest this food.

Q 6  Is that the only food they have, if they have that?

A    They can only get beans. Their parents have been out of work this summer. Families have had to depend on the Red Cross. The Red Cross put out some beans and corn.

Q 7  Did they supply any proper food for the babies such as milk?

A    No milk at all.

Q 8  Were there many families that depended on the Red Cross?

A    I believe there is a lot of families that depended on the Red Cross. I didn't. Those families could tell you more about the Red Cross. There is a family by the name of Lechard; he is a working man and had a large family.

Now Thea Bennett could also tell you about the Red Cross, what they are allowed a week.

Q 9    Was it enough to keep them?

A    No, it was a small amount.

Q 10    What did it consist of?

A    Just beans and potatoes.

Q 11    Do they give to every one that asks?

A    No, the Red Cross does not give to every one. I always thought they was selfish; they didn't have the right kind of heart.

Q 12    Do they give to members of the National Miners Union?

A    No, they stop it when they know a man belongs to the union.

Q 13    What did they say about it?

A    The Red Cross is against a man who is trying to better conditions. They are for the operators, and they want the mines to be going so they won't give anything to a man unless he does what the operators want him to. For instance, I will explain this. My husband took pneumonia and flux for three months. He has not been able to work since this strike. I have to carry back something for my husband to eat from the soup kitchen. The Red Cross won't give anything. We are really in destitution. I talked to the Red Cross lady over at Pineville.

Q 14    Do you know her name?

A    No, I don't. I said, "There is a lot of little children in destitution. Their feet are on the ground. They have come so far. They are going to get pneumonia and flux this winter that will kill the children off."

Q 15    Did she offer to give you any relief?

A    No, because they was members of the National Miners Union. They said, "We are not responsible for those men out on strike. They should go back to work and work for any price that they will take them for." That was last week.

Q 16    How many children die a month or a year under these conditions?

A     Now in the summer, it would be three to seven each week up and down this creek.

Q 17  Did they have any insurance to take care of the funeral or burial expenses?

A     No, sir. They cut off the men's wages to bury them. But all the miners buries their own dead. They cut $2 a month, and you cannot get this money.

Q 18  Do they cut for doctor?

A     Yes.

Q 19  Can you get him when you call him in sickness?

A     This Dr. Stacy in Pineville, you can call him—the men pay $2 for him a month—and then you will call, and sometimes four or five days later he will come to see you. That is the service we get.

Q 20  Are these houses sanitary and healthful to live in?

A     These houses bring grip, flu and pneumonia.

Q 21  Is this a company house?

A     Yes.

Q 22  Does the company fix it?

A     They do not fix it. Just plainly speaking they are no more interested in the men, in the miners, they have not got the sympathy that people has for stock, for the mules.

Q 23  Much less, because a man who owns stock knows he must take care of it or he loses money. They don't feel that way about the miners, I believe you.

A     If I had a milk cow or a horse I certainly would be more interested in them than the coal operators is in these people.

Q 24  Is your husband a member of the N. M. U.?

A     My husband is a member of the National Miners Union, and I am too, and I have never stopped, brother, since I know of this work for the N. M. U. I think it is one of the greatest things that has ever come into this world.

Q 25  Who are the operators of this mine?

A     O. L. Goodman. They highly insulted me.

Q 26  He is the owner?

A     Yes.

Q 27 What did he say?

A    My son that is at home, he advised the young man to go and ask for a job at the same rate. Goodman said, "Well, Joe, if you will leave home and not put any support of them for the benefit of your parents, and get you a new boarding house, I will work you. . . ."

Q 28 Is that what he said, "work you"—that's the proper expression?

A    Yes, he said that; "get you a new boarding house," he says, "for your parents have taken too much interest in this union." And he says, "Your mother spoke to about 300 people and exposed me, so I don't want no more to do with her." He says, "If that is the chance for a job for me, I won't go to work." He says, "You haven't got any work for me then."

*Mr. Walker questions:*

Q 29 You know all the people in this village are suffering from lack of food?

A    Yes, they are destitute of food and clothing.

Q 30 You have been a nurse in this community?

A    Yes, just charity.

Q 31 You have brought children into this world?

A    Yes, sir, 65. My poor husband, he did all he could do. They took their wagons and they would beg for these pumpkins and corn and that would be all they would get. without any seasoning and many days they had nothing but those pumpkins. It's all right if we had the other things to fix the pumpkins up but we had nothing and it is very hard to digest that way.

Q 32 What do they do with the pumpkins?

A    They feed their hogs. If you had the flavoring, you could fix up something good.

*Straight Creek, Kentucky, November 7, 1931*

Testimony of CALLOWAY HOBBS given in his cabin

Q 1 What is your name?
A  Calloway Hobbs.
Q 2 You are a miner?
A  Yes, sir.
Q 3 Whom do you work for?
A  For the Glendon Mine. I was on strike for three weeks.
Q 4 Under the National Miners Union?
A  Yes, sir.
Q 5 How long have you been working now?
A  I have been working about a week.
Q 6 Do you work regularly?
A  I ain't got work much.
Q 7 How much do you make?
A  I don't know what I am making now.
Q 8 How much do you get a ton?
A  We get 38 cents a ton.
Q 9 How much do you make a day on that?
A  About two dollars a day.
Q 10 When did you start to work?
A  We went back on Wednesday.
Q 11 How much do you make a month on the average?
A  I made from $14 to $20 a month.
Q 12 This is a company house?
A  Yes.
Q 13 How much rent do you pay?
A  Three dollars a month when I make it.
Q 14 Do you pay when you are not working?
A  If I don't make it I don't pay them.
Q 15 Do they take it off your pay when you work?
A  They don't hold it against me.
Q 16 They don't take back rent off?
A  No.

Q 17 How many are there in your family that you have to support?

A     There is the wife and seven children, nine of us.

Q 18 Do you support them all?

A     Yes, sir.

Q 19 What do you live on?

A     We manage to get by the best we can. We live on what we can get.

Q 20 When you didn't work did you get anything from the Red Cross?

A     I didn't get anything from them.

Q 21 Anything from the neighbors?

A     No, sir.

Q 22 What do you eat?

A     We have a few beans and a little meat some times.

Q 23 How much can you get from the company store?

A     I don't know.

Q 24 How much will they allow you before they refuse to give you anything?

A     Some get nothing at all when they ask for it. I get some scrip.

Q 25 How about the children, how are they?

A     The children, they don't get any milk. One baby died, the doctor said nothing was wrong with her. All the children have had flux, one is sick now.

Q 26 How about this child, doesn't she get any milk?

A     Yes, she gets milk now. Mr. Warren, that's my brother-in-law, has a cow and she gets that milk, but nobody else gets any because there is some only for her.

Q 27 Is Mr. Warren a miner?

A     No, sir.

Q 28 How much does your son-in-law make?

A     He doesn't make anything.

Q 29 Doesn't he help you?

A     We have to feed him too.

Q 30 Do you have a two dollar reduction for doctor?

A     Yes, sir.

Q 31 When your baby was sick, did you get the doctor for her?

A   Sometimes we got him. We called him many times. When he used to come around here, I would watch for him and then he would come in but otherwise he would not stop in to see her. He said there was nothing the matter with her. When she died, he asked, "Did that baby finally die?" That is what he said.

Q 32 How much do you owe the company store?

A   When I went back to work I owed $5.45.

Q 33 How much did you draw this week?

A   I drew a dollar a day.

Q 34 For seven people? What do you do for entertainment, for fun?

A   We go to church.

Q 35 Do you ever go to the movies?

A   I don't take no interest in that.

Q 36 What church do you go to?

A   I belong to the Missionary Baptists.

Q 37 Does that help you to live?

A   Yes, sir, if a man belongs to God, he is all right.

Q 38 You believe you will get your reward later on in the beyond?

A   I know I ain't never going to get nothing here. My children has got no clothes. The little girl here, she has got no underwear on.

Q 39 Do you belong to the Democrat or Republican Party?

A   I was a Republican all my life but this time they made a Democrat out of me.

Q 40 Do you think the Democrats will be any better?

A   If they don't, they can't be any worse.

While Dreiser is questioning old man Hobbs, one of the militia officers is standing on the back stoop looking out into the gathering dusk and remarking that as a military man he felt the absence of sanitation very keenly. Somebody explained that during the summer they'd had a cow for a while. The militia officer went on to wonder whether anything could be done to teach these people sanitation.

Afterwards some of us drove up a heavily rutted road up one of the forks to a tumbledown shack where an old man lay dying.[1] It was nearly dark. The little cabin was crushed under the steep black of the hill and the ramshackle structure of a mine tipple jutting up into the sky. The first step I took into the cabin the floor creaked so I put my hand against the wall to steady myself. The rotten boards gave. With several people crowding into it, the crazy cabin looked as if it would crumple up at any minute. The floor of the kitchen had already caved in. In an inside room, in front of a brightly burning coal grate an old man is lying back in a low chair, half supported by two women. His clothes are pulled apart so that you can see an open suppurating gash on one side of his abdomen.

*Straight Creek, Kentucky, November* 7, 1931

Testimony of ALEX NAPIER taken in his cabin

Q 1    Did you carry any company insurance?

A    No, sir.

Q 2    What is your name?

A    Alex Napier.

Q 3    Where do you work?

A    I worked for the Coleman mine before the accident for about five years. I was injured in the stomach, as you can see. A piece of coal fell on me and cut it. You can see here it was all swelled up and there is stuff comes out like water. It swelled up so I thought it would break.

Q 4    How long have you been hurt?

A    It is seven weeks since I got hurt. About the 16th of September.

Q 5    Has the company done anything for you?

A    They haven't done a thing.

Q 6    How much rent do you pay?

---

[1] He died a few days later.

A    Five dollars a month. The company they say they are not carrying my burden.

Q 7    You have no insurance?

A    No, we live the best we could. My sister helps a little bit.

Q 8    Does not any charitable organization help you?

A    No, sir.

Q 9    Have you asked them?

A    No, sir.

Q 10    Why not?

A    You see, sir, I can't get around at all. I can't move hardly.

Q 11    Why don't you ask some one to ask help for you? Would you like us to?

A    I would appreciate it very much.

Q 12    You have never asked the Red Cross for help?

A    No, sir.

Q 13    This house is pretty bad.

A    Yes, sir. I pay five dollars a month. They raised the rent two dollars and promised to fix it but they didn't do it.

Q 14    Did you pay the burial fund?

A    Yes.

Q 15    Are you a miner?

A    I am a day man. I was working at the tipple or power house doing day work for five years.

Q 16    You have how many children?

A    Six children.

Q 17    How old are they?

A    The oldest is 23 years. He was operated on, he busted something in his back when he tried to lift something. He can't do heavy work. Then I have another who is 17 years. He can't get a job. He isn't strong. He has a weak heart and gits fainting spells. Next is this little girl.

Q 18    Do you get any clothes?

A    We only have the few rags we have to stick to.

Q 19    What do you eat, when you do eat?

A    Anything I can get.

Q 20    Do you get it from the company store?

A    My sister helps me sometimes; nobody else.

Q 21  Where do you get the coal?

A    Down at the mine; we pick it up.

Q 22  What about the lights?

A    We burn oil my sister gives me.

Q 23  Who pays your doctor?

A    I do, with the money my sister gives us. We don't pay him regularly now, but he has not quit coming. He saved me.

Q 24  What does he say?

A    He said he thinks I will get well. There is a little place here that swells so big and water comes. I always paid my doctor bills.

The hollow was completely black. To get to the Glendon Baptist Church, where the meeting was to be held, we had to cross a high swinging bridge above the creek-bed. Young miners in their best clothes had been posted by the N. M. U. to guard the approaches to it. The low frame hall was packed with miners and their wives; all the faces were out of early American history. Stepping into the hall was going back a hundred years (or perhaps forward a few years). These were the gaunt faces, the slow elaborations of talk and courtesy, of the frontiersmen who voted for Jefferson and Jackson, and whose turns of speech were formed on the oratory of Patrick Henry. I never felt the actuality of the American revolution so intensely as sitting in that church, listening to these mountaineers with their old time phrases, getting up on their feet and explaining why the time to fight for freedom had come again.

The chairman was a young preacher named Meek. He spoke of the crowd as a congregation and of the meeting as a service. The old slogans of religion seemed to serve him just as well for the new hopes of unionism. The comic relief was afforded by a fat woman who stood in the aisle with her arms akimbo during many of the speeches glaring at the speakers. She finally broke into something the chairman was saying to remind him he'd never paid her ten dollars he'd owed her for two years.

She was the local agent of the Red Cross and the bookkeeper at the Carey mine.

It's a shame that all the speeches were not taken down as the miners who spoke put the situation far better than I can. Here's what Mistress "Sudy" Gates had to say:

## MISTRESS "SUDY" GATES' SPEECH

In the name of the Women's branch of the National Miners Union of Straight Creek, we welcome the writers' committee. We are glad to know that some one outside of Straight Creek is interested in the conditions of the miners in Straight Creek and we thank them very much for this interest.

It is hard to explain to them just exactly the conditions of the lives of the miners here. Our wages are so small that we cannot buy anything, just barely what we have to have and just what we can exist on. We . . . the miners' wives have to go to the stores to draw the scrip what their husbands made the day before; probably they could get some and probably not. If they got any they only got a small allowance.

The biggest part is taken out for carbide.

They cannot get much to eat because they have to buy this.

We are glad to have this writers' committee to investigate these things and probably it will be known and help us in time to come.

When we go to the company stores the prices are so high, we cannot buy our groceries or anything. Our children, they go without lunch. Sometimes they have a little beans and corn bread but without anything on it.

We have all kinds of disease because of that. No nourishment or food. That is the reason why we have Flux. There are many cases of Flux. We don't even know how many. We have had many deaths because of the conditions of food.

The conditions of our drinking water is so impure that the county nurse reported that it was very bad and impure, yet we have not better water yet. The nurse, when she took a test of the water, the doctor asked her what she was doing taking the test of the water. The doctor asked her what she was doing taking the test, why she was taking this test and that it was his business to take this test. She said it was not his business but hers and she was going to do it.

The conditions of our houses are very bad. We have to pay $3.00, $5 to $6.40 a month rent for them. The houses are so bad they are about to fall down. So rotten and cold, we nearly freeze to death. You can ask the boss to fix the house but he tells us he cannot and won't do it.

Also I have something else about the doctor. There was a case of a little kid. The doctor saw it and said nothing was wrong, to give it a dose of castor oil. It was sick for many weeks and one day they asked the doctor what was the matter with the baby and he said there was no chance for the baby to live, and then when he saw the funeral of the kid he said, "Did that kid finally die and git out of the way?"

That is the kind of a doctor we have here.

We are cut wages for the doctor; the men are cut two dollars a month for the doctor. You get very bad service from the doctor.

What's the good of calling a doctor, if he doesn't come around when you call him? You call him one day and he doesn't come around for a few days. You can be dead in the meantime.

And the company, if they know a man is honest and pays back his debts, then they give him a scrip and get him into debt and then he works and works and pays the debt. And then if he refuses to get in debt then they won't let him work.

We go to Pineville to buy where the stuff is much cheaper but he doesn't want us to go there, but he wants us to buy in his store and if we refuse, he doesn't let us work for him; so we have to do it. When we git scrip we have to buy in his store and we have to pay much more for everything and then we can't buy anything after we pay for the carbide.

The National Miners Union, which has come into this country, we never realized what it was to have some one help us until they came in here and got us poor miners together.

There are so many miners here that we don't know what wages is. They have gotten up to four dollars or five dollars a day, but now they get two dollars to three dollars and the miners must organize and must organize their wives. The wives must be organized because she has to suffer, she and the children has to go without clothes and she has to see her children starve. It is time for the miners to organize and to stick together to fight these conditions.

The miners yet cannot see when they won't need their bosses.

The thing for every one is to unite and stick together and fight these conditions and fight for better wages and better food and more of it and milk and stuff for the children.

The children are so cold, they turn blue. They try to go to school and try to learn but they have not got the energy to learn.

We have to fight these wage cuts. Every time you turn around you get a wage cut. Every time they cut the prices in the store a little, we know that we are going to get a wage cut. They cut the prices a little bit and give us a big wage cut.

That is the reason we must organize a union and stick together to fight this thing.

The wives here, you don't see a one that has sufficient clothes to go out in public. Their shoes is off their feet. They have them tied with strings. In the summer, if they happen to have a pair of shoes, they don't wear them, they save them for the cold winter. The kids they go around with no shoes and no food, do you wonder why we are losing children?

I don't see how they can stand it. It is hard for grown persons to stand.

Many people say, Why don't you buy? We have nothing to buy with. If we git some money, we go to the store and when we buy, we can't buy less than 25 cents worth of carbide and we have to buy the carbide.

I ask all the women and all the men of this place to stick together. All the wives must join with us. Now is the time that the women has some right to fight with her husband and by both fighting we can win in time to come.

The good thing about the National Miners Union is that they don't leave the women out and so, not like in the other times, many times the wives would make the husbands go back to work. The wives must meet with their husbands and together plan, because it is as much to the wives as to the miners. In the National Miners Union the wives know just as much what is going on. We are not going to say, "Go on, Johnny, go back to work."

We are going to stand right along with them and fight.

We are thankful to the National Miners Union for this. It makes you have a sensation you hardly know what it is all about. We never had nothing to do before but cook some beans. Now we have something to do. Now we have something else to do. We are going to have John win the strike. We were naked long enough and we are going to fight for something. We are going to keep this organization and we are going to fight.

I appreciate the writers' committee so much, I don't know how to express it.

Then Aunt Molly Jackson sang her now famous Hungry Miners' Wife's Blues and her younger brother, Jim Garland, made a very funny speech about why the Coal Operators called the miners reds. He said folks might maybe call him a red because his people, father, grandfather and great grandfather had been so long in that country that if you went any further back you came to Cherokee injun blood and that was red all right. Then he said maybe another reason you might call the miners red was that they'd gotten so thin and poor, from the small wages they got, that if you stood one of them up against the sun you'd see red right through him. Then George Maurer of the I. L. D. made a speech asking for solidarity and Harry Gannes of the *Daily Worker* reminded everybody that that night was the fourteenth anniversary of the Soviet Union and that this was probably the first time such an anniversary had been mentioned in the mountains of Kentucky. One miner summed up the general feeling by saying, after he'd described how a march of a thousand men going out on strike under the

U. M. W. of A. that spring had been broken up in spite of tne fact that they came out with five American flags, "By God, if they won't let us march under the American flag, we'll march under the red flag."

The speakin' at Wallins Creek next afternoon took place in the gymnasium of the handsome High School on the hill above the town. The High School seemed to be the only visible sign left of the boom period of '20-'21. We'd been told that there might be trouble at Wallins Creek and that the deputies were threatening to break the meeting up. Nothing happened, however, but you could see that the miners in the audience got nervous as it got dark, and many of them left before the meeting was over. It was a surprise to us on arriving in the town to see a banner strung across the main street reading:

WELCOME, Writers' Committee, International Labor Defense, National Miners Union.

In Wallins Creek as in Evarts the small store-keepers and the townspeople generally seemed to be in sympathy with the rednecks, as they call the members of the N. M. U. One taxi-driver told me, "Ma neck got so red this summer I reckon its about ready to turn brown."

At the meeting one more man came up to say he wanted to tell us about the Red Cross.

*Wallins Creek, Kentucky, November 8, 1931*

Testimony of CHRIS PATERSON, resident of Day Hoit, Ky.

Q 1   Where did you work?
A       I last worked at Lenurup (?) I worked there up to last winter.
Q 2   Did the Red Cross feed you?
A       Yes, they feed men with large families.
Q 3   How much does the Red Cross give?
A       They give two to two and a half to you according to the size of the family.

Q 4  Does the Red Cross help all those who need it?

A    No, sir. Every time a man joins a strike the Red Cross
     stops giving support. They don't give any help to you
     if you are a member of the union. They ask you whether
     you belong to the union first.

Q 5  Anything else?

A    No, sir.

It takes a brave man to stand up and speak his mind, when
he knows that his opponents are taking down everything he
says so as to twist it into the basis for an indictment, when he
knows that his opponents have at their command all the force
of the law, of the state, the money power, and hired gunmen
besides to fight him with. The miners and the miners' wives
who spoke at Straight Creek and at Wallins Creek were brave
men and women; they knew what they were up against. This
is what a tall blackhaired miner named Donaldson, who stalked
up and down the platform pounding the table with his fist like
an oldtime hellroaring evangelist, had to say at Wallins Creek.


*Wallins Creek, Kentucky, November* 8, 1931

## DONALDSON'S SPEECH

I am surprised of an opportunity of standing before you in
behalf of this great struggle that we are now attempting to
fight against mass starvation.

We are now really going through a terrible time. I have
been a miner for the past 33 years. During this time under the
ground, I have had some terribly trying times.

In this period of time I have shot at gun thugs and been
shot by them.

As for me to tell you that I have always been a good boy,
I would be misrepresenting things.

I spent some days in the prison because of violation of corrupt laws read in the constitution. The results of these laws

against the laborers is that it is impossible to live in Kentucky without violating some of the laws.

I love the flag of United States and America but I hate the men who handle this country; these men have so taken away our privileges that it is impossible to live.

The men we have elected to make our laws have been corrupt.

During the time that we had a livin' wage, we could support our families but that has been taken away by the unjust laws and the way our nation has been handled. I love my children ten thousand times better than I love Hoover or the coal operators. . . .

The coal operators say the Roosian red has been down in this here country. A man that won't support and stand by his children is ten times worse than an infidel.

There is no place for a capitalist sympathizer but Hell.

I want to say that the miners are today worse off than slaves during slave time. You go to work in the morning and you leave your wife and your children, but the mines you go into are not the safe and sanitary mines you used to go into. You go into the mines to slave for $1.00 or 80 cents a day. You eat pinto beans and corn beans. Is that true?

("Yes, it's true. Yes, it's true," comes from the audience.)

You go to bed in a bag of rags but the hellbound Criminal Syndicalist law forbids you to speak.

You are denied every privilege by Judge Jones and Brock. I spoke to Brock and he said to me, "If you stick to me, I will do the best for you and your labor troubles."

He forbids us every privilege that the constitution gives us.

Hoover says he is unable to handle the situation.

The thing I say is the National Miners Union is ready to handle it, to give you the same livin' conditions you had before the government put in these laws that were unjust. The National Miners stand for the principles that our forefathers fought for us.

The United Mine Workers in their day was a success but we got traitors in and they sold us out. I want to say that there is a delegate here that was in the Convention in 1927-28. At that time I was not a member of any union but I was sent down there to vote the Lewis issue, and they gave me $75. I took the money. That's what they take the money for, and they have the money and you have the bread and beans.

The labor leader has led you into captivity.

I know some time men will have to make a complete sacrifice; hundreds of men's lives will be sacrificed; but nothing good ever came without somebody making a sacrifice. I love my children but this is the only reason that I would leave my children and make the great sacrifice.

I may be victimized for this but if Judge Jones thinks I am better in jail, then let it be so because I will get better food there than at home. The company for which I now work refuses to reduce my rent one dollar because they say they cannot do it. Yet that man has been able to pay a gun thug (I know because he is my own brother-in-law) to patrol the street.

I am going to feed my children. I am going to kill, murder, rob for my children because I won't let my children starve.

If you give me a show, I will work it out.

The National Miners Union is the only thing that has not failed us. We don't have to pay $12,000 a year for a man to sell us out and to send us back to scab. In that 1928 convention we voted a raise for Lewis from $8,000 to $10,000 and then we came back home and told the men that they would have to take a cut in wages. Is that fair?

Whatever you get you have to take from the capitalist. We beg and beg and tell them our starving conditions but it don't do no good.

I just made up my mind that I won't work and go hungry any more. Last winter was a cold winter and I want to say to you that during the winter I worked every day at such poor wages and could hardly buy food for my children, who had to go out without a bit of underwear.

And then you say that this is a good country. I say that it is not a good country that denies a man a good fair wage.

We don't want to get rich. We want to eat. If you put a man into poverty then you send him down to Hell and sin. Believe me, it would not take much for me to go down and steal a good square meal.

# XII. I WANT TO BE COUNTED [1]

## by Sherwood Anderson

I AM intensely interested in this meeting and have come up here from my home in Virginia for that reason.

First of all I have a simple desire to stand up and be counted on the side of Theodore Dreiser, John Dos Passos and the other men and women, mostly I think writers, thinkers, perhaps poets and dreamers, who had the guts to go on this trip down into a little Kentucky mining town. I have been in mining towns myself, I know what most of them are like.

In the mining town in question there had been an attempt to organize a union. I believe the Supreme Court of the United States has said men have a right to form unions, even a communist may run for Congress or for the Senate, or for President—legally—I believe.

A few years ago I was on a visit to France—not considered, I think, an unenlightened country. Even then there were communist deputies sitting in the French house of Deputies.

But in Kentucky they are afraid of unions—so they fight them. They shoot men who join unions—hunt them like rabbits. Now I do not know who owns the mines at Harlan, Kentucky. It is some big company.

There are men in that town, county officials, lawyers, doctors, preachers, store keepers and workers. The workers are, I daresay, quite miserable. I do not need to go to Harlan, Kentucky. I can believe that. I have been in coal mining towns myself, in England, in France, in America, in the North and in the South. I was myself from a small town of the middle-west, a farming town. I remember when, as a boy, I first saw,

[1] An address delivered before a meeting held by the National Committee for the Defense of Political Prisoners in New York City on December 6, 1931, to protest the legal and illegal terror in the Harlan, Kentucky, coal fields.

from a train window, a coal mining town of that country. I remember the shudder that ran through me. There were men and women living like rabbits in dirty holes. I remember how the sight frightened and startled me.

So nowadays everywhere workers are out of work. They are poorly paid.

It is so with all workers in all trades now. With the industrial workers it is worse than with any other sort of workers.

Why? It seems to me very simple. Nowadays, because of our human mechanical genius, the building up of the modern machine, you can manufacture five times, ten times, in some fields perhaps 100 times as many goods per man employed as you could 25 or 50 years ago.

So nowadays, if you want to cut wages in any plant, any industry, if you want to lengthen hours to speed up the work, keeping the workers always keyed up to an intense pitch, breaking down the nerve force, breaking by persistent speeding the spirits of men and women, it is easy. Are there not thousands of men waiting for jobs outside the factory gates?

I am a worker in a factory, you come to me. Being my boss, you tell me. "You will have to take another cut. Your hours will have to be lengthened, etc." There I stand by my machine. I turn my head and look out a window into the street. There are all of those other men and women standing down there in the street by the factory gate, unemployed men with families. Do I take what you, my boss, choose to give me? I usually do.

This happens not only in industry. In my own country, in the South, in Virginia, I am told there are farm laborers now glad to get work at 50 cents a day.

I remember what a man said to me a short time ago. I was on a train and talking to this man. I knew him. He was a large manufacturer. "You are a writer, Anderson," he said. "You write stories and novels, books, etc.?"

"Yes."

"Well," he said, "I could not do that. I could not write any books. Do you want to know why?"

"Yes, I would like to know."

"Because," he said, "I could not go on talking like that—what it would take you a whole book to say I could say in two words."

I was telling a friend about this. "Sure, he could," my friend said. "He could say, 'You're fired.'"

So you have got labor driven into a corner now subdued, defeated.

Occasionally something breaks out—a strike. Were you ever in on one? The experience is something never to be forgotten. There are these men, the workers, in a machine age, all controlled by a few men up above—far, far up above, by men who perhaps never visit the factory. Oil controlled absolutely by men who never drilled an oil well, soap controlled by men who never made a pound of soap. The same with food, all kinds of foods, with steel, with textiles. Do you think that farmers, who raise our food, have any control over the food they raise? It is to laugh.

You workers are caught down under there. Suddenly, with your fellow workers, you strike. Something runs through a shop. A surprising number of our strikes nowadays are like that. They are operatic, unexpected, often uncontrollable.

A kind of tremor runs through a plant, or mine. There are cries and shouts. The workers pour out. Meetings are held. Something happens. These little individual units the individual workers, lost down there in that amazingly beautiful and terrible thing—the modern world of the machine—these units, so tied, so bound to the machines, suddenly fly off the machines.

Why, it is something uncanny, something to the onlooker a little strange.

There are these units, tied thus to the machines. If you go nowadays much into great modern factories, you cannot escape the feeling that men and women in industry are in a queer new way tied, bound, to their machines. They seem to have become a part of the machines.

It is, I say, strange to see them fly off thus, separate themselves even temporarily from the machines. It is even pathetic this little struggle of individual men and women to free themselves a little, go again toward one another, touch, feel for each other, in this strange new machine world we have made.

Men come out into the light, into the open. Words long suppressed come to the lips, hand touches hand.

"You here, Jim, and you, Fred, and you, Joe? You are going to stick, to fight?"

"Yes, by God."

"And you—Maude and Helen and Kate."

A strange new sense of brotherhood, of sisterhood.

"Do you think we have a chance?"

"Yes. Yes."

Hope, fight.

"What the hell can we lose? Our lives? Hell, they've got our lives."

Light coming into dull eyes, hope into brains dulled by long years of toil. Men are marching now. They are singing. The strike is a marvelous thing. Win or lose it is a marvelous thing.

There is this sense of brotherhood come back, shoulder touching shoulder, at last in these lives a period of aliveness and of hope, of warmth, of brotherhood in struggle.

Ask any man who has been to war. Did he get anything out of it? Ask him. Did he get new hatred of his so-called enemy?

Never. I'll tell you what he got, if he got anything. He got flashes of a new sense in men—the sense of brotherhood. He got that or he got nothing.

Why the strike is like that to workers. In these days usually it doesn't last long. The same brains that have organized all of this big strange new thing in our world, modern industry, have also organized the means of crushing these outbreaks.

That is a machine too. The machine that crushes these new hopes. How deftly, how powerfully, it is organized. It has organized the press, the schools, the churches, the preachers, pretty much the whole middle and professional classes of lawyers, doctors, merchants, salesmen, newspapers, newspaper reporters, editors of newspapers. It has pretty much got them all.

As for the politicians. It is shameful to mention it to a crowd of intelligent people, it is so obvious—I mean the organization, the control of our modern so-called public men, by the machine, by money, by the money brains that control the western world now.

And all of this for what?

Who is served by it? I mean by this modern crushing organization of modern society? Has it been built up to serve an aristocracy men and women of blood lines, an intellectual aristocracy—an aristocracy of taste, of refinement? Are there gods nowadays walking the earth who must be served by all of the rest of us, by the common man or woman, by his brains, by his talents? Are these new gods, specially refined; intelligent, kind and thoughtful beings? Are they themselves even served by it? Are they made happier, are their children better off, are they better off?

Why they are caught and held by the machine as we are.

Are they special men, specially endowed by some strange god?

Why no—none that I have seen.

Who is served?

A refiner of oil.

A maker of steel.

A soap maker.

A hog killer, out in Chicago.

A weaver.

A money changer.

What, all of this for these men?

Money brains.

Soap brains.

Wheat brains.

Shoe brains.

Clothing brains.

This beautiful new majestic thing in the world, the machine, now crushing millions of people under its iron heels, this thing that sprang out of the brain of men, out from under the cunning fingers of men—this thing all for these men.

Soap brains.

Wheat brains.

Coal brains.

Shoe brains.

Money brains.

Is that what our people came to America for? Was it for this we built all of our railroads, cut down the forests, opened up the land, conquered the sea, conquered the air—that these men, with specialized kinds of brains, meat brains, oil, soap, shoe, iron, coal, money brains . . . was it all only to set up a new kingdom for these?

Why, I will tell you something. There is something wrong. We men and women of our day are in a strange, an odd position. Do you know what I think is wrong? We are, all of us, men and women living on one world while we think and feel, most of us, in an old and an outworn world. We are living on one world while we try to think and feel in another. Do you wonder there is confusion?

There is a new world. It is here. It is a machine world. I do not believe there is anything wrong with the machine. Often it is a beautiful, a powerful, a strange and lovely thing in the world.

It has got out of our hands. We are not controlling it now. It has really frightened us, unnerved us. We are in a time of transition now, men and women passing out of one world into another. Beyond a doubt, before we again get into the clear, out of the fog of fear and hatred we are now in, out again into an open road where we can go forward, if it is in us to go forward, before that, beyond a doubt new forms of government will have to be made, new kinds of cities built, there will have to be new kinds of agriculture, new kinds of control in every department of life.

Well, and so, what of it?

Are we afraid? Is that what makes us so cruel to one another just now? Of course we are afraid!

We are afraid of one another. Millionaires are afraid, workers are afraid, merchants, doctors, lawyers, school teachers, preachers, newspaper writers and publishers—almost without exception we are all afraid. Fear is what is ruling now in Harlan, Kentucky.

This meeting is being held here today to voice a certain protest. Something has happened in the life of a certain community in the State of Kentucky. It did not happen because it was Kentucky. It might have happened in California, in Florida, in Maine. The ordinary man or woman who lives now in Harlan, Kentucky, is not a different sort of man or woman from one who lives in Chicago, in New York, in San Francisco, in Kalamazoo.

There is just a town in Kentucky, sunk yet in an old world, living, thinking, breathing, feeling in an old world and by an odd chance confronted suddenly by a new world. That is all.

And there is something else. There are certain individuals here confronted with something too. There is Mr. Dreiser here, Mr. Dos Passos, and these other men and women.

Now look—this is what happened. There were all of these cries, rumors, tales of brutal things being done down there. There was a strike. Why no one in America is alarmed much by communism in Russia. That is far away. Our newspaper cartoonists have fixed it all nicely for us. We can think of Russians, of the Russian people as something strange, as far away, as not quite human.

The Russian is a great bewhiskered brute. He is dirty and heavy. He scratches himself and out jumps a Tartar.

But what is a Tartar?

Oh, he is a kind of a wild and lousy cowboy on a horse who dashes through streets, tramping children underfoot.

All a little savage, a little wild, a little crazy.

This in spite of Turgenev, Chekov, Tolstoy, Dostoevsky, Gorky, Gogol, Russian painting, Russian dancing, the Russian theater, all tremendously civilizing influences—all coming out of Russia.

Well, it's all right, I guess. Does not the average European think of us Americans as all rich, all riding in high-priced auto-

mobiles, throwing money about, living in palaces? You ought
to know how true the picture is.

So there was all this ugliness down there in Harlan, Kentucky. Newspaper reporters going down there, to find out if
all the stories told were true, were beaten and driven out of
town. The mine owners had got their hired gunmen in there.
You ought to know about that in New York. Chicago knows
about it. There was apparently a reign of terror.

Well, what about it? Were the working people of that community being terrorized, thrown into ugly little jails, beaten,
was Harlan, Kentucky, really being made into a kind of Siberian
penal camp, under the old Tsars?

It was a fine question. Would some one go out there and
find out?

Mr. Dreiser did not want to go. Mr. Dos Passos did not
want to go. Why, I know this type of man. I'm one of them
myself.

I know what these men want. Mr. Dreiser is a story teller.
He is a man who had never sought and does not want the
limelight. He wants to wander about talking to people, to
workers, to millionaires, to merchants. He wants to go talk
with women. He is a story teller. He has a tremendous searching constant hunger in him to find out about lives.

It gnaws at him, bites at him, will not let him alone.

Dreiser has been that way all of his life. He wants the truth
about people. He is tender about people. When something
hurts some one it hurts him too. He doesn't want to be that
way. It would be much more comfortable for him if he was
indifferent, self-satisfied, could take life merely as a game, play
to win.

Why this is a grand chance for me, as another American
writer, to say something about my friend Theodore Dreiser.
I myself began writing after Theodore Dreiser did. I guess
you all here know what has happened to American writing.

It is like this. As soon as a man here, in America, shows some
talent as a writer they pounce down on him. They want to buy
his talent.

They usually do too, I'll tell you that.

So they offer him money, position, security.

All he has to do you see is to corrupt slightly everything he does.

They want to make a clever man of him, a cunning little twister of words and ideas, soiling his own tools, going crooked you see, selling the people out.

Oh, it's nice, some of the implications of being a successful writer in this country.

You don't even have to lie. You can just keep still. Shut your eyes.

So Dreiser wouldn't do that. He had a curious hunger for truth. He was in love with truth. They say he is an immoral man. By the gods, it's true. He has been blatantly, openly, immorally in love with truth all of his life. He has fought for her. He has fought for her, coaxed her, put his hands on her, raped her.

He hasn't let the magazine editors run him, the publishers tell him how and what to write. He hasn't written any leg shows for the movies. Most of his life he has been poor. Long after he was famous he was poor.

And what did that mean? Let me tell you what it means to American writers. I know.

Let us say that the average young American writer comes from a poor family. Most of them do. I don't know why. They are lucky if they do. They may get a little real education that way. My Heavens, if the average American millionaire knew what, in accumulating his millions, sweating it out of working people, scheming and lying and cheating often enough to get it, if he knew what he was doing to his own children, to his own sons and daughters, how he is cutting them off from real contact with life, from real education, dwarfing them (the daily newspapers ought to tell him that story but he won't see it) if he knew he would be the first man to throw his millions into the river and go Bolshevik. . . .

Why there is something in being of the proletariat too. I was one once. I was a common laborer until I was 24 or 25

years old. I swear I would have been a better artist, a better
story-teller now if I had stayed there. I might then have had
something to say here as coming up out of the mass of people,
out of the hearts of common everyday people, out of poor
farmers and poor factory hands, always growing in numbers in
this country. I say that if I had stayed down there, never tried
to rise, had earned my bread and butter always with the same
hands with which I wrote words I might have had something
real to say with the words I wrote.

Mr. Dreiser has stood out against this, against the corruption of American writers with money, with promises of social
distinction, with all the subtle promises that can be given such
men. He has stood out. He has been honest and fearless. He
was the first downright honest American prose writer.

Do you think that has not meant a lot to the rest of us? It
has meant everything.

So there is Mr. Dreiser. He is naïve. He has never had
success enough to make him smart, make him clever. Why I
have been called naïve myself. I remember coming to New
York once, some years ago. It was after prohibition so I was
invited to a cocktail party. I went.

A certain well-known American critic came up to me. He
staggered up. Well, he was drunk. "I don't like your work,"
he said. "You're too naïve."

"Oh, yes? You think so?"

"You are naïve. You believe human life amounts to a damn.
It don't amount to a damn," he said.


And so there was this Harlan, Kentucky, situation. The eyes
of the whole country had become focussed on that little spot.
It had become a little ugly running sore, workers being beaten,
women thrown into jail, American citizens being terrorized,
newspaper men trying to investigate, being shot and terrorized.
When you have got a disease inside the body it has a nasty
little trick of breaking out in little sores of that sort.

So it was thought some one—a body of men and women
of more or less authority—should go down there to investigate,

to find out the truth, if possible. Why, Mr. Dreiser did not want to go.

And here let me step aside a moment to say something. I was recently, since this Dreiser thing came up, at a certain American College. I had gone there to talk about country newspapers.

So I was in a room afterwards with half a dozen young American men—fine young fellows too, two or three of them on the college football team, one of the famous teams of the country, and we were talking. The boys spoke of Mr. Dreiser.

"Why did he go down there?" one of them asked, and another answered, "Oh, I guess he wanted some publicity."

Ye gods. Even in the young. Refusal to believe any man can do anything for clean reason. Taking it for granted that men of the artists' class are also business men, thinking always and only of money, publicity, what is called fame. A man of Mr. Dreiser's world reputation, and an honest artist, being put instinctively on the footing of some little publicity grubbing movie actor. It makes your flesh creep to think of it. We pay through the nose for our glorious American money civilization, now don't we?

When it comes to Harlan, Kentucky, Mr. Dreiser and the others who went down there with him went as a last resort.

Others were publicly asked to go. There was a call sent out. Men of prominence in the educational world, college heads, statesmen, so called, humanitarians. There was a long list of big names.

Not a man would go.

They all got sick suddenly, or they had appointments, or their sisters got sick, or they had a cousin coming to visit.

It was a hot spot, you see. They all wanted to keep nice and cool.

And then too, the word had gone out that some one might get hurt.

But there is something more than this. We, in America, are in a queer time. It is a speak-easy generation.

You will find this sort of thing everywhere now. They will talk to you in private.

Why, there are some men like that Judge down in Kentucky, that prosecuting attorney down there. I know a lot of such men.

Sometime ago I was in the South, in another town when a strike was going on. It is always the same story. The company whose plant is being struck employs what they call a detective agency, to guard the property. I'll tell you they do a lot more than guard it. They are strong-arm men, thugs, racketeers. It is the business of these men to make trouble.

Why? I'll tell you why. Once you have made trouble, set off a few sticks of dynamite, the soldiers may be brought in.

It's easy after that. Now you get an injunction against picketing, against parading, against what they call, "unlawful assembly." It's a line-up, isn't it? The United States Government, the courts, the whole middle-class, the newspapers, the churches, the state governments, county government, and to round it off these hired gunmen—all of these against what? Against a few miners with their blackened eyes or a few pale, consumptive cotton mill workers.

In this court to which I went a few tired men and women, confused as such people always are when confronted with what we call "the majesty of the law," in that big strange room— I'll never forget their confused faces—so they were being tried for what was called, "unlawful assembly." They had gone into a vacant lot. They hadn't any permission to go into this vacant lot. They were gathered together there, huddled together, talking.

If I remember correctly they even had resisted arrest. A woman had, I believe, scratched the deputy sheriff's or a soldier's cheek. Some frightened mill hand had cursed. So they had been dragged into court. A jury had tried them. While the jury was out in that case the judge went into his chamber. I followed him in there. I had been curious about this thing. I introduced myself. We had cigarettes. We talked. Why I believe Theodore Dreiser who is accused of what is called criminal syndicalism, is also accused of being a communist. He isn't, any more than I am. He couldn't be if he wanted to be. They wouldn't have him. As I understand it the Communist Party is a working class party. Mr. Dreiser belongs to another class, the class to which I have the honor of belonging—the artist class. Why, I do not know nowadays whether it is or is not an honor to belong among us. As a class nowadays, we have become as weak-kneed, as money-hungry, as afraid to speak out as most of the men of the press, the church, the courts and the schools.

If you think Mr. Dreiser a communist, you should have heard the conversation in that judge's chamber that day. You see the door was closed. We were alone in there. That judge thought the coming of communism absolutely inevitable. He said so.

Then he went right out and sent those men and women to jail for unlawful assembly. There you are.

You find it among college professors, preachers, school teachers, men in the offices of big companies, you find it everywhere.

I do not know how many newspaper men and women I know personally. A good many. Perhaps fifty, perhaps a hundred, perhaps two hundred. But this I do know. In private conversation, over a drink, in a speak-easy almost to a man they are what is called radical. The profession, everything considered is miserably paid. A clever advertising writer will make four times what even a first-rate reporter makes.

But the radicalism is usually all private. It is private almost everywhere. It is under the rose. In public—in the public prints —well, you know what happens.

It is characteristic of our whole American attitude just now —that is what I am trying to say. We are a speak-easy country. That is what makes me glad for Theodore Dreiser. That is what makes me glad for these young communists. Why, a friend of mine down South asked me recently—"What is the difference between a Communist and a Socialist?" he asked me. I couldn't tell him the technical difference. I didn't know. I am myself a story teller, not a political economist. "I don't know," I said. "I guess the Communists mean it."

So there you are. Mr. Dreiser and these other people have had the nerve and the manhood to go down there into Kentucky, when there is apparently this reign of terror. They went openly and only after other men and women had refused to go. What they found there I will naturally leave for them to tell. They went there and asked questions. Mr. Dreiser made no speeches. He doesn't make speeches. He wanted, the others wanted, to call public attention to what was going on. He wanted truth. And then too, he spoke aloud in a speak-easy country. He said in public what millions of Americans are thinking in private.

For that he is accused of criminal syndicalism.

So that's what criminal syndicalism is? I am glad to know. Now I know at last what is the matter with this country. We need less speak-easy citizens and more criminal syndicalists.

And they say Mr. Dreiser is immoral. He has loved women. Isn't it terrible? When it comes to Mr. Dreiser's immorality— Do you remember the story of Abraham Lincoln and General Grant? Why, there it was. It seems General Grant drank whiskey. So that upset the preachers. A delegation of them went to Abraham Lincoln. They told on Grant. "Horrors. He drinks whiskey."

"What kind?" asked Abraham, "what brand? I'd like to know," he said. "I'd like to give it to some of the rest of my generals."

Why, that is all I have to say here. There is this accusation of criminal syndicalism now standing against Mr. Dreiser. They would like to take him to Kentucky, try him down there, throw him into prison. Well, I have just this to say. That if they can do it, if they do it, it will be the shame of all decent American writers if they do not to a man go out at once and commit criminal syndicalism. They ought to find out how it is done and go and do it. They ought to go to jail with him.

It is time for writers, college professors, newspaper men, for every one who has the public ear to speak out. As for the communists, if there is any little vestige of freedom left in the country they should be allowed to speak and agitate too. They may have found the true solution to our economic difficulties. I don't know.

I think the writers of this country ought to quit pandering. It is a troubled time, an uncertain time. I think we writers ought to quit thinking so much of money and fame and social position and safety and line up with the underdogs.

That's why I'm here. I don't like public meetings and public speaking. I'd rather be in a quiet hole somewhere, bent over a desk or going about quietly, talking to people.

I'm here because I think that Mr. Dreiser has got a rotten deal. What he has done has been twisted in some places into something it wasn't at all. I think the press, the pulpit and all of us are to blame. As I said before, I think that if they can take Mr. Dreiser out there to Kentucky and try him in that court for criminal syndicalism then we ought all to begin committing criminal syndicalism as fast as we know how to do it. I don't believe we ought to be satisfied or condemned to live all of our lives in a speak-easy country.

# A HEARING IN WASHINGTON

THE material in the following pages is a result of a hearing held before United States Senators Costigan, Cutting, and Logan, in Washington on Friday, February 12, 1932.

Mr. Waldo Frank had led an independent delegation of writers into the Kentucky mine regions for the express purpose of distributing food to the miners and their families there. With him were Malcolm Cowley, Edmund Wilson, Mary Heaton Vorse, Polly Boyden, Benjamin Lieder, Dr. Elsie Reed Mitchell, John Henry Hammond, Jr., Liston M. Oak, Quincy Howe, A. M. Max, and Harold Hickerson.

They were accompanied by Mr. Allan Taub, who previously had been retained as a lawyer for some of the miners indicted in Bell County. On his arrival in Pineville, he had been summarily arrested for Criminal Syndicalism. Later, during the visit of the writers' delegation, he had been expelled from the state.

The events which led to the kidnaping of the delegation by business men, armed mine guards, and deputy sheriffs, and the assault upon Mr. Frank and Mr. Taub, are revealed in the following pages.

At the time of the hearing before the Senators this book was already in type. However, the editors felt that the testimony at the hearing helped to give a complete picture of conditions in southeastern Kentucky. Although the demands of space and time have made necessary certain excisions from the testimony as given, these are confined to non-essential material—either statements concerning the personalities and occupations of the witnesses or their companions, or else repetitions of evidence already in the volume. Mr. Frank's testimony follows:

Mr. Frank. As the Chairman of this Committee, I would like to state, as succinctly as I can, what the Committee is and what happened to us. This will be a narrative, and I will make it as brief as possible. Then I presume the Senators will wish to ask questions, and the rest of the committee will enter into the discussion.

This committee consisted of writers, editors, journalists, doctors, and other professional people, and it had no existence before this little crusade into the mining fields. I presume it will have no existence after we get back to New York. The individuals making it up are of different political and intellectual faiths, although I presume all of us are closer to the left than we are to the right. However, so far as I know, none of us is in any way affiliated with the Communist Party.

Each member of this committee, individually, had been informed of the terrible condition of the striking miners in the Kentucky fields, and had been informed that the bringing in of food and other relief had been denied them. We individually were appealed to, were asked whether we would be willing to escort a number of trucks of food in, not merely to distribute this actual relief, but in order to establish the precedent of the right of individual American citizens to help other American citizens in the legal exercise of their right to live and to organize, if they wished, in order to be able to live.

Senator Costigan. Mr. Frank, the record should be made clear as to the reason for this meeting. It is true, is it not, that you or others associated with you, requested an opportunity to make this statement?

Mr. Frank. Yes.

Senator Costigan. You were not requested by the Senators who are here, to appear, but are appearing voluntarily for the purpose?

Mr. Frank. Yes.

Senator Costigan. For the purpose of advising us of certain experiences you have recently had?

Mr. Frank. Yes.

Senator Costigan. And we have appeared in response to the request.

Mr. Frank. Well, that being in the record, I will now proceed with what happened.

As soon as we reached Knoxville, we decided that our first visit in Kentucky would be to Bell County, of which the county seat is Pineville. We therefore informed the Mayor of Pineville, as well as the Governor of Kentucky of our purpose.

Senator Cutting. How long ago was this?

Mr. Frank. When was the date of this?

Mrs. Walker. We arrived in Knoxville—

Mr. Frank. When did you send the telegrams?

Mrs. Walker. Saturday.

Mr. Frank. Last Saturday. We got an answer immediately from the Mayor of Pineville, which I will read, with your permission:

"No objections your distribution of food. No public meetings allowed without permit from City authorities [signed] J. M. Brooks, Mayor of Pineville, Kentucky."

We received no answer from the Governor. We answered Mr. Brooks, the Mayor of Pineville, as follows, by telegram:

"Your telegram respectfully acknowledged stop In order to make distribution of food effective the striking miners must be able to come into Pineville and meet us stop We therefore expect a permit be granted for meeting called by local strike relief committee for purpose of receiving food. [signed] Waldo Frank, for the Independent Miners' Relief Committee."

We received an answer to that telegram from ourselves to the Mayor, the telegram from the Mayor, making his second telegram, reading as follows:

"Waldo Frank, Chairman, Independent Miners' Relief Committee. Positively no speeches, meetings, parades, or demonstrations of any kind will be permitted in Pineville tomorrow or at any other time by your committee or any other committee of this type stop Distributors of food will be given courteous treatment stop Food may be distributed only in camps outside of Pineville where you deem relief is necessary stop No relief from you or your committee is needed in Pineville."

We thereupon had a meeting of our Committee, and decided that since we had permission to come into Pineville to distribute food, it was unnecessary to communicate any further with the Mayor. We decided, however, that we had better clearly and concisely establish precisely what we were going in for, more precisely than heretofore, and we decided that we would go peaceably into Pineville and immediately read the statement to the Mayor so that he would understand. We, therefore, drew up this statement which I am going to put into the record now, although it was later read to the Mayor:

"We insist upon our rights, our Constitutional rights as American citizens, distributing relief to fellow American citizens, to come in personal contact with the striking miners, entering Pineville, their county seat, to meet us, and to hold meetings with them in such places as are not forbidden by city ordinance, in order (a) to learn of their situation, difficulties, and grievances, and (b) to confer with them on legal and equitable methods of relief distribution. [signed] The Independent Miners' Relief Committee."

We showed this, after consultation, to John Randolph Neal, a well-known constitutional lawyer in Knoxville, who told us that we were completely within our rights.

We then sent a second telegram to the Governor, as follows:

"Independent Miners' Relief Committee plans to go into Pineville tomorrow in accordance with program stated in previous telegram stop We would appreciate privilege of conferring with you Friday afternoon stop Kindly wire reply Pineville Hotel."

We then, on Wednesday morning, proceeded to Pineville. A few of us, including myself, who acted as the spokesman, went ahead of the trucks, arriving in Pineville at about one o'clock. We sought the Mayor, who is a dentist, and asked him for an interview. He told us he was busy for an hour, at the end of which time he would see us. We explained that we wanted to see him before the trucks came in, so as to avoid any possible trouble, and persuaded him to see us in twenty minutes, which he said was necessary in order to get rid of his patient, at the hotel.

At the end of twenty minutes, our advance committee went to the hotel, where we found Mayor Brooks, together with about twenty-five citizens, to whom we were introduced. They consisted, so far as we could make out, of lawyers, coal operators, and other leading citizens of the town.

Senator Costigan. Who were the members of your committee?

Mr. Frank. The members of our committee who had come in advance, were Dr. Elsie Mitchell, Edmund Wilson, Malcolm Cowley, and myself. Before the end of this meeting, however, I think several other members had come in.

Senator Costigan. Were the persons mentioned by you all residents of the City of New York?

Mr. Frank. I think we all are. All these four who came in in advance are residents of the City of New York.

To make a long story short, and only to mention the essentials, we read this statement to the Mayor, making it clear, however, that we were not going to insist on having our Constitutional rights, but we were merely going to assert them, and that we would obey all orders by the local authorities.

Our demands to have meetings in the city, or to distribute food in the city, were forbidden absolutely. We were also told that if there was any distributing of literature of any sort, or any attempt to get in contact with the miners in the city in any way, either to speak with them or to give them food, we would be immediately arrested. The meeting ended with certain threats which are of no importance.

I then asked whether we could meet the miners outside of the city limits. We were told this was in the hands of County Attorney Smith. We therefore went immediately to the office of County Attorney Smith, who at once received us. We again explained who we were, and the gist of our meeting, and after a long conversation were told we could distribute the food outside of the city limits. As to the question of whether we could meet and confer with the miners, County Attorney Smith said that he was not certain about that. He did tell us, however, that any speeches which were inflammatory would result immediately in arrests. I asked him to give us an example of what he meant by inflammatory speeches. Since he hesitated, I said, if any miner said to us that he had been interfered with in the receiving of food by gun thugs, would that be considered inflammatory, and County Attorney Smith said, Yes, that that would be considered an inflammatory speech.

We left him and immediately afterwards he came out into the street and told us that he had decided that no speeches could be made, even outside he city limits. In the meantime, we had discovered that the trucks had come into the town, had been boarded by deputy sheriffs and the local police officers, paid by the operators and the town, and that the trucks had been run out of the city at once.

Testimony was given at this point by Benjamin Lieder, a news-reel photographer. He told among other things how "an accredited Paramount news-reel photographer was denied permission to make a photographic record of events"; how the food trucks were shunted to a mud road where the distribution of relief began, the miners and writers "practically surrounded by deputies." He testified too that "there was no disorder until a deputy began heckling one of the miners. 'If you will come down here,' the testimony records the deputy as saying, 'I'll show you. . . .' The deputy then drew his gun and ran forward to the front of the trucks toward the striker. He was joined by several other deputies, who with drawn guns pushed aggressively through the crowd." Mr. Lieder notes that "during the confusion no miner offered any resistance whatever." It was at this point that Harold Hickerson, a writer and a member of the Committee, and Doris Parks, a relief worker, were arrested and

taken to jail. The rest of Mr. Lieder's testimony is concerned
with the actual kidnaping, described elsewhere, and with an
account of the beatings of Waldo Frank and Allan Taub and
the confiscation of motion-picture and camera films.

Mr. Frank. Now, while this was going on, we had been having our conversation, first with Mayor Brooks, then with County Attorney Smith, and
as we came out from Mr. Smith's office, I learned of the meeting and of
the arrests. Mr. Smith, as I said, joined us in the public square. We told
him we were sorry this had happened, that we had no intention of in any
way disobeying orders, but that these orders that there should be no
speeches had come too late for us to have any control over what happened
outside. Mr. Smith said he understood and knew that this was not our
fault, and assured us that we would get complete protection in every way.
I again assured him, as I had assured the Mayor, that although we felt
our Constitutional rights had been flouted, that we intended to obey
strictly the orders of the local authorities, because our purpose was to learn
whether our Constitutional rights were going to be honored, and not to
insist on them against local authorities.

The end of the scene out at the trucks is as follows:

All of us went out there, and while there, we managed to sustain order,
although there was constant pressure on the part of the deputies and of
their henchmen, on me and on the other members of the committee, to
make trouble, and to get us to hand the relief, the food, out to them. It
was getting dark and we decided that we could not stay for the rest of the
work to be done. We decided that since the miners were in considerable
force, and since the distribution was going on peacefully, that we could
leave. We therefore left just about dark, and called a meeting of our
committee.

We learned afterwards from a miner, whose name was Mason, that
almost immediately after we had left, the deputies brought out their guns
and took over what remained, which was not much, of the relief food.
Frank Mason estimated that about 150 pounds were all that was left. This
food was confiscated by the deputies and handed out to their own henchmen.

As soon as we left we were accosted by the sheriff and his men, who
told us we must go to the police court and have our suitcases searched for
literature. This was done and all of our literature was taken away from
us, we being assured we would get it back in perfect condition the following day.

We then all went to the hotel, and I think immediately after dinner, a few of the committee went to the jail to visit the one member of our committee who had been arrested, Hickerson, and the various relief workers, who were in jail there. We stayed with them a few minutes, being very courteously treated by the jailer, and then we went back to the hotel and called a meeting. We decided at that meeting that we had established in Pineville all that we had come for.

Senator Costigan. You called a meeting of what?

Mr. Frank. Of our committee, and we decided at the meeting that we had established in Pineville all that we had come for, namely, that our Constitutional rights were not to be honored.

We decided therefore that the following day half of our committee would purchase another truckload of food for Harlan, while the second half went around the mining camps to speak to the miners out in the outlying country. We had decided, in other words, to do nothing further in Pineville in any way, but to accept the decision of the local authorities, although we were convinced that these decisions were contrary to our rights as American citizens, and to the rights of the miners as American citizens.

The meeting broke up at about ten-thirty. Prior to its breaking up, one member of the committee left to visit an outlying hospital where a miner was lying who had been shot that morning, and was supposed to be in a dying condition.

We broke up and the two ladies had retired. I stayed behind a few minutes with the other men, and then also decided to retire. I think Cowley had retired in the meantime, and, on my way to my room in the half-darkened hall, I found a number of men who were obviously waiting for me. I did not like their looks and therefore decided I had better not face them alone, and so quietly walked back to the committee room. They called out to me to stop, and, since they said nothing about the law, I did not stop. I went into the committee room and had no sooner gotten into it, where Quincy Howe and Edmund Wilson and several others were, than there was a knock on the door and the deputy sheriff came in and informed us that we were under arrest.

I asked to see the warrant, which was shown to me, and found that all of us were under arrest on the charge of disorderly conduct. I said to the deputy, "Do you know what this is about?" They said, "We know nothing about it, but come ahead down to the police court." They were very courteous and very friendly. We had no difficulty with them, and they had no difficulty. In fact, there was a good deal of joking about this. We did not pack our suitcases, but went and got out overcoats and hats, and in the meantime the two ladies were awakened, and within a half hour we were all filing across the village square to the county court house, in the basement of which was the police court. When we got there, we found the court full of men, most of whom were deputies, and there was a crowd of people outside.

To make a long story short, when the judge came—oh, yes, Allan Taub, who was not a member of our committee, but was a lawyer representing the International Labor Defense, was also arrested and went with us. He was the one lawyer in our group, and got up as our spokesman and demanded a local attorney. This was granted, and the local attorney, Mr. Stone, soon joined us. As soon as the court was called to order, the, I suppose, prosecuting attorney, moved that the warrant be quashed for lack of prosecution. Those were his exact words. This was granted, and thereupon Mr. Taub got up as one of our attorneys—he had not been our attorney before, but he constituted himself with our permission our attorney on the moment—he got up and asked that we be granted safe conduct back to the hotel. This was granted us. The purpose of Mr. Taub in doing this was doubtless that there was a large crowd outside, and he wanted to be sure that we would be safe.

Nothing further was said of any sort, and there was no passing of words, beyond what I have exactly stated to you. We were informed that the warrant against us, the charge against us, of disorderly conduct, had been quashed, and that we had been granted safe conduct back to the hotel, so we filed out again with the deputies at our side, and into the lobby of the hotel.

In the lobby of the hotel, there were a number of citizens of Pineville, and, as soon as we got in, we were informed brusquely to pack our suitcases, that we were going to be run out of the state. From now on, I can only speak for myself, because from this moment until the end I had no opportunity to speak with a single other member of our committee. I was unable to see any of them. I spoke to a man whose name I do not know, and I said, "Let me see our local attorney, Mr. Stone." I was told to shut up.

I then said, "Under what—by what right do you run us out of the State?" I was again told to shut up. I then said, "Let me confer with my fellow committee members." Thereupon, I was pushed upstairs and told immediately to pack my suitcase. As soon as I was in my room, the door opened and in came nine men who, I assume, were deputy sheriffs. One man was under the influence of liquor, and he said he was from Harlan. He began abusing me, and I immediately saw that the men behind him were on his side, and if I wanted to come out alive, I had better be quiet, so I did not open my mouth, but went and packed my suitcase. I was then taken downstairs with my suitcase, and was put into the dining room, where the other members of the committee and other men of the town were standing. I had no possibility even then of speaking to any of my group.

I was immediately taken by the arm by a man who said, "Here, you get into the car with Allan Taub." Allan Taub, as I said before, was not a member of our committee, and we had had no connection with him, except that we had met him there at Pineville in the office of the local attorney, Mr. Stone, whom we had met in the afternoon.

In our car were Mr. Taub and myself and the driver, and two other men. I asked the men who they were, and they said they were merchants. When we got to the border, which is at the top of what is known as the saddle of Cumberland Gap, the cars were stopped. At this place, right on the border, the road is very wide, and there is a place where evidently cars can be parked—I suppose for the convenience of people who wish to climb up to the pinnacle. It is sort of a sight-seeing place.

The cars were grouped together there, and I noticed, although it meant nothing to me at the time, that the car in which Allan Taub and myself were, was on the periphery of the group of fourteen cars. This, however, meant nothing to me at the time.

As soon as the cars had stopped, several voices rang out, "Put out the lights." Immediately all the lights were put out, and we could observe, because there was some dim light there, it being a clear night, that most of the men were getting out of the cars. Our three escorts got out of our car. I said to them, "Shall we come too?" They said, "Stay where you are." So, Taub and myself remained alone in our car in the dark. We remained there perhaps a couple of minutes and then some one came back to our car, but I cannot swear that the man that came back was one of the three men who were in our car as our escorts, because, after all, I did not know these men, and could only recognize one of them who sat next to me. He said, "Get out." I got out first and walked a few steps. As soon as I had done so, and had gotten a few feet away, I heard a yell of pain, which I immediately assumed was from Allan Taub, and instantly after this yell of pain, I myself was attacked from the back. At no moment did I see my assailants. Blows were rained on me, I do not know how many. All I remember is one severe blow that hit me on the back of the head. No one hit me from the front. While the blows were being given, voices were saying, "Will you ever come to Kentucky again?" "You will know enough to stay out of this state," etc. This blow on the head was the last one, I think. It stunned me, but I was not unconscious. I assumed everybody was being beaten up. However, the blows stopped and I was glad to see I was still alive, and when I came back to my senses, I heard men yelling, "What is this? They have been beating each other up. What does this mean?" and other vague remarks of that sort. A man came up and said, "What have you been doing, you and Taub, have you been having a fight?"

Some one yelled, "Switch on the lights," and they were switched on. A man came up to me threateningly, "So this is it, you and Taub have been trying to get us into trouble. You have been having a fight." I said, "Beat me up or kill me, but you won't make me admit anything of that sort. You know I was beaten up," and there were words of that sort.

That is more or less the end of the story, except that we were then all gathered together and our suitcases were searched for films, and the party then left us, with, as a parting shot, "Now, you can listen to a speech on Constitutional law from Lawyer Taub." Whereupon, we proceeded to go down the hill where we met a couple of boys in a car coming from a dance. They took us in, since we had no car of our own, and so we got down to the bottom of the hill.

Now, that is the story, and of course—although the climax of it was that a couple of us were beaten up—I want to assure you gentlemen, from our standpoint, that this is the least important part of the story. We invited this sort of thing, and we can feel very lucky we were not worse treated. I hope this episode of one or two of us having been thugged will not make anybody lose sight of what still remains, the main purpose and the main idea for our visit and our motive, in coming to you, and presenting this thing to the people of the United States, namely, that we, as a peaceful group of citizens, had come into a state of our own union in order to help the citizens with whom we are in sympathy, in view of the fact that they are struggling, we are convinced, for life and for decent living conditions, legally struggling by means of an organization of their own choosing and of their own kind, and we discovered that in order to distribute this relief, and in order to make possible the further distribution of relief, it was necessary for us peaceably to confer with these miners in a central place, the central place being logically the county seat of these miners; that our Constitutional rights were absolutely cynically flouted; that we were given no opportunity to meet with the miners, and were forcibly ejected from the state, in spite of the fact that we had assured the authorities that we were going to obey not only the laws, but their own orders; that we were peaceful, and had no intention of doing anything contrary to any order of any sort.

Now, perhaps I had better stop, and let you gentlemen speak—I want to add one other thing. We sent a telegram to the Governor appealing for him to sustain us, after we had been denied Constitutional rights. We sent it that night, and saying that silence on his part we would be forced to take as a tacit admission that he sustained the behavior of the local authorities of Pineville and of Bell County. We have received no answer from the Governor of Kentucky.

Senator Cutting. Mr. Frank, just what do you think that we, as United States Senators, can do under these premises?

Mr. Frank. Mr. Senator, I do not know. I feel that you know that better than we do, but I do feel this. We were convinced before we went in there that conditions of these miners were bad. The little contact that I have had with the miners convinced me that their condition is literally that of peonage. I know, as a student of Mexico, for instance, what the conditions of the Indian peons were in Mexico, before the revolution in 1910. I am willing to go on record that the condition of these American citizens working in the mines—so far as I know, the situation in Kentucky where we were is nearly typical—the condition of these American citizens is as bad as was that of the Mexican peons in 1910.

I feel that the United States, and that you as the Senators of the United States, should know about this. Whether something can be done about it, I do not know. I am not a lawyer. I am not an agitator. This is the first time that I have ever been in anything of this sort. I am a writer of books, and I am not equipped to do any more than to tell you the truth as I have spoken it.

At this point, Mr. Frank was asked for the titles of some of his books, and Mr. Liston Oak gave his eye-witness account of the kidnaping.

Mr. Frank. If I may add just one word, gentlemen, it is this—that you bear in mind the emergency which I feel we can state to be this: Here are a group of men who are literally being starved. Their resistance is being killed by terror and starvation, and it is perfectly clear that these local authorities are not going to permit any relief to come in there, except in their own hands, which means, of course, that they will distribute it in such a way as not to help the very men for whom it is proposed. In other words, here is a question of American citizens, who have been starved back into peonage, from which they have in desperation rebelled.

Mrs. Elizabeth Baldwin, whose husband, a striking coal miner, was shot and killed by Deputy Sheriffs, at this point described some of the conditions of a miner's life in Kentucky and the abduction and killing of her husband at the swimming pool near Harlan. This material is covered in full in the earlier portions of the book.

Senator Logan. Mr. Frank, I want to make this statement before asking anything, that I approach the subject absolutely impartially in asking for some information for the benefit of Senator Costigan and Senator Cutting. Probably I am more familiar with the situation than any of you who have just gone in there.

You went down to Kentucky, as I understand, because there was suffering and distress down there among families of the coal miners? Is that correct?

Mr. Frank. No, that is not correct. It is not a complete statement.

Senator Logan. The real reason then, was to test out, as you said awhile ago, the Constitutional rights that you thought you had to go there and do certain things.

Mr. Frank. I think we went there, not merely because of the suffering, although of course that was the basis of it. If we had merely been interested in alleviating suffering, we could have stayed in New York City.

Senator Logan. And found plenty of it?

Mr. Frank. Yes.

Senator Logan. A lot of babies there have not any milk?

Mr. Frank. I do not know about that, but at any rate there is plenty of suffering.

Senator Logan. Well, then, what was the real reason for your going to Kentucky?

Mr. Frank. I thought I—I tried to make that clear, that we went because the suffering that was going on in Kentucky was the result of a labor problem which interests us very much, that is, we were informed that the miners in Kentucky were suffering, were starving, were in a condition of peonage practically, and that they were attempting to alleviate and better their condition by organizing, and that their fight to organize in order to live was being fought by the preventing of relief being given to them, by the preventing of food coming in, and I think we went in especially in order to see if we could not open a way so that food could go into these men so that they could fight their fight.

Senator Logan. Do you think the condition is worse in those two counties in Kentucky than it is in certain districts in Pennsylvania?

Mr. Frank. Of course, I am no authority on that, Senator, but I, myself, was interested in this because I was convinced that the situation in Kentucky has in it the essence of a situation which may very well become national, and I think that is what interested us.

Senator Logan. The National Miners Union, to which you have referred, is not in affiliation with the United Mine Workers of America, is it?

Mr. Frank. I .can answer nothing except by hearsay. I have never had any contact, nor, so far as I know, ever talked with any—

Mr. Walker (interposing). I can answer that. There is not any connection.

Here Mr. Frank, questioned by Senator Logan about the relation between the National Miners Union and the United Mine Workers of America, referred the Senator to this voluue, which he stated would shortly be published.

Senator Logan. You do know that the question of Communistic doctrine seemed to be agitating some of those native Kentuckians there, about Pineville and Harlan, do you not?

Mr. Frank. Yes.

Senator Logan. And, the basis of their actions, as they claim, is with reference to the matter of Communism. Did you hear that?

Mr. Frank. Yes, I did. In ·fact, I asked some questions about that before I went, simply because I was interested, and was informed that the same type of oppressive methods had been applied against the United Mine Workers earlier.

Senator Logan. I understand, but now this National Miners Union, that is rather a radical organization, is it not?

Mr. Frank. I know nothing about it. But I understood it was radical in its leadership in the east. I do not know myself.

Senator Logan. It is closely akin to the Communists as far as the political beliefs are concerned.

Mr. Frank. As I told you, that is mere hearsay on my part.

Senator Logan. You know nothing about that particular phase of it?

Mr. Frank. So far as I know, I have never met any member of the union, except those that I met in Tennessee and Kentucky.

Senator Logan. Do you know whether the basis of all this trouble down there comes out of the fight between the United Mine Workers and the International Miners Union in the coal fields there?

Mr. Frank. Why, my understanding is that the National Union got its foothold because of the failure of the United to sustain a strike which was begun in the spring of 1931. Is that right?

Mr. Walker. Could I say a word on that?

At this point, Senator Logan asked Mr. Walker who were the members of the Dreiser Committee, and Mr. Frank gave some information about the personnel of Bell County sheriff's office.

Senator Logan. You mentioned a Mr. Smith. What type of man did Mr. Smith appear to be, the County Attorney?

Mr. Frank. What do you want?

Senator Logan. Did he appear to be a man of some education and refinement, or was he rough and uncouth and uneducated?

Mr. Frank. He was extremely courteous, and even courtly, I should say. He impressed me as being a man who had extremely good manners and a very fine manner.

Senator Logan. A young man, is he not?

Mr. Frank. Yes, he impressed me as being a very keen young chap.

Senator Logan. I know him very well. He is a brother of the United States District Attorney for that district. Did you meet Judge Jones, the Circuit Court Judge, in that district?

Mr. Frank. I met Mr. Van Beber. Since I am characterizing Mr. Smith, do you not think it fair to let me say something else?

Senator Logan. Yes.

Mr. Frank. I have given you so far a picture of his surface. He impressed me as being a very charming gentleman. I found we were members of the same fraternity, Phi Beta Kappa, and I said to him that I was sure we would get along very well if we met at a club. He impressed me as a man who was not his own master, who was completely given over to carrying out the commands, the set commands of the oligarchy, of the system which he represented. He impressed me in a word as being a man who had made up his mind to be as courteous with us as possible, whose mind was completely made up, and who, while courteous with us, would grant nothing—who had his orders and was determined to carry them out, those orders being, as I have told you, orders which made it impossible for us to do what we had come there to do.

Senator Logan. Did you discover the names of any of those who constitute the oligarchy down there?

Mr. Frank. Yes. I do not remember them, but Mr. Oak has them.

Mr. Oak. The names of those whom you visited?

Senator Logan. Mr. Frank mentioned an oligarchy down there, and I asked him if he knew the names of those who constitute the oligarchy in that country.

Mr. Oak. Some of them took us on the ride. Of course, I found it extremely difficult to get names. I tried to get names of coal operators who were present in the reception committee that Mayor Brooks organized to talk to us when we first entered the town, but no one would give me his name, and I could not find out who they were. I did get a few names, just a very few, besides Walter Smith, the County Attorney, and I got the name of Dr. Hoskins, and a man named Calvert, a lawyer who is attorney for the Straight Creek Coal Company, I was informed.

Senator Logan. That is right.

Mr. Oak. Some one gave me the name of Mr. Patterson, another lawyer, and attorney for one of the coal companies. But upon inquiry I found that he was not in Pineville at the time. I believe he was outside the state.

Mr. Frank. Several other men, speaking at the meeting, said they were operators.

Mr. Oak. I also met a Mr. Evans, editor of the local paper, and the Associated Press correspondent and Chairman of the local Red Cross, who was a member of the mob which kidnaped us—

Senator Logan. You mean Mr. Evans was a member of the mob?

Mr. Oak. Yes, he was a member of the mob and he said to Mr. Taub, while blood was streaming down Taub's face, just before they left, "Well, Taub, why don't you make us a speech on Constitutional rights? It is the last chance you will ever get to make a speech in Kentucky. After this you can make all the speeches you want to to the members of your committee, but we are tired of hearing about Constitutional rights."

Mr. Frank. May I say just one other word about this use of the word oligarchy? Let me tell you from my own standpoint that word is justified by our actual experience as follows: As I told you, the first thing we did when we got to the town was to see the Mayor and the Mayor refused to see us at that time, saying he was busy with a patient for an hour, and we eventually persuaded him to see us in twenty minutes. He said that was the least he could see us in because he was busy with a patient. He is a dentist. We wanted to wait in the office, but he said that we should go to the hotel, and he would meet us there. Now, all that we had done was ask to see him in order to give him a clear statement of what we wanted. In twenty minutes when Mr. Cowley and Mr. Wilson and Dr. Mitchell and myself got there, we found this large committee consisting of the leading citizens. It was perfectly obvious the Mayor did not want to see us alone, but wanted these men to be at the meeting. Moreover, the Mayor said almost nothing during the first forty-five minutes of the meeting. All the active talking was done by the other men, and the other men told us where we got off.

Senator Logan. That is what I am trying to get at. Who were those other men? I know most of those people there. You mentioned Mr. Patterson and Mr. Calvert. They are attorneys, right prominent attorneys.

Mr. Frank. Some of the most active ones in telling us where we got off, as it were, said they were coal operators.

Senator Logan. Do you have their names?

Mr. Frank. No, I am sorry.

Senator Logan. Who owns the mines now in operation down in that section? There are only a few in operation as I understand it. Did you come in contact with any of the Ashers?

Mr. Oak. A man by the name of Bob Asher was pointed out to me as one of the deputies, I believe, if I remember correctly. I would not be positive about that.

Mr. Frank. It was perfectly plain to me, Mr. Senator, and we as a matter of fact felt that we were going to have no trouble of any sort, and when Mr. Smith offered us guards at the hotel, I myself laughed it off and said, "No, we do not need guards at the hotel." We thought, since we had made it clear that we were in no position to insist on our rights, and were merely asking for our rights, and were going to take the orders of the authorities—we thought, in view of that, there was no possible danger, and I myself believed in the good faith of these men before I went. It. is a bad habit of mine, perhaps, but I do not disbelieve a man until I am forced to, and the whole proceeding was one amazement after another to me.

I have never in my life gotten a clearer impression than this, that the Mayor was an abject tool of these other men and of these interests, and that Mr. Smith was a more independent tool, but still essentially as abject.

Senator Logan. You mentioned a while ago that they knew the Bible. I want to disabuse your mind on one thing. You will find no followers of Thomas Jefferson in that entire section. They are all Republicans of the most ardent type.

Mr. Oak. I found that out. I said to Mr. Smith, "I presume you are a

Jeffersonian Democrat, and if so you have read what Thomas Jefferson had to say about Constitutional rights," and he said, "I do not believe in granting Constitutional rights to Bolsheviks."

Senator Logan. I do not know whether Bolsheviks would be more popular there or Democrats. I am an old-fashioned Jeffersonian Democrat. Politically, those people have always been opposing that in all matters down there, but the gentlemen you have mentioned, some of them, are as high-type citizens as we have in the state of Kentucky. I do not think there is any higher type than Mr. Patterson, whom you mentioned, and I am surprised and think there must be some mistake in identity also about Mr. Evans.

Mr. Taub. I met Evans, Patterson, Calvert, and all the leading officials of the town, as well as the attorneys for the coal operators, and I think I can relate to you without much comment a story that will be eloquent, and I am sure Mr. Patterson would not deny what I said, and what occurred. It is in the court record.

There follows here the testimony given by Mr. Allan Taub before Senators Logan, Cutting and Costigan, some two and one-half pages of testimony, which cover Mr. Taub's legal education and background.

Mr. Taub also testified that "I am an independent in politics and am not affiliated with any party. I was affiliated with the Democratic party, but now I choose the man I want to vote for whether he is affiliated with one party or the other."

Mr. Taub. I am only too glad to have questions asked, Senator, and I respectfully invite them, and I will respectfully answer them.

Senator Logan. I know nothing about their problems with regard to the Communist question, as they denominate it. I have read it in the newspapers in the last year, but I am not personally familiar with that angle of it. I do know this, and probably you have discovered it, that those people in eastern Kentucky are great people. Notwithstanding their politics, I must insist that there are no greater American citizens on earth, or on this continent, than our mountaineers in Kentucky. They are rather suspicious of anybody who comes from the outside, and they resent it very much. They think it is a reflection on their community and on them for people from New York City or anywhere else to come in and tell them what they ought to do, and I think you would feel the same if they came into your community.

I have nothing more to say just now.

Mr. Taub. Senator, I am very glad you brought up that question about the type of person, and the type of citizen one finds in Kentucky. Nothing, I am sure, that was said here was meant to cast any reflection on the people of the hills or the cities of the fair state of Kentucky.

As a matter of fact, I have dealt with the workers, the coal miners and others in Bell and Harlan Counties. I have been in Louisville, Lexington and Frankfort, and I say here frankly, that I have met no finer and cleaner and more peaceful type of citizens than I have met in the hills and cities of Kentucky, and this is no indictment against the people, the workers, the average run of men, women and children in the State of Kentucky. They rank as high as anybody else. The only issue we want to bring up is as to those who are responsible for a savage reign of terror among the coal miners, and for creating a condition of starvation which is absolutely incredible and is unprecedented in any country.

I want to go briefly into my experience, and I want to put myself very squarely on the record in the presence of all the newspaper men.

I am the attorney for the International Labor Defense. The International Labor Defense is what its name implies, a labor defense organization. . . .

Mr. Frank. The other Senators are going to read Mr. Taub's record very carefully. They are sorry some engagement takes them away, but they will read the record when it is typed.

Mr. Taub. The reason I asked them to be present is that I did not come in as an investigator, or a member of the committee, or of these two organizations. I came there as counsel, as a professional man, to carry out my duties, and I thought my testimony would be of especial interest to the other Senators, and yourself, Senator.

The International Labor Defense, as I have already said, is a labor defense organization that is not affiliated with any political party or religious sect. Its members are made up of Republicans and Democrats, and Independents, and Socialists, Communists, any other political party—prohibitionists will be accepted also, Senator Logan, and any religious denomination is accepted.

I left New York on January 5th, Tuesday, and on January 6th at four o'clock, within twenty-four hours after leaving New York, I was inside of the jail, the county jail, looking out of the bars.

I arrived in Pineville at two-twenty and walked. directly to Mr. Stone's office, and at two-twenty-five o'clock I was in Mr. Stone's office. Judge Stone is a local attorney who represents the International Labor Defense.

He has been retained to represent the defendants in Pineville, and Bell County generally.

I was with Attorney Stone from two-twenty-five until four o'clock, when, in his presence, and seated with him in the car, I was dragged out of the automobile by the chief of police of the city of Pineville. They produced no warrant of arrest, although I demanded that a warrant be produced, and I was led to the county jail located in Pineville, and as I was placed in the jail, the chief of police said, "Book him for criminal syndicalism," and I was in that jail for eight days.

Senator Logan. Without any warrant?

Mr. Taub. There was no warrant. I demanded to see a warrant several times, and I got in touch with the County Attorney and could not see the warrant. I demanded to find out what the bail was, or what law I had broken. All law had broken down. The Constitution and all rights were thrown out of the window. A lawyer had no standing. I was declared a felon, and was treated like a downright criminal after coming into that county as an attorney.

I was in jail until January 14th, that is, I was in jail eight days. I expected to face a stack of charges. The original charge of criminal syndicalism was changed to conspiracy to overthrow the United States Government in the State of Kentucky. Now, on January 14th, the date of my hearing, I did not know what to expect.

Senator Logan. Before whom did you appear?

Mr. Taub. I appeared before County Judge George Van Beber, and the prosecutor was Walter B. Smith, County Attorney. The case was scheduled for nine o'clock in the morning. It was postponed until one o'clock, and I was in court at one o'clock, and at one-thirty-five precisely, County Judge George Van Beber entered the court room, accompanied by Mr. Patterson, who turned out to be special prosecutor, and County Attorney Walter B. Smith. The County Attorney hastily made a motion to dismiss the charge against Allan Taub, the defendant, and the Judge said, "Motion granted. Court adjourned," and started to walk out. I arose and asked to be given an opportunity to make a statement to clear my name as an attorney. I had been in jail for eight days on a pretty serious charge, the most serious imaginable for a citizen, and particularly for an attorney. That motion was not granted, and as I left the court room, deputies on each side walked up to me, men whom I knew to be deputy sheriffs, and asked me how long I expected to hang around Pineville. One of them actually walked up to me and said if I hung around a week the chances were I would be a dead man. He was either a deputy or a friend of a deputy, standing with a deputy. That was on January 14th. Subsequent to that, I went to Frankfort, and entered my protest with the Attorney General of the State of Kentucky, Bailey B. Wootton. I related to him my experience, as an attorney, as a member of the Bar of New York, who had merely gone into Pineville to consult with local counsel. I told him that I had not gone to Pineville to take any cases away from local counsel, and in fact engaged local attorneys, and that I merely came to consult with them and offer any assistance that I could, having had some experience in other labor cases. Attorney General Wootton listened to the outline of my experience, and when I was through said, "There is nothing I can do." That seemed like a very surprising statement for the head of the legal department of the State of Kentucky to make, and I tried to see the Governor of the State, and I waited two hours, but was not granted an audience.

After the interview with the Attorney General, and my failure to see the Governor, I thought it was my right, in fact my duty, to go back and help these defendants who were in jail, and I tried to enter Pineville on Sunday, January 24th. As my taxi approached the city limits, seven armed men who carried high powered shot guns stopped my taxi. They recognized me at once, as I had been in jail eight days, and had been active in the hearings in court of the other defendants. They said I would have to wait, and they would check up and see if I could enter Pineville. They told me they would call the Mayor and I asked if I could speak to the Mayor myself, and explain who I was, and what my mission was in entering Pineville.

I spoke to a man who said he was the Mayor, and I explained to him I was an attorney who had been to Pineville, and now I was coming back to consult with Attorney Stone. He said, "Just wait there, and I will be out in a few minutes." In about five or ten minutes, two cars rolled out to the city limits, where I had been stopped by the seven armed men. Out of the first car came Mayor J. M. Brooks of Pineville, and the second man out of the car was the Chief of Police of Pineville, and behind him were ten men armed with sub-machine guns, high powered shot guns, automatic pistols and revolvers. They surrounded me. I was alone except for the taxi driver, and I told them again what my mission was, and that I wanted to enter Pineville. They said I could not enter Pineville, and I protested as an American citizen. I protested as a member of the Bar. They did not seem to get my point of view, and they said I could not enter Pineville, and Mayor Brooks pointed his finger specifically at me and said, "You cannot enter Pineville, and don't you dare come in on any road today, and if you want to come to Pineville, first call me up on the telephone, and then see me, and I will tell you whether you can come into Pineville."

Well, of course, there was nothing to do after orders like that and we turned our car around and left. I returned to Knoxville, Tennessee, which seemed to me the safest vantage point from what local miners told me.

On January 29th, after receiving several calls from defendants in person, and from local miners, to come in and assist local counsel on a writ of habeas corpus, I returned to Pineville. I had to ride all night long like a fugitive or felon, and to sneak into the City of Pineville, in the State of Kentucky, and I arrived there after five hours of riding in the dead of night, at six o'clock in the morning, and I had to surreptitiously go to the home of Attorney Stone, and I practically hid there until the certain hour when court convened. The house was watched to see that nobody was trailing my footsteps.

I remained in Pineville without asking the permission of the Mayor or anybody else to go in there, and I stayed there up until February 10th, the night of February 10th.

Now, on February 10th, I went to consult—

Senator Logan (interposing). That was the day before yesterday?

Mr. Taub. Yes. On the evening of February 10th, I consulted with the committee, of which Mr. Waldo Frank is the chairman, and found it necessary to remain at the hotel a few hours. I engaged a room there, and thought that I would hold consultations with various members of the committee, as any attorney would do. I had a conference with Attorney Stone and with one of the coal miners.

While sitting in this room, at about the hour of ten-thirty at night, about seven deputy officers walked into my room and told me I was under arrest. This was my second arrest. I was charged with disorderly conduct in a public place, and was told that I was only one of many defendants; that everybody else in the building who had come down as a member of the committee was now a defendant, so I was led out with the entire committee. It looked like an odd procedure.

Senator Logan. Well, you had company, did you not?

Mr. Taub. I certainly had plenty of company, but it looked very much as if this was not going to be a trial. I frankly thought that this was a night ride from the start, because I had been in and out of Pineville for five weeks, and this looked very suspicious, these seven deputies up on the third floor of the hotel getting us out at this hour of the night.

Senator Logan. Did you just have their word that they were deputies?

Mr. Taub. I knew some of them. I had seen them in court, and in and around the town.

I was then led to the police court from the hotel. While Mr. Frank has already gone into the details of this, I would not be doing justice to my clients or myself not to describe them, because I am an attorney and should speak these facts, and give an attorney's interpretation and explanation of them.

We were brought down to the police court and were surrounded in the court with deputies and officers. A warrant was shown to us, charging us with disorderly conduct.

Senator Logan. About what time was that?

Mr. Taub. That was about eleven o'clock. We stayed in that room until about eleven-fifteen, in the presence of Mr. Evans, the editor of the *Pineville Sun* and the head of the Red Cross in Bell County, and in the presence of Mr. Calvert, attorney for a number of coal companies, together with a number of coal operators, and a number of attorneys being present, I do not have their names, and in the presence of Judge Page.

Senator Logan. I did not get the name.

Mr. Taub. Judge Page. He finally ordered that everybody but the defendants and the officers be excluded from the court room, and this certainly was a violation of the rights which we as defendants had, because we had a right to a public trial, and then the windows and the doors were ordered shut, and it was a most amazing scene presented to me as an attorney, and I did not know what to expect at that time. I arose and demanded protection for all the defendants. As a matter of fact, Senator, a young fellow sitting in the court room reached for a cigarette and a 45-caliber pistol fell out of his pocket to the floor. I do not know whether that was accidental, or was done as a hint to us as to what to expect, and in that closed, darkened room—not dark, the lights were on—I did not know whether we were to expect a star chamber proceeding or a third degree beating.

Afterwards the special prosecutor, whose name I do not know, but who seemed to be a special prosecutor, rose and said that there were no charges to be preferred, and in view of the lack of prosecution, moved a dismissal of the charge, and the Judge said he would dismiss the charges.

This made the whole situation look more suspicious. I submit to you, Senator Logan, and any other gentleman of the United States Senate, I submit, what would you think of a situation like that, the defendants being brought out of a hotel in the dead of night with not a word said against them, charged with disorderly conduct in a public place, and then told to walk right out.

Senator Logan. Would you be kind enough to mention the names of any that you recognized that were present at that night meeting in the court room?

Mr. Taub. Yes. The Judge was Joe Page.

Mr. Frank. Mr. Calvert was there.

Mr. Taub. Yes, I mentioned that. Mr. Evans, head of the *Pineville Sun*, and head of the Red Cross in Bell County, the representative of the United Press and the Associated Press, in fact, the big mogul who sends out all information in Bell County, was there. I recognized Officer Jack Bingham, and I recognized Officer Walter Baker, and also Mr. Calvert, attorney for the Straight Creek Coal Company. Attorney Stone later came into the room. He only came in and was allowed in as we twice insisted on having local counsel present.

I am sorry I do not have the names of the others. Nobody would have liked to have the names more than I would.

Senator Logan. Was Walter Smith there?

Mr. Taub. I did not see Walter Smith. He was not there, I guess.

Mayor Brooks was in the adjoining room. I saw him as I came out. As the defendants were led out of the court room, I again insisted on protection for them, and placed the responsibility directly on the court. I went out and demanded the right to see the Mayor that time. It was very plain to anybody that foul play was about to take place, and men have to speak up at times. There are times when one cannot quibble. One must speak up.

This thing was planned and set. I saw Mayor Brooks in Judge Page's chambers, and I said, "I am putting it up to you, the entire responsibility. Are these defendants and myself going to be taken out for a night ride, lynched, or murdered? This is a procedure I have never yet seen in my legal training, in all my experience at the Bar in the State of New York, or any other State, and I have practiced in about eight States already." Mayor Brooks said, "You can just go out." I said, "We demand the right of protection, and I place upon your shoulders the responsibility of giving these men safe escort from the court house to the hotel." Well, he simply said, they would be protected. Finally, after these protests, they were accompanied out by officers. Two officers accompanied me, one of whom was Special Deputy or special police officer Jack Bingham, and they walked to the Pineville Hotel with me. While walking over, Mr. Evans accompanied me. He was always eager to accompany people who came into Pineville, to distribute relief or to represent defendants. He said, "Why don't you advise these people to get out of Pineville tonight. Tell them to go away." I said, "You have no right to make that request of them. They have a perfect right to be here as American citizens, and neither you nor anybody else can molest them or threaten them." He said, "You know feeling is running high." I said, "It is not running high with the miners. It is running high with you and with Calvert, and a handful of men, and you are starting this reign of terror, nobody else."

When we got to the hotel we were then advised again we ought to get out of town. While going up to our rooms a few minutes later, word was given to me to get my things and get out of town. I was told that all the other members of the committee, as well as myself, could get the hell out of town. I asked what was meant by that, and they said they would take us out of town. There was no use talking back at that time. The lobby of the hotel was crowded with deputy officers, special officers, with crowds of hangers-on, men obviously who were armed. The street was crowded outside of the Pineville Hotel. We were then led to the back of the hotel, and the officers specifically pointed to Mr. Waldo Frank and myself, Allan Taub, and said, "Take these men into one car."

That was a very definite procedure, and let it be set down now with all these letters and affidavits coming from Pineville. Let it be stated clearly that the officers said, "Take Waldo Frank and Allan Taub in the one car."

An officer held on to me as tight as he could. I was led into a car, and the driver of that car was Mr. Isaacs, a merchant of the city of Pineville. There were two other officers. I could easily recognize the officer who sat in the front of that car.

Mr. Frank. I could recognize the one in the back.

Mr. Taub. Then, we were sitting in the car, and we asked where we were being taken. He said, "We are going to take you out to see John Henry Blair, and Blair is going to greet you, and after he is through with you, he will take you out where he wants to." We protested at that.

Senator Logan. John Henry Blair is sheriff of Harlan County?

Mr. Taub. Yes, he is more than the sheriff. He runs the county. He is high sheriff and high chief, and there is no other government in Harlan County than he. I speak somewhat indignantly, and I think I have a right to speak so. I think an American citizen would not be worth the name if he did not feel indignant at this time. Why quibble about it? The thing smells to high heaven. We were going to be turned over to John Henry Blair, high sheriff of Harlan County. We protested and finally the deputy said, "Well, I will tell you, there is a car up in front and we will follow that car. Wherever that car goes we will go with it."

We rode down the road to Middlesboro and from there we rode to Cumberland Gap, and on the saddle of Cumberland Gap all the cars were pulled up in one formation. I saw the lights being turned out. Orders were given to turn them out. Everybody came out of the cars, but the deputies in our car told Mr. Frank and myself to remain seated in the car. We could look out on the right side of the car, and we saw one of their men pull a revolver out of his pocket. He was standing about ten feet from my car. Then, Mr. Frank and I were ordered to step out. Mr. Frank stepped out first. I was the last to step out. As Mr. Frank walked away, some men stepped up behind me and attacked me. I was beaten and dealt fourteen blows. I did not count them, but I should say I was dealt twelve or fourteen blows, and some hard substance was used. I will say frankly I do not know who hit me. My nose began to bleed, and I think I was also bleeding from my head or my eye, and after a few minutes transpired, one of the officers walked up to me after flashing his light in the car, and said, "Who hit you with that jack?" pointing to an automobile jack, and that was the base of the jack. Well, that was the first time I had any inkling I was hit with an automobile jack. I have never made that charge, and I only quote an officer who said I was hit by an automobile jack. If it had not been for the fact that I was very fast in covering my face, head and body, and in twisting in all shapes, the chances are I would have been cut up as badly as Waldo Frank, or perhaps much worse.

After that, we stayed around awhile. The luggage of the various members of the committee was searched carefully. They went through everything. Evans, the same Evans who is the editor of the *Pineville Sun*, and the head of the Red Cross of Bell County, walked up to me while my face was smeared with blood and said, "Taub, give us a speech on the Constitution now. Tell us all about the amendments. This will be your last chance in the State of Kentucky. Later, you will be able to tell it to the members of your committee." Calvert, who was very prominent, walked straight up to me. This was Calvert, the attorney for the Straight Creek Coal Company, whom I had opposed in an injunction against 102 defendants in Lexington County, when he tried to sue out an injunction against coal miners, literally throw them out of their homes, and we argued the injunction in the Federal Court. Now he had an opportunity to see me beaten up and taken for a ride. His car was used. I remember the number of the car was 27-040, Kentucky, 1932. It was a Packard automobile, brown in color.

We were informed, Senator, by some men, apparently natives of the neighborhood, that this incident took place in the State of Tennessee and not in Kentucky. I, frankly, do not know whether we were in Kentucky or Tennessee. I could point the place out, I am sure, but I was told by taxi-men and by other boys in the neighborhood that this was in the State of Tennessee.

I do not want to go into too great detail, and yet I would be failing in my profession as an attorney here if I did not.

I have tried, in every legal way, to appeal to the courts of the State of Kentucky. I have gone to the police court. I have appealed to the County Court. I have appealed to the Circuit Court. I have gone to see Judge D. S. Rose, a Circuit Court Judge, of Whitley County, Kentucky. I have asked him as a judge, as a lawyer, and as a citizen, to come into Bell County, and to listen to a writ of habeas corpus, and he said he was too busy.

We had no other course. I had seen the Attorney General of the State of Kentucky, and he said there was nothing he could do, and the Governor refused to see us. Where else were we to go, if not to the Federal Capital at Washington, and to see the United States Senate? This writ of habeas corpus that I have touched on was a writ that was sued out two weeks ago, two weeks ago this very day, and that was the day I was called back into Bell County to assist local counsel. We allege various grounds for the writ, excessive bail being one, unconstitutionality of the act of criminal syndicalism is another; the fact that bail was not accepted when we offered it to the county judge, and there are other grounds.

I know of nothing that is so high in law, among the rights guaranteed and given to American citizens, as the writ of habeas corpus. It comes down to us from Anglo-Saxon jurisprudence, and it has been revered. That writ is still to be argued. It is still pending, and Bell County, and everybody in Bell County who is an official, does not want that writ to be argued, and they have avoided that, and we know that, and that there is a lawless state of affairs in the County of Bell, and that this is a challenge to the United States Senate.

You asked us what we ask you to do about it. Are not the facts plain, and eloquent? Let anybody go down there and find out if that is so.

Senator Logan. You mentioned a thing I wanted to ask about. What can the United States Senate do? You are a lawyer. You are familiar with the laws, Federal laws, and State laws. You are talking about a matter that took place in a sovereign state. What jurisdiction has the United States by any process of reasoning, to go into one of the counties in a state of the union and attempt to take charge of matters? What if they should do so? What could they do after they made an investigation?

Mr. Taub. I will answer that question this way, Senator. I am an attorney. I have never yet answered a question on legal procedure unless it was something extremely elementary, that I had gone over a thousand times, without consulting the statutes, and the code on it. I am sure I can very quickly check up on the procedure to be followed by a committee of the United States Senate. I will say this further. The Senate has sufficient precedent to send a United States Senate investigating committee into the State of Kentucky. It has been done before.

Senator Logan. In what case?

Mr. Taub. I understand that investigating committees have gone into the State of Pennsylvania. I believe that was in 1922.

Senator Logan. Probably that related to interstate commerce.

Mr. Taub. The point is this. If the Constitution of the United States Government has ceased to function in any state, I think that Federal authorities have a perfect right, I am sure they have a right, and it is their duty to go into a state and see why law and order has completely fallen down and why the Constitution has been thrown out of the courts, and it is basic and elementary to every lawyer that the Senate has the right to go in.

Mr. Frank. We are insisting, not on any state rights, but on American constitutional rights. . . .

Mr. Taub. May I go on, Senator?

Senator Logan. Yes.

Mr. Taub. The further point is this, again and again. Senator, this issue has been raised, and I am glad that you brought it up. I certainly, as an attorney, do not want to hedge on it and avoid it. The question has been raised, are there radicals, Reds, or Bolshevists in Bell County? Well, if there are, or there are not, Senator Logan, the fact is that law and order have been broken down, and have been cast aside, not by the so-called or alleged radicals, but by the very men who have been chosen to uphold the law.

I want to say here, in the presence of the press, that nobody in Bell or Harlan Counties, so far as I know, particularly in Bell, has been able to point to one instance to members of the National Miners Union, which is alleged to be a Communistic organization, or affiliated with the Communist Party, and alleged to have radicals in it—nobody can point to them and say they ever committed one act of violence, that one of their members ever took a gun out of his pocket, or pointed it at an officer or anybody else, and threatened to murder him. There is not one such act. What do we find Calvert and Patterson saying today? They are saying that these men are radicals, that they are Reds, and that they come down here to tear our government down. That is a smoke-screen, and let the entire country know it. Let this go over the wires that they are trying to bring up here a smoke-screen to cover up a state of starvation and terror never known heretofore in this country. Fifty years ago, Senator Logan, when workers organized to demand basic elementary rights, they were shot down as they are now in Kentucky. Honest leaders and honest organizers were shot down, and locked up. This is a false issue.

In the hearing that was held in Bell County in the cases of the nine defendants, several of whom were reporters and others relief workers, again and again we said this issue was a false one, and that the only issue here is: Do the defendants, Senator Logan, have a right to distribute relief to starving men, women and babies, free of charge, and to give it to them? That was done by the Workers International Relief. Secondly: Does a labor organization like the International Labor Defense have a right to send a lawyer and legal representative down into Bell or Harlan County, Kentucky, and assist in the defense of defendants who have been arrested on such charges as criminal syndicalism, and conspiracy? Does the National Miners Union have a right to maintain an office, openly, publicly, legally, and lawfully? And where do they open their office? At 105 Virginia Avenue, City of Pineville, County of Bell, Kentucky, and where was that office? Opposite the court house. They did not hide away in some side alley, or slip away in the dead of the night. They operated out in the open where everybody could see them. Any officer could come up there and visit the headquarters.

Mr. Walker. May I interrupt?

Mr. Taub. Go ahead.

Mr. Walker. On the occasion when this committee went in, some nineteen miners were arrested and the warehouse of the Workers' International Relief, to which the trucks, for which we bought food, were bound, was destroyed. One miner, Harry Simms, who was assembling miners to receive their food, was shot down by a Deputy Sheriff. Just one more point and I will stop. A driver, driving a truck from Cincinnati, bringing food, who was to meet us and go with our trucks, was shot, and is now in the hospital. I cannot give you the details from my own experience. That will have to be investigated.

Mr. Taub. Just one more statement, and I think I am through. It has been charged—and I want to be perfectly fair, and give you what the charges were against the unions, and against the miners—it has been charged that relief was brought in on the one hand by the relief organization, while with the other hand, the same body or group of men behind them were encouraging miners to violence. Of course, nothing like this has ever been proved. There has been no statement to that effect. I want to give the lie to that charge, and it is typical of others I could give and if I did so, I would keep this committee here all night.

Last May, Harry Appleman, a groceryman of Kentucky, a man socially minded, and pretty decent, agreed with his wife they would take the money they had saved to buy an automobile with, and they would use that money to buy flour and food, distribute that flour and food to the starving miners in the county. Senator, after they did that, and distributed that flour to the starving men, women, and babies of the county, Appleman was indicted for criminal syndicalism, and had to flee from his home, and left his wife and children, and was declared a fugitive from justice. That is the story of Harry Appleman, reported in the Knoxville *News Sentinel* on December 24, 1931. . . .

Section 1 of the Constitution of the State of Kentucky reads:

"Bill of Rights. Section 1. Inherent and inalienable rights. All men are, by nature, free and equal, and have certain inherent and inalienable rights, among which may be reckoned:

Sub Division 4—the right of freely communicating their thoughts and opinions.

Sub Division 6—the right of assembling together in peaceable manner, and for common food, and of applying to those invested with the power of government for redress of grievances or other proper purposes by petition, address or remonstrance.

Sub Division 8—freedom of speech, freedom of the press. Every person may freely and fully speak, write and print on any subject, being responsible for the abuse of that liberty."

I say, if you try to exercise those legal constitutional rights, and do it openly and publicly, before a mixed group of coal miners and anybody else in town, anybody who does so will be held for criminal syndicalism, and on this basis we ask that law and order be reëstablished in Bell County.

I am an attorney, and it is my duty to go back there. Why should I not go back and help in the defense? Is the United States Senate not going to say anything to me? Are you going to follow what the Attorney General of Kentucky said: that there is nothing you can do?

I say, Senators, Bell County today is looking to Washington, D. C., and if nothing is done, they will break out in the most ferocious form of terror. They will stop at nothing at all, and this responsibility now is plainly on the shoulders of the Federal Government. We said we were going to the United States Senate. We, as American citizens, have tried to follow the law at every point.

Senator Logan. Now, Mr. Taub. Before you could make a case, what should you and Mr. Frank have done, before you could find out that justice has flown from Kentucky? I personally know, having served as a Justice of the Court of Appeals of Kentucky, until I resigned to come to the Senate, if they were interfering with any Constitutional rights, you could have gone into court and have sought an injunction. You might have obtained it locally to prevent their interfering in any way with you distributing this relief, or doing anything you had a right to do under the Constitution of the United States.

Mr. Frank. We were not allowed to stay there long enough to do it.

Dr. Mitchell (interposing). May I bring out a point that has been over-looked? At the time the local attorney was talking to us he said, "Perhaps you had better not sit there with your back to my windows because the machine guns in the upper part of the court house are directed right this way."

Senator Logan. I understand that, but you had a right to go to the courts. That you did not do.

Mr. Frank. We did not have time, Mr. Senator, we were run out of town and the court was not sitting.

Senator Logan. What happened to you is indefensible on the state-ments which you have made, I mean on the part of those who thus treated you. There can be no justification for the conduct shown to you down there by those whose actions you have narrated, but I know the courts of Kentucky, and particularly the Court of Appeals. I know every member on it, and I do know that if you had tried your cause there, that you would have received justice, the justice that is guaranteed to you by the Constitution of Kentucky, and by the Constitution of the United States. Now, you say you did not have an opportunity. That is true, but that is not the fault of the law. That was the fault of those who violated the law, if they did. The courts down there in that particular section may be what you say. I know Judge Jones very well. I have known him for a good many years. He is not a native of that section of Kentucky. He came from Louisiana, I believe, and I think Judge Jones did attempt to construe the law as he understood it.

Mr. Walker. May I interpellate at this point?

Senator Logan. Yes.

Mr. Walker. Regarding Judge Jones, I made quite a study of the history of the courts in the cases of the miners that have been brought up there. When the former committee, Mr. Dreiser's committee, went down there to investigate, Judge Jones stated publicly that he was going to advise the miners to form a mob and chase Theodore Dreiser and his gang away from the state.

Senator Logan. A statement of that kind, of course, was very unbecoming, or it showed the Judge was not qualified. As you said a while ago, you have to be practical about all those things. We cannot get anywhere by becoming over-zealous, over-excited about them. It is a practical question that must be determined according to good, common, sound sense. I am not so well acquainted with that particular section of Kentucky, my home being four hundred or five hundred miles away. We have rather an extensive state down there. Their charge—I mean the officers—is that some of the miners are encouraging those who are banded together in an effort to overturn all government; that they get together and hold meetings and make speeches, in which they take the position that the Government of the United States and of the State of Kentucky is a complete failure, and that it ought to be overturned. Now, I do not believe that any of you would go that far. I do not believe you would endorse a sentiment of that kind.

Mr. Frank. The group that are fomenting revolutionary sentiments in Kentucky are the operators, and their political henchmen.

Senator Logan. In other words, the mistreatment of the miners would naturally foment a feeling of that kind.

Mr. Frank said further that he believed revolutionary sentiment was caused by the stupidity and brutality of the operators and authorities.

Senator Logan insisted on the patriotism of the inhabitants of Eastern Kentucky.

Mr. Walker. May I say that the Chairman of the National Miners Local which I visited down there—and I believe he later became the General Chairman for the whole Union down there, at the time of the conference to call the strike—a man named Billy Meeks, was a local Baptist preacher and an ex-service man. I heard the miners say repeatedly, "They call us Russian Reds down here. I wonder why they call me a Russian Red? My grandfather was a Red Cherokee Indian. Maybe that is the reason." I asked another man, a member of the National Miners Union, "When did your family come to Kentucky?" He said, "My great-great-grandpappy came to Kentucky just after he helped George Washington win the war." He said, "We fought one fight for freedom, and by God, they have taken it away from us and we will fight another." That is the kind of people they are.

Mrs. Walker. That is the inflammatory speech for which he was arrested for criminal syndicalism.

Senator Logan. Those people down there would very much resent anyone's attempting to set up any organization that looked toward doing anything to the American Union or the Government. They have it inbred in them. They are the purest stock in America, almost. They have lived there since 1775 or 1776, or about that time, when they came over from Virginia and North Carolina into that section.

Now, the treatment that you received down there is something that you, of course, feel very indignant about. I can well understand that.

Mr. Walker. We do not want to disassociate ourselves from the similar threats made to those who coöperated with us and with whom we coöperated, namely, members of the Workers International Relief and others. I do not think they should be differentiated.

Senator Logan. I do not either. I agree with you on that but you have folks down there in that section, not illiterate men, not men that do not know anything at all. There are college men. There are men who have had training, but they are rabid on that one question of Communism. They just go as crazy as possible. I want to say this. I do not want you to think I am in sympathy with any such treatment as you received down there. I think it is reprehensible, and if there is anything that I can do as a United States Senator to bring about better conditions down there, no one in the world would be more willing to do it. I know we have had those difficulties before, and I would be glad to see them ended. But the one thing that I have not been able to understand, and maybe you can help out some on that, is that I know of no power, I know of no jurisdiction that the Senate of the United States has to interfere in the affairs of a sovereign state when there is no charge that any Federal Law has been violated. They were charged too with having committed criminal syndicalism. I was Attorney General when that was passed. I have always been opposed to the law. I think it is wrong. Wrong in principle. It only brings trouble.

Mr. Frank. May I ask you one question, as a lawyer?

Senator Logan. Yes.

Mr. Frank. I am not a lawyer, and do not know. I have read the Constitution of the United States, but I confess I have not got that very clearly in my head. As I remember it, there are a group of amendments to the Constitution, the first amendments which were passed, really being a Bill of Rights.

Senator Logan. That is right.

Mr. Frank. Is the enforcement of this Bill of Rights, is that vested entirely in the States, or is that vested in the Federal Government?

Senator Logan. That would be a little difficult to answer, Mr. Frank, to a layman. The Federal Government only has certain delegated rights. There are certain things that the Congress may do, but it must look, for its authority, to the Constitution. It cannot go into a state and have anything to do with the enforcement of purely state laws, unless those laws are in violation of the Constitution of the United States or some of its amendments. Now, if you should judge for instance, that this law that they have been using against you violates some provision of the Constitution of the United States, you could bring any prosecution that might be instituted against you, it might be brought to the Supreme Court of the United States on a writ of error, and the matter be determined there, but only the question of whether the act was unconstitutional or not. You would have to look to the State of Kentucky for the protection of the rights which you have in the State of Kentucky. Now, as you say, you had a mob forcibly eject you from the State of Kentucky, or from Bell County. That is what it amounts to. You were assaulted and beaten and bruised and probably left for dead.

Dr. Mitchell. No, let me tell you the last words they said to me. "Where is this Doctor?" I said, "I am a Doctor, but I retired some years ago." "Oh, well, I think you are enough of a doctor to fix this head." I had not seen the head.

Mrs. Walker. I want to know if, as has been charged here today, all our laws and our civil rights have been abrogated in these two counties, if counsel sent in to defend people in those rights have been jailed and arrested and beaten, is it your opinion that the Federal Government can do nothing about it, that this state of lawlessness, the complete abrogation of the law, of the Declaration of Independence, upon which this country is substantially founded, must be allowed to continue?

I went down there and was asked to make a speech. I said, "We have come down here because we have heard a great deal about your conditions, and what you are suffering and we are interested, and we are in great sympathy with you." I was indicted for criminal syndicalism.

Senator Logan. If I were your attorney, I could tell you very readily what I would do. I would do what the laws of Kentucky give me a right to do. I would move for a change of venue. I would ask for every legal right that I had. Then, if I were tried and should be convicted, I would appeal to the Court of Appeals of Kentucky where I know you would receive justice. I know that court. Then, if you think the law is in violation of the Constitution of the United States, I would appeal, come up on a writ of error from the decision of the Court of Appeals, to the Supreme Court of the United States. Now, no citizen on earth can have any greater protection than that. We cannot get away from courts. There is where our rights should be determined.

Mr. Taub. You speak about going into court, and issuing out writs. I have to call up Pineville to find out if Attorney Stone is still alive. We were told when we left, by the deputies in the court, the same treatment accorded to us would be accorded to Stone. We have three lawyers. We are trying to get all the local counsel we can. How can we possibly get an injunction or follow up on a writ of habeas corpus when we do not know whether our local counsel and their families and wives and children are not going to be attacked? I was in the home of Attorney Stone when it was considered unsafe for me to stay in the hotel. I lived at his home in Pineville and they barred the doors and the windows. I received mysterious telephone calls, and at times cars circled the house. I was confined to the house every night and warned not to go out. . . .

Here there was a brief discussion between Mrs. Walker, Senator Logan and Mr. Taub regarding the Criminal Syndicalism law, the fact that nobody had been brought to trial under this law in Kentucky and that it was used simply to keep people out of the State.

Mr. Taub and Senator Logan discussed the proper method of picking the grand jury and certain alleged illegality in Bell and Harlan Counties.

Mr. Walker. To come back to the issue which we ought to be discussing at this point—what can a Federal investigation do and how can the Senate help in this matter—I would like to say we have been getting together a great many details about the way the law operates. That is not the only thing. The basic thing is the economic condition of the people out of which this abuse of the law arises. Obviously, if the coal mines were operated prosperously in Kentucky, there would be a different condition. The basic fact of the starvation there is at the foundation of all this, and then we have abuses, and suggestions as to how to mend it. We are not without precedent, I believe, in asking for a Federal investigation of conditions similar to this.

Senator Logan. I do not know about that. Senator Cutting may know about that, as he has been in the Senate longer than I have.

Senator Cutting. We did have an investigation in 1928 of conditions in the coal fields in Pennsylvania. It went before the Interstate Commerce Commission and they appointed a sub-committee on which Senator Gooding of Idaho was Chairman. . . .

Senator Logan. There is no member of the United States Senate that would not do all that was within his power to prevent an injustice being done to any American citizen. That is, if he were deprived of his legal rights. I think I can safely say that there is not a man in the Senate who would not, as far as he could, within the laws that control him, do what he could to see that justice is done. Suppose you prepare for us, and submit it to Senator Cutting and Senator Costigan, a memorandum showing just what you think can be done. Mr. Taub is a lawyer.

Mr. Taub. I will be very glad to prepare that, Senator.

Mr. Frank. That will be prepared, Mr. Senator, and I feel we have kept you too long, and that you have been awfully good, and I feel that the meat of this thing is on the record, and I just want to add one word, after which, as far as I am concerned, I think there is nothing more to be said, and that is this. We have presented to you, and there will be a further presentation to show you, the state of lawlessness in Kentucky—in certain sections of Kentucky—a lawlessness of which the vested city and county officials seem to be the chief instigators. We have brought this to the attention of certain members of the United States Senate, and will have our findings written in such a form that other members of the United States Senate will know of it; and we have shown with all these records that there is a large community of American citizens who are starving, and who are rebelling against the state of virtual peonage, and who are being starved in order to force them back into a state of peonage.

Now, you gentlemen have said to us, "What can the United States Senate do about it?" and I would like to turn that question back on you. I would like to say, "What does the United States Senate feel that it should do about it?"

Senator Logan. I feel like you should have addressed your complaint to the Kentucky Legislature. To make myself perfectly clear, here is the situation. If the Senators of the United States who are more experienced than I am show me the right the Senate has to go into it, then as a Senator from Kentucky, I will ask for an investigation of the entire matter, and we will find out whether there is any Communism down there trying to overthrow the Government, and we will find out whether there exists, for the want of a better name, we will call it an oligarchy that is absolutely destroying our Government down there. I will ask that myself, if you will show me where we have any authority. The only thing that would make me hesitate about it—I believe you will testify that I have paid as high a tribute as I can to the people in eastern Kentucky—there is only one thing that would cause me to hesitate, and that is doing what I think is my plain duty. These people in that section of the state, Senator Cutting, politically, are almost without exception, of the opposite political faith to myself. They are all Republicans, and I would not want them to think that I was doing it because of my political affiliations, and I would not do it for that reason.

At this point, reference was made to affidavits by various committee members supporting the testimony given before the Senators. Senator Logan again repeated that this was a purely informal meeting and questioned the jurisdiction of the Senate in this matter.

Senator Cutting. I want to say this, Mr. Frank, when you put the question back to us as to what the United States Senate feels it ought to do under the circumstances, you must remember that we feel that we ought not to do anything that we are not allowed to do under the Constitution, and that is the only reason I have asked these questions as to what you felt could be done. I am sorry I missed the argument of Mr. Taub, but I had a very important engagement which was made some weeks ago. I assure you, it has been extremely interesting to me and I think to the other Senators who listened to the account of the situation, and certainly if it is in my power, I want to go the limit within the authority which we possess to see that the right thing is done.